AMERICAN
BUSINESS
VALUES

THE PRENTICE-HALL SERIES
IN ECONOMIC INSTITUTIONS AND SOCIAL SYSTEMS

S. Prakash Sethi and Dow Votaw, *Editors*

THIRD EDITION
AMERICAN BUSINESS VALUES

Gerald F. Cavanagh
University of Detroit

Prentice Hall
Englewood Cliffs, New Jersey 07632

Library of Congress Cataloging-in-Publication Data

Cavanagh, Gerald F.
   American business values / Gerald F. Cavanagh. -- 3rd ed.
      p.   cm. -- (The Prentice-Hall series in economic institutions
   and social systems)
      ISBN 0-13-025529-7
      1. Business ethics--United States. 2. Industry--Social aspects-
   -United States. 3. United States--Commerce. 4. Free enterprise.
   I. Title. II. Series.
   HF5387.C379 1990
   174'.4'0973--dc20   89-37484
                                                            CIP

Editorial/production supervision: WordCrafters Editorial Services, Inc.
Cover design: 20/20 Services, Inc.
Manufacturing buyer: Ed O'Dougherty

Previous edition published under the title of *American Business Values in Transition.*

Printed in the United States of America

10 9 8 7 6 5 4 3 2

ISBN 0–13–025529–7

PRENTICE-HALL INTERNATIONAL, INC., *London*
PRENTICE-HALL OF AUSTRALIA PTY. LIMITED, *Sydney*
EDITORA PRENTICE-HALL DO BRASIL, LTDA., *Rio de Janeiro*
PRENTICE-HALL CANADA INC., *Toronto*
PRENTICE-HALL OF INDIA PRIVATE LIMITED, *New Delhi*
PRENTICE-HALL OF JAPAN, INC., *Tokyo*
SIMON & SCHUSTER OF SOUTHEAST ASIA PTE. LTD., *Singapore*

CONTENTS

x   *Contents*

FOREWORD

After having been a part of the curriculum in many schools of business for twenty years or more, the field now vaguely described as "business and society" seems at last to be coming into focus. A common core of interest has begun to evolve and to give promise of providing the integrating concepts of teaching and research that have been so conspicuous by their absence in the past. Evidence of this long delayed crystallization can be found in new course descriptions and outlines, in the research interests of those working in the field, and in the proceedings of conferences convened for the purpose of examining the proper content and parameters of this important area of practical, as well as academic, concern. The field and its integrating theme appear very clearly, as suggested above, to be the complex, dynamic, two-way relationship between the economic institutions of our society, with which most schools of business are primarily concerned, and the social systems in which those institutions now operate and are likely to operate in the future.

It would be incorrect and misleading to suggest that the interaction between business and society has not been part of the business school curriculum in the past. In one form or another, this interaction has played an important role in business and society courses for many years. There are, however, several basic differences between what has been done in the past and the new rallying point we now see evolving. The old, and still dominant, approach has been very narrow in its emphasis and in its boundaries and has all too often been limited to little more than an instructor's own specialty in such areas as social control, business and government, or antitrust. Even where an instructor's narrow predispositions are not present, the "social" side of the relationship is often viewed as being static, or relatively so, and external to the current decision or situational context; and the primary goals of the course are those of explaining the phenomenon of business to the students and of analyzing the requirements of business-like, efficient, or responsible behavior in a rather loose social sense. Furthermore, the emphasis is almost wholly the private, large, and industrial aspects of the economic sector, with little, if any, attention devoted to the public, small, or nonindustrial variables.

The flaws in the approach are obvious, and changes are already begin-ning to take place. What appears to be evolving, and what we believe should be evolving, is a much greater interest in the dynamics of the whole system. What is needed is a systematic analysis of the effects (noneconomic as well as economic) of business on other institutions and on the social system, and of the effects of changes in other insitutions and in the social system on the economic sector. Most important, perhaps, the stage should be set for an understanding of the basic assumptions, attitudes, values, concepts, and ide-ologies that underlie a particular arrangement of economic institutions and social systems and of how changes in these assumptions affect the arrange-ments and the interactions among the various parts of the whole system.

Two other points ought also to be made here. *First,* although most schools of business do not behave as though it were so, they are actually engaged in training of managers of tomorrow and not the managers of today. As the relationships between economic institutions and their social environ-ment become more intimate, and as each part of the whole system becomes more sensitive and more responsive to changes in the other parts, how much more important it is going to be for the manager to understand the dynamics of the system as a whole than it is for him to know what the momentary conformation happened to be when he was in school. It seems to us, further, that one of the manifestations of an industrially mature society will be the economic sector's diminishing importance and, as a consequence, a reversal of the flow of influence from the economic sector to society as a whole. The manager of the future will need to be more sensitive to changes in society than he ever was in the past. His training will have to include a very different congeries of tools and ingredients than it now does.

Second, we think note should be taken of some evidence now beginning to accumulate that suggests that in the future schools of business may come to play the same sort of influential role in the profession of management that schools of law and medicine now play in theirs. If this change should come about, it will become ever more important that managers, during their period of formal education, be provided with those conceptual and analytical tools that best meet the needs of their profession and of the society as a whole. If present forecasts prove to be accurate and "continuing education" be-comes a much more important aspect of higher education than it is now, among the first academic institutions to be profoundly affected will be the schools of business. The influence of the schools upon the profession of man-agement will become more immediate and the need for pragmatic training in the interactions between economic institutions and social systems greatly enhanced.

While there is no great disagreement on these general issues, it would be a mistake to assume that there is consensus on the details. We believe that this series takes into account both the agreement on some of the broader points and the lack of consensus on many of the more specific aspects of the changes taking place in the environmental field. For example, there are people who believe that comments like those made above dictate the integration of social materials in all parts of the business curriculum rather than their use in specialized courses devoted to the field; there are many who feel that the bulk of such work should be done in specialized courses; there are many views in the area between these two extremes. We feel that this series is designed in such a way that it can cater to business school curricula of all varieties.

We visualize this series evolving in a set of concentric circles starting at the core and expanding outward. The innermost circle consists of those books that provide much of the basic material that is usually included in the introductory courses in "business and society," including the insitutional role of large corporations; government interaction with business; business ideology and values; methodological approaches to measuring the social impact of business activities; corporations and political activities; and the influence of corporate management on the formulation of public policy.

The next circle is made up of books that deal with the impact of corporate activities in specific functional areas. The issues covered here include marketing and social conflict; accounting, accountability, and the public interest; corporate personnel policies and individual rights; and computers and invasion of privacy.

The outermost circle consists of books that are either interdisciplinary or cross-cultural in nature or both. Here we are concerned with the synergistic effect of various economic activities on the society as a whole. On one dimension we are concerned with issues such as how technology gets introduced into society; the economic effects of various types of social welfare programs; how various social activities like health, sanitation, mass transit, and public education are affected by the actions of business; and the social consequences of zero economic growth or population growth. On another level, studies will include comparison between corporate behavior in different social systems.

The concentric circles are not intended to be mutually exclusive, nor do they reflect a certain order of priority in the nature of problems or publication schedule. They are simply a convenient arrangement for thinking about the relationships among various problem areas.

In addition to their role as part of the training provided by collegiate schools of business and management and other social science disciplines, most of the volumes in this series are also of use and interest to managers and to the general public. The basic purpose of the series is to help provide a better understanding of the relationship between our economic institutions and the broader social system, and it is obvious that the need which the series hopes to satisfy is not confined to students of business and management or for that matter even to students. The ultimate goal, we suppose, is not just better corporate social policy but better public policy as well, in the formation of which all citizens participate. Consequently, we have urged the authors of these volumes to keep in mind the broad, in addition to the narrow, targets and to couch their work in language, content, and style that meet both kinds of requirements.

S. Prakash Sethi
Dow Votaw

University of California
Berkeley, California

PREFACE

In this book we will examine the values, ethics, and beliefs of American business and businesspeople. Business values and ethics have a profound impact on new products, product quality, productivity, workplace design, on-the-job relationships, and government regulations. Values thus have a great influence on the manager and the firm. Conversely, the business firm and work are so central to our lives that they strongly influence our personal values, goals, and life styles.

The purpose of this book is:

1. To examine the values, ethics, and beliefs upon which the free market system of production and exchange is built;
2. To provide the language and tools for, and some practice in actually doing, ethical analysis;
3. To aid readers in clarifying their own personal values and goals;
4. To help provide a foundation of values and ethics for managers who design products and work environments;
5. To help all men and women clarify their expectations of business and government.

Most people agree that both business and government must take a long-range view in order for the United States to compete in the world marketplace. Long-range planning demands ethics, values, and beliefs that respect the needs of all stakeholders.

Creating policies and plans to provide long-term benefits for a firm requires a consensus of people within that organization. That consensus can be built when we understand the roots of traditional American business values—especially those that can be nurtured to deal with present challenges. While flexibility has always been a strength of Americans, we recognize the equal importance of our historical traditions, values, and beliefs. To facilitate understanding of these values and beliefs, both traditional business values and the challenges to these values will be presented here.

I have great respect and affection for the free market system. The productivity of American business depends on the energy, creativity, and cooperativeness of its entrepreneurs, managers and workers, all of whom must have a long-term perspective. I confess another bias, but it is one shared with most Americans: the central importance of *each* individual person. Every business decision, action, and policy made should consider the best interests of *all* who are touched by that decision. The concerns of customers, associates, neighbors, suppliers, and the larger community must be weighed along with the traditional concerns of shareholders and management. Not to be forgotten are those most often neglected: the poor. Each of these parties are *stakeholders* of the firm.

This third edition of *American Business Values* retains the best elements of the second edition and adds many important new features. This edition has nine shorter and more manageable chapters. Chapter 1 examines current business problems such as productivity, takeovers, advertising, and self-interest. Chapters 2 and 3 probe the historical roots of American business. Chapter 4 outlines the most telling critique of free markets: the Marxist indictment. Chapter 5 presents the influence of the organization on the values and beliefs of the individual. Chapter 6 examines the stress that many face at work, as well as how personal moral development takes place. Chapter 7 provides the language, concepts and models useful for doing practical ethical analysis. Chapter 8 shows how values and ethics, or a lack of either, affect the performance of the firm. Chapter 9 examines business beliefs, mission statements, and projected change in business values and beliefs.

Thus, the content can be summarized as follows: Chapter 1 focuses on contemporary business values and ethical dilemmas; chapters 2 through 4 are historical; chapters 5 and 6 are behavioral; chapter 7 treats business ethics; and chapters 8 and 9 discuss implementation and future values.

At the end of each chapter are questions for discussion, brief cases, and some exercises. When used in a class, this book is often supplemented with other books that contain additional cases.

This book is the result of research and enriching dialogue with businesspeople, teachers, students, and brothers in the Society of Jesus. It has benefited from the insights of fellow faculty who have provided helpful comments on this and earlier editions: Otto Bremmer, Kirk Hanson, Manuel Velasquez, Leroy Plumlee, Earl Alberts, Alene Staley, Martin Calkins, Bruce Paternoster, Kristin Aronson, Philip Cochran, John Fleming, and Bill Stewart. Graduate assistant Paul Turnbull researched, provided critiques, and created the index; Tracy White researched material. Dean Gregory Ulferts and the College of Business and Administration of the University of Detroit provided support for this project. Thanks to Heather Adams and Christian Milord who edited the manuscript, and special thanks to senior editor Alison Reeves at Prentice Hall who shepherded this third edition through its many stages.

Gerald F. Cavanagh, S.J.
University of Detroit
Detroit, Michigan

CHAPTER ONE
VALUES AND ETHICS
OF FREE ENTERPRISE

He who owns the most when he dies, wins.

Bumper sticker

A firm's values influence its treatment of customers and workers and determine operations and success. Financial bankers and merger specialists exercise great power in the United States, yet some of their values are questionable. Defense contractors such as General Dynamics, General Electric, and Northrop have acknowledged receiving kickbacks, producing poor-quality goods, and overcharging the government—all considered unethical acts. Whether one can trust an unwritten promise or how one will be treated as a worker depends on managers' values and ethics. Values and ethics hold together the fabric of the corporate culture, and that culture ultimately determines a firm's success or failure.

This first chapter will explore some ways in which values and ethics affect our lives and businesses. In Chapters 2 through 4, we will examine the historical roots and critiques of business values. Chapters 5 and 6 investigate how the organization affects and is affected by our personal values and ethics. For a definition of some important terms, see Figure 1–1.

Values heavily influence personality and actions. They undergird and often determine the important decisions that an individual makes. Either acknowledged or implicit, values are always present and profoundly influence our lives and choices. To probe and to know one's values allows one to

---

Ethics: A system of moral principles and the methods for applying them.
Ideal: An ultimate aim of an individual or a society; a standard of perfection.
Ideology: A cluster of values integrated into a comprehensive, coherent, motivating statement of purpose.
Moral: Dealing with or capable of distinguishing right from wrong.
Value: A lasting belief that a certain mode of conduct or goal is better than the opposite conduct or goal.

FIGURE 1-1   Values and Ethics Terms

understand those values better and hence possess greater control over one's own life and actions.

A value system forms the foundation of decision making with regard to both personal and business matters. Values become so much a part of us that we are often unaware of their precise content and impact. An analogy might help. Consider the way we drive an automobile. As we learn to drive, the procedure becomes increasingly automatic. Gradually driving becomes so much a part of us that we become explicitly aware of it only when we take time to reflect on our actions. Yet without our knowing that procedure, it would be impossible to drive. Similarly, without a value system or ideology, it is impossible to make consistent and reasonable decisions on important alternatives. To deny the importance of values is shortsighted and prevents one from understanding fully one's actions and those of others. This chapter will examine some current business practices and some business firms, focusing on the values that undergird those activities.

FREEDOM AND MARKETS

Free enterprise values are familiar to each American. Freedom is a foundation value of our economy: free markets, free movement of people, free entry into new businesses, freedom to take or leave a job or a business. This freedom parallels the freedom that Americans find and cherish in political democracy. The American free enterprise system, stimulated by freedom and other values, provides many benefits to people:

1. the immense output of goods and services produced over the last century
2. high standards of living available to the majority of Americans
3. the considerable rewards that come from the new ideas, skill, and initiative of entrepreneurs
4. the 27 million new jobs that have been created in the United States in the last decade

5. encouragement of flexibility and innovation among people
6. the reinforcement of personal freedom

Yet in spite of these successes of the U.S. economy over the last century, signs of trouble appear. An unflinching, honest examination of these difficulties will give us additional insight into ourselves and our current business values. Examining our values and ethics will enable us to be better equipped to improve ourselves and our performance.

LIVING FOR TODAY

Americans value consumption more than saving. Advertising and our perceived need to have things and to demonstrate to others our success encourage us to buy goods. We purchase cars and televisions and go into debt to pay for them. A better life is measured in greater consumption: a bigger house, more travel, and more club memberships. Since we save so little, we have too little capital for investment in critically needed new plants, equipment, and research. We are far behind other developed countries in our rate of saving. The Japanese save more than three times the proportion of their personal income as do Americans; the French, Germans, British, and Italians save more than twice as much as Americans.[1] We are a "buy now, pay later" culture, handing the bill for our current purchases to future generations. Excessive consumption and increasing debt result from short-sighted attitudes.

Productivity and Debt

Productivity increases in the United States, which had been rapid in the 1950s and 1960s, slowed considerably in the 1970s and 1980s. If one ranks countries according to the rate of their increase in productivity, the United States trails not only Korea and Japan but also Great Britain, Norway, Germany, Sweden, Belgium, France, Canada, the Netherlands, and Denmark. Of developed countries, only Italy had lower increases in productivity from 1981–1985.[2] This partially stems from the fact that the United States lost manufacturing and shifted more of its business activity to services—inreases in productivity are much harder to achieve in services. The values of American managers also contribute to the problem. These values lead them to

1. try to achieve profitability in the short-term and thereby often neglect the long-term

[1] *Statistical Abstract of the United States—1987*. Washington, D.C.: U.S. Department of Commerce, 1987), p. 420.

[2] "Productivity: Why It's the No. 1 Underachiever," *Business Week*, April 20, 1987, p. 54-55.

2. fail to invest sufficiently in research and development
3. allow poor communication and confrontational labor-management relations to continue

When such behavior occurs, it stems from the pressures on and the values of managers and from the underlying values that are encouraged in American business.

We use more capital in the United States than we are able to provide ourselves. The national debt that accumulated from 1981 to 1988 is 1½ times greater than the total debt accumulated during the previous 200 years. Added interest costs since 1980 are greater than the cumulative amount of the large tax cuts in 1981. Our children undoubtedly will resent paying the interest on that debt, from which they will gain no benefit. They will be paying the debt for the overspending of *this* generation. From 1982 to the present, the United States went from being the world's largest creditor to the world's largest debtor nation. Now foreigners "lend us vastly larger sums so we can buy their goods, consume more than we produce and invest more than we save."[3] Not only the federal government but also corporations and individuals have accumulated immense debt to foreign interests. Each quarter both federal debt and private debt increase. Evidence seems to indicate that Americans care more about their own comfort and consumption than about the future of their country or their children. Each American's priorities appear to be centered on his or her life, career, and leisure. The fabric of our society is being torn, as indicated by a feature article in a leading news magazine entitled "A Nation of Liars?"[4]

Americans have watched the wealthy become wealthier and the poor become poorer. Fifteen years ago the richest 1 percent of American families held 27 percent of the nation's wealth; today that percentage approaches and may soon surpass the peak of 36 percent attained before the Great Depression of 1929. Moreover, during the last fifteen years, the annual income in real dollars of the poorest 20 percent of American families dropped one-third. While financial bankers complain that they cannot maintain their life styles on $400,000 per year, two out of five Hispanic children and three out five black children live in poverty.[5]

Examples of the focus on convenience, comfort, and short-term prosperity abound. In the wake of the Arab oil embargo in the 1970s, Americans realized that they had a voracious appetite for the finite supply of petroleum that exists in the world. Among a variety of attempts to lessen our use of

---

[3] Peter G. Peterson, "A Summit on the Budget," *The New York Times,* February 3, 1987, p. 87.

[4] "A Nation of Liars?" *U.S. News and World Report,* February 23, 1987, pp. 54–62.

[5] Jim Hightower, "Where Greed, Unofficially Blessed by Reagan, Has Led," *New York Times,* June 21, 1987, p. E25.

petroleum, we legislated better mileage standards for autos and a lower speed limit. In spite of these efforts, a report commissioned by President Reagan notes that an increasing dependence on foreign oil, from 27 percent of the total used in the United States in 1986 to 38 percent in 1987, poses a security threat and adds considerably to the imbalance of payments.[6] Nevertheless, better mileage standards for autos were delayed and the speed limit was raised. Each of these actions increases petroleum use. In addition, higher speeds will probably result in ten thousand more highway deaths each year.

Restructuring American Business

American business has restructured; it has reduced costs and become "lean and mean" to better meet foreign, low-cost competition. Layers of line management and many staff people have been cut, bringing better communication and greater efficiencies. However, restructuring also has some long-term negative effects. Investment in research and development (R & D) benefits a firm in the long-term. However, one of the effects of restructuring is a decline in R & D. In fact, overall investment in R & D declined in 1987. As one analyst put it, "Short-term profits have simply become too important to most companies."[7] When firms are acquired, R & D is most often cut to help pay the outstanding debt resulting from the acquisition. Moreover, even when managers succeed in defending their firms from hostile takeovers, they often must sell off assets and take on additional debt. This generally demands decreases in the R & D budget. Decreasing R & D is like eating your seed corn. While it is a way to meet current problems, it mortgages the future.

Second, the low priority given to technology and innovation by American society and business is indicated by the proportion of scientists and engineers in the United States compared with Japan. For every 10,000 citizens, the United States has 70 scientists and engineers whereas Japan has 400. On the other hand, for every 10,000 citizens the United States has 20 lawyers and 40 accountants whereas Japan has but 1 lawyer and 3 accountants.[8] Moreover, our brightest young scientists and engineers work on military projects; Japanese scientists work on civilian projects. Again our actions bespeak our values.

A third negative effect of corporate cost cutting is the decline of business contributions to private sector charitable organizations. Recall that when federal funds for education and for the disadvantaged were cut in 1981,

[6]"U.S. Urges Cut in Dependence on Foreign Oil," *New York Times*, March 17, 1987, pp. A1, D9.

[7]"Corporations Are Putting Less into Research," *Business Week*, August 10, 1987, p. 18; "Research Spending Is Building up to a Letdown," *Business Week*, June 22, 1987, pp. 139–140.

[8]James Fallows, "American Industry—What Ails It, How to Save It," *Atlantic*, September 1980, pp. 35–50.

President Reagan called for private contributions to meet the resulting need. Corporate contributions did not increase but actually declined.[9]

A fourth and broader effect of restructuring is that many firms have also cut other internal efforts at balanced long-term growth because of the pressure to keep impatient shareholders happy and corporate raiders at bay. Now executives "are focusing their efforts on trimming operations and shuffling assets to improve near-term profits, often at the expense of both balance and growth."[10] Even though a top manager's own priorities might call for long-term planning, institutional shareholders, portfolio managers, and corporate raiders often deprive managers of this option. Goodyear Tire and Rubber, to escape corporate raider James Goldsmith, dropped plans to go into energy and aerospace to balance its huge but slow-growing tire business. Let us examine this attempted takeover in more detail.

TAKEOVERS AND SPECULATION

When British financier James Goldsmith made the hostile bid to take over Goodyear (see Figure 1–2), the firm had a 9.1 percent return on equity, well above the industry average of 6.8 percent. Shortly before, it had diversified into aerospace and energy to balance the cyclic tire business.[11]

Goodyear managed to repel the hostile takeover bid, but at immense cost. To maintain its freedom, Goodyear spent $2.6 billion to buy back 41 million shares of its own stock, including $657 million to raider Goldsmith for his shares (purchased a few weeks earlier for $500 million) and his expenses. Goldsmith had exacted greenmail from Goodyear's management.

To retire the debt that Goodyear assumed at high rates of interest, chairman R. E. Mercer points out,

> We've closed three marginal plants we otherwise might have been able to save. We've also sold for slightly more than $1 billion our motor wheel subsidiary, our aerospace subsidiary, a five star resort and other properties near Phoenix, Arizona. We still have our oil and gas subsidiary—Celeron—on the selling block.
> We've reduced our payroll by approximately 10 percent and undertaken other stringent cost-cutting measures.[12]

---

[9] "Corporate Pressures Slowing Gifts to Charity," *New York Times,* July 8, 1987, p. 1.

[10] See Jeff Madrick, *Taking America* (New York: Bantam, 1987); "Trying to Streamline, Some Firms May Hurt Long-Term Prospects," *Wall Street Journal,* January 8, 1987, p. 1.

[11] "More Than Ever, It's Management for the Short Term," *Business Week,* November 24, 1986, p. 93.

[12] R. E. Mercer, "Terrorists in Three-Piece Suits," *Vital Speeches,* May 1, 1987, p. 421.

Acquisition: The acquiring of one firm by another.

Friendly takeover: A takeover that occurs with the cooperation of the management and board of both firms.

Golden parachute: Guaranteed payment to top executives enacted as a disincentive to a hostile takeover.

Greenmail: When a raider requires a target firm to purchase the raider's stock at more than market value so that the raider will cease attempting a takeover.

Hostile takeover: A takeover that occurs in spite of the opposition of the target firm's management and board.

Institutional investor: Institutions (e.g., pension funds, endowments, trust funds, insurance firms) that hold common stock. Most have professional financial managers.

Junk bonds: High-yield, high-risk bonds sold to finance a leveraged buyout or the activities of a corporate raider.

Leveraged buyout: Purchase of outstanding shares on borrowed capital, often by the firm's own management or by workers.

Merger: The joining of two firms.

Poison pill (also *shark repellant*): An action that makes the target firm a less attractive target for a takeover.

Put into play: Signaling that a firm is undervalued and ripe for a takeover.

Raider: The person or firm that initiates a hostile takeover.

Stakeholder: One who holds a stake in the firm; a constituency of the firm (e.g., customers, employees, the local community, shareholders, suppliers, the local government).

Stockholder: One who holds stock in a company; an investor who is considered an owner of the firm.

Takeover: The taking of ownership of another firm.

Target firm: The company being considered for takeover.

FIGURE 1-2   Investor and Takeover Terms

Like other firms forced into cost cutting, R & D was also reduced at Goodyear. So, whether the defense succeeds or fails, note the costs: reduced employment, the selling off of less profitable assets, and vastly increased debt.

Raiders Goldsmith, T. Boone Pickens, Carl Icahn, and many financial economists maintain that takeovers occur only when the target firm's stock price is low. This happens when the market judges that the firm is not using its capital resources efficiently. A major cause of inefficient use of resources occurs when the parent company diversifies into less-familiar and less-profitable operations. Defenders of takeovers maintain that the target company executives have invested shareholder funds inefficiently. Such funds would

TABLE 1-1   Completed Mergers and Acquisitions, 1980–1987

YEAR	NUMBER OF TRANSACTIONS	VALUE IN MILLIONS OF DOLLARS
1980	1,560	$ 32,882
1981	2,329	70,064
1982	2,298	60,698
1983	2,391	52,691
1984	3,164	126,074
1985	3,437	145,464
1986	4,381	204,895
1987	3,920	177,203
1988	3,487	226,643

Source: "1988 Profile," *Mergers and Acquisitions*, May-June 1989, p. 45. Quoted with permission.

be more efficiently used if they were merely returned to shareholders. According to T. Boone Pickens, the oil industry provides many examples in which the cash generated in the 1970s when the price of oil went up was used for unwise diversification: Mobil purchased Montgomery Ward, Exxon bought Reliance Electric, Atlantic Richfield and Standard Oil of Ohio bought into mining and minerals.[13] Since they were unprofitable, these acquisitions have already been sold.

The external takeover market protects shareholders when the corporation's internal controls and board-level control mechanisms are slow, clumsy, or break down completely.[14] Note that the greatest advantages of takeovers accrue to shareholders. Stakeholders—terminated employees, affected local neighborhoods, and suppliers—bear the costs. Long-term planning in the firm, including R & D, also suffers.

Mergers and acquisitions have increased dramatically over the past decade (see Table 1–1). Most attempted mergers are successful. Goldsmith's failure to take over Goodyear is one of few exceptions. Of the mergers attempted in 1986, 4,024 succeeded and only 318 failed.[15] That means that firms are becoming larger and hence more bureaucratic and most often less productive.

Greenmail and Golden Parachutes

To defend themselves against hostile takeovers, executives resort to numerous short-term strategies to make their firms less attractive to raiders.

---

[13] T. Boone Pickens, Jr., "Professions of a Short-Timer," *Harvard Business Review*, May-June 1986, p. 78.

[14] Michael C. Jensen, "The Takeover Controversy," *Vital Speeches*, May 1, 1987, p. 427. For another view, see Robert F. Bruner and Lynn Sharp Paine, "Management Buyouts and Managerial Ethics," *California Management Review* 30 (Winter 1988): 89–106.

[15] "1986 Profile," *Mergers and Acquisitions*, May-June 1987, p. 57.

Executives will therefore sometimes dispose of assets, sell a division, take on a large amount of debt, and generate golden parachutes and poison pills. Golden parachutes are guarantees of compensation for top executives even if the firm is taken over. Top management benefits greatly. Even though their firm may be dismembered and many employees fired, top executives receive substantial compensation. These defensive strategies are often as questionable as those used by the raiders themselves. They pose a conflict of interest for top managers.

When a raider has already purchased a substantial portion of a target company's stock, the raider then threatens to seize control of the firm and to then "restructure the company." The raider will undoubtedly sell less-profitable operations and fire current management and many staff people. Management may protect itself and the firm by offering to purchase back the raider's stock at a price greater than the price the raider paid for it. Thus the raider in a few weeks makes a large profit, as did Goldsmith in the Goodyear case. Other shareholders often are not able to sell their stock at this higher price. In addition, the firm generally must liquidate some of its assets or borrow substantially in order to purchase these shares from the raider. This leaves the company in much greater debt, and the rest of the shareholders and other stakeholders pay the bill. Greenmail results in ransom being given to the raider at the expense of other stakeholders.

Institutional Investors

Institutional investors now own most of the outstanding common stock in the United States.[16] These institutions hire professional portfolio managers whose success is judged by the amount the total portfolio of stocks increases in a given quarter. Hence the portfolio manager acts to insure that the stock continues to increase in value. Corporate raiders have brought about dramatic increases in share value, so portfolio managers carefully follow the activities of raiders and often support them. Moreover, an institution will switch from one portfolio manager to another if the rate of return is not what the fund manager thinks it should be.

Two decades ago, before computers and when most common shares were in the hands of individuals, markets were more stable. Few individuals had the time or inclination to watch the market daily. Investors also tended to look on their investments as longer-term ownership and thus were concerned about the future of the firm.

Today portfolio managers care little about a given firm itself. They are

---

[16]James E. Heard, "Pension Funds and Contests for Corporate Control," *California Management Review,* Winter 1987, p. 89–100; see also "Evening Odds in Proxy Fights," *Business Week,* July 4, 1988, p. 37.

interested only in the rate of return generated by dividends and capital gains. With the aid of computers, their full-time occupation is to watch the market. They can thus buy and sell a block of stock many times a day to make incremental gains, sometimes large gains.

This, in turn, puts considerable pressure on top managers of firms to keep their stock price up. Indeed, that is the only sure way to keep the raiders away. When the stock is undervalued, a firm becomes a ripe target for a raider. However, keeping the stock price up can lead to sacrificing long-term health for short-term returns, as we saw earlier. This can have negative effects on jobs, new products, and long-term prospects for the firm. Moreover, the stock price reflects the perceptions of analysts; it is not always an accurate indicator of the current and future health of a firm.

Insider Trading

Ivan Boesky, David Levine, and Martin Siegel acknowledged using confidential information obtained from clients to amass personal fortunes. Of Wall Street firms, several members of upstart Drexel Burnham Lambert were early indicted.[17] But the old and respected houses of Kidder, Peabody & Co. and Goldman, Sachs & Company were also involved.[18] Financial bankers and other businesspeople agree that confidentiality is essential to Wall Street firms and to their clients.

One by-product of the widespread insider trading scandals is that clients are now more guarded in what they reveal to outside financial advisers. Whatever managers tell these advisers can be used against them; their firm may be "put into play" by the very advisers they approach for help to avoid just that. The ethics of insider trading is clear: It is a breach of confidentiality. It is unfair to current shareholders to use information to which even they as owners do not have access. Those with inside information thus purchase their shares at an artificially low price.

The insider trading scandals grew in concert with increased merger and acquisition activities. When a takeover is planned, information of the takeover is valuable because the stock of the target company will surely rise when the news becomes public. So, if one has early notice of a takeover, one can make large profits quickly, at little risk, and with no real effort. It is the American dream: to become rich without much effort or risk.

---

[17] For a view of Drexel's junk bond author, Michael Milken, see Connie Bruck, *The Preditor's Ball* (New York: The American Lawyer and Simon & Schuster, 1988); see also "Who'll Be the Next to Fall?" *Business Week*, December 1, 1986, pp. 28–35.

[18] "The Wall Street Career of Martin Siegel Was a Dream Gone Wrong," *Wall Street Journal*, February 17, 1987, pp. 1, 30; "Suddenly the Fish Get Bigger," *Business Week*, March 2, 1987, pp. 28–35.

Some Ethical Issues

Although illegal, insider trading does take place on Wall Street. Many careers of bright, capable, but greedy people came to an end because of insider trading. In spite of the arrests, insider trading is difficult to police. Even though every purchase of stock leaves a record of who buys and at what time, it is still hard to prove that the purchaser had information from a confidential source. Wall Street brokers, financial bankers, and risk arbitrageurs live on recent, accurate, sometimes gossipy information. Nevertheless, passing inside information is both illegal and unethical. Greenmail and poison pills are legal, but most agree that they abuse the system and are unfair.

With regard to mergers and acquisitions, both supporters and critics of takeovers agree with the following:

1. American firms are often too large, complex, and bureaucratic and are therefore inefficient.
2. If American firms are to survive and compete in the world marketplace, they must streamline and become more efficient.

It is at this point that the agreement stops. Proponents of hostile takeovers would opt for turning capitalism loose to eliminate the inefficiencies of American business. The free operation of current capital markets has and will continue to force American firms to restructure and become more efficient.

Critics of hostile takeovers acknowledge the necessity of greater efficiencies through restructuring but hold that restructuring should be for the long-term benefit of the firm and its *many* stakeholders. Critics maintain that raiders are merely seeking a quick financial killing and are not interested in the firm they takeover; nor do they usually make a firm more efficient in the long-term. The record shows that firms that have been raided cut R & D and cut staff. Firings undermine the loyalty of workers who are important to a firm's long-term future.

A takeover battle pits the raider and the bright young analysts at their computers calculating return on investment against the top management of the target company. Many argue that experienced top management, with the input of various stakeholders of the firm (if there is time for such input), is in a better position to decide the best strategy for the future of the firm and the disposition of its assets. On-site management knows the stakeholders better and has face-to-face relationships with the people who work in the firm. This helps to insure the loyalty of the workforce and results in products of better quality. Is the bright, ambitious financial banker in a better position to decide how and when to restructure the firm?

A recent study of takeovers concludes that "based on historical data, negative returns to shareholders from acquisitions are more prevalent than the prevailing folklore on the subject admits."[19] While some shareholders benefit, most do not. "While the acquiring firm shareholders are losing overall, the individuals they have hired to manage their assets are benefiting from their loss. Takeover promoters are not the champions of the small shareholders as so often claimed."[20]

On a broader scale, rather than develop new and better products and engage in basic R & D, our economy has encouraged "paper entrepreneurs." Takeover experts, financial bankers, lawyers, and accountants do not devise better products, production processes, or marketing techniques; they do not provide new goods or new jobs. Rather, they shift existing assets and often cause a reduction of jobs and a plummeting of morale. Moreover, their fees and salaries add to overhead costs and drag down productivity. We will return to the issue of unfriendly takeovers in Chapter 8, where some suggestions for participants will be offered.

MANAGEMENT SELF-INTEREST

Management, when faced with blue-collar workers' absenteeism, tardiness, unwillingness to work hard, and lack of pride in work, puts the blame on worker attitudes of short-term self-interest. Nevertheless, the focus on immediate and personal goals often begins with managers. Many a manager's criterion for success is the achievement of a large return on investment and a large increase in market share for the current quarter. These are often achieved at the expense of long-term profitability.

The larger and more diversified a firm is, the less able top management is to know specific products, markets, or employees. Given the greater distance from production, new product ideas, consumers, and the public, management turns to what it *can* understand—the only control mechanism that is then available—"the numbers." Management then relies on return on equity, market share, and other numerical indices of success. This tends to put the focus on short-term results. This focus in turn tends to reduce productivity, research, and risk-taking, and it also undermines efforts to integrate ethics into management decisions.

Mergers are not new. Between 1955 and 1980, fully 166 of the largest 500 firms had vanished as independent corporations; they had been acquired by *other* firms. Fortune 500 firms acquired roughly 4,500 firms during this period. The number of employees of the Fortune 500 firms has increased 105 percent.[21] The increase in employment and the concentration of power have

---

[19]Murray Weidenbaum and Stephen Vogt, "Takeovers and Stockholders," *California Management Review*, Summer 1987, pp. 157–168.

[20]Ibid., p. 166.

[21]Linda Snyder Hayes, "Twenty-five Years of Change in the Fortune 500," *Fortune*, May 5, 1980, pp. 88–96.

resulted from mergers. Today there are fewer entrepreneurs and fewer "family firms" because of mergers. A large diversified firm must be managed "by the numbers." This encourages abstract, impersonal, short-term thinking that is done in relative isolation from products, employees, and customers. Sometimes the newly acquired firm is closed, its assets liquidated, and its employees thrown out of work simply because the distant parent company judged it had better use for the assets acquired.

In sum, the principal underlying cause of lessened productivity is the shortsightedness of management. Managers too often take the easy way out; they prefer measurable, short-term results so that their personal record looks good. Note that this underlying motive also often leads to unethical behavior. Therefore, it is fair to conclude that the shortsighted values that lead to lower productivity are the same values that undermine ethics in the firm.

Public Confidence in Corporations and Executives

Americans do not have much confidence in either business executives or the firms they lead. This is not surprising given the evidence of the short-term perspective of many managers and their concern with their own careers that we have already examined. Attitudes toward our economic and business system have been probed in opinion surveys. Some of the items pertinent to our inquiry are shown in Table 1–2. There is currently less dissatisfaction with the distribution of income and wealth than there was fifteen years ago. On the other hand, two-thirds of today's graduate business students still feel that "business is overly concerned with profits and not concerned enough with public responsibilities." A majority also continued to maintain that U.S. foreign policy "is based on narrow economic and power interests." Supporting this, 89 percent feel that the real power in the United States rests with the "giant corporations and financial institutions." That is, the public perception is that there is a locus of power but that it is being exercised by corporations for their own interests.

A Harris Survey found that only 40 percent of Americans thought that the ethical standards of business executives were good, whereas 58 percent thought that their ethical standards were only fair or poor. This same survey found that 90 percent of Americans thought that white-collar crime is a common phenomenon.[22] Confidence is essential for the survival and health of social institutions. Americans now have less confidence in the leadership of major institutions than they did before (see Table 1–3). Over the last twenty-five years, confidence in society and its institutions has dropped precipitously. If only 19 percent have a great deal of confidence in corporate

---

[22] "Is an Antibusiness Backlash Building?" *Business Week*, July 20, 1987, p. 71.

TABLE 1-2   Attitudes of Graduate Business Students on Issues Underlying the Business System

	PERCENTAGE AGREEING*			
	1974	1981	1983	1988
1. Business is overly concerned with profits and not concerned enough with public responsibilities.	75%	70%	51%	66%
2. Our foreign policy is based on narrow economic and power interests.	70	75	54	53
3. Economic well-being in this country is unjustly and unfairly distributed.	80	34	34	42
4. The real power in the United States rests with				
a. the Congress.	52	61	69	61
b. the giant corporations and financial institutions.	81	88	87	89
c. the public.	43	45	56	50

*Graduate business students from author's classes at Wayne State University (1974) and the University of Detroit (1981, 1983, 1988).

executives, that is not good news. It means that the average American perceives these leaders not to be working in the best interest of the people as a whole. However, it should be noted that citizens of European countries (France, Great Britain, Spain, and West Germany) have even less confidence in their social institutions and leaders.[23]

The Contemporary Corporation: Cornucopia or Citizen?

Focusing narrowly on profits and productivity provides both theoretical and psychological support to those businesspeople who "look out for number one first." Colonial Pipeline, jointly owned by nine of the largest American oil companies and itself owner of the largest oil pipeline in the country, was finishing the construction of its line into New Jersey in 1962.[24] A site for a petroleum storage area (a tank farm) was needed, and tank farms were not popular with the people of Woodbridge, New Jersey, the area selected. Although public hearings were required by law, both the mayor and the president of the town council said they would see to it that Colonial received its building permit if the firm would give a $50,000 "campaign contribution." To look for another site would delay the project and to lay

[23] "Americans More Trusting of Institutions, Poll Finds," *Washington Post*, May 15, 1987, p. A32.

[24] Morton Mintz, "A Colonial Heritage," in *In the Name of Profits*, ed. Robert Heilbroner et al. (New York: Warner Books, 1973), pp. 59–96.

TABLE 1-3   Confidence in the Leadership of Major Institutions

	1966	1971	1976	1981	1986	1988
Great deal of confidence in leadership of:						
Major companies	55%	27%	16%	16%	16%	19%
The White House	X	X	11	28	19	17
U.S. Congress	42	19	9	16	21	15
The press	29	18	20	16	19	18
Television news	X	X	28	24	27	28
Higher education						
institutions	61	37	31	34	34	34
Medicine	73	61	42	37	33	40
Major oil compa-						
nies	X	X	X	11	X	X
Wall Street	X	X	X	12	X	X

Source: Louis Harris, "Confidence in Institutions is Down, Led by Sharp Decline in Trust in White House," *The Harris Poll*, May 8, 1988, p. 2. Used with permission.

additional pipeline to another spot would cost millions, so Colonial paid the $50,000 (and later an additional $100,000).

It is illegal for a firm to contribute to political campaigns. In addition, the firm and the local leadership conspired to deprive citizens of their right to be heard on the issue. Nevertheless, it was a far less expensive alternative for management. Management counted on not being caught, having decided it was better for the firm to break the law than to incur additional costs. In spite of cleverly hidden accounts and transfers of funds, however, the scheme was accidently exposed. Ensuing events showed that similar campaign contributions by large firms are not uncommon. Self-interest leads firms to seek the lowest cost alternative.

When a firm emphasizes profitability exclusively, it then attempts to push some of its own costs of production off onto innocent third parties. Pollution, whether from production facilities or moving vehicles, is a classic example. Others who may or may not benefit from the product pay the cost by ingesting disease-causing pollutants. There are many other examples. A large-scale dump for toxic chemicals was established by Hooker Chemical (now a division of Occidental Chemical) in the old Love Canal near Niagara Falls, New York. Homes and a school were built over the dump, and various physical ailments began appearing among the residents—miscarriages, birth defects, and mental retardation. Hundreds of people were forced to leave their homes.

In another case, the pesticide Kepone was manufactured by a firm under license from Allied Chemical (now Allied Signal) in Hopewell, Virginia. The highly toxic chemical was handled casually, and waste was flushed into the river. Serious illnesses among employees and the contamination of the entire James River and the Cheseapeake Bay resulted.[25] The National Cancer Institute estimates that between 60 to 90 percent of all cancer in men and women in the United States is caused by chemicals introduced into the environment by human beings.

The central point is that self-interest, especially the desire to cut costs, can lead a firm to dump its toxic materials and thereby adversely affect innocent third parties. It is cheaper to do so. Users of pesticides, rubber, autos, and plastic products thus do not pay their full cost. Those who ingest the toxic substances pay by suffering ill health and having months or even years taken off their lives. An evenhanded and just system would require manufacturers to "internalize" these very real costs of production and pass them on to those who actually use the products.

The Environmental Protection Agency (EPA) was set up to help accomplish this. Whether or not the EPA is efficient, it is clear that the unrestrained free market has no mechanism for controlling pollution. In fact, it encourages firms to pollute as long as they are not penalized. When it comes to pollution, the challenge to government is not whether to regulate but how to regulate efficiently, effectively, and equitably.

ADVERTISING AND MULTINATIONALS SHAPE VALUES

Advertising is the communication link between producer and consumer. Without advertising, the prospective purchaser would not be aware of the various prices and qualities of goods and services sold. A free market demands a free flow of information, and advertising provides a major portion of the information that is so essential to consumers.

From the standpoint of the consumer, the purpose of advertising is to obtain information that will help in the making of purchasing decisions. From the standpoint of the seller, the purpose of advertising is to influence people to purchase products or services. The success of advertising is demonstrated by the fact that sellers spend $60 billion on it each year.[26]

Advertisers use a variety of approaches to influence the purchasing decisions of consumers. Some advertising is informative, tasteful, and supports the values of individual responsibility, family, and community. Recall the Gallo TV ads, which feature birthdays, weddings, baptisms, and a variety of family-oriented activities. On the other hand, some advertising is sexist,

---

[25] For an account of the Love Canal, Kepone, and other cases, see "The Chemicals Around us," *Newsweek*, August 21, 1978, pp. 25–28; see also "Who Pays? Cleaning up the Love Canals," *New York Times*, June 8, 1980, sec. F, pp. 1–5.

[26] *Statistical Abstract of the United States—1981*, p. 572.

individualistic, and self-oriented. Note cigarette and beer ads in college newspapers, ads targeted at individuals who are susceptible to peer group pressure and who cannot purchase beer legally. Still other ads, though a minority, are deceptive, crude, and demeaning. Not surprisingly Americans are suspicious and cynical about the messages they see in advertising.[27]

Young children constitute one group not yet suspicious of advertising. They have not had the experiences necessary to build critical judgment. Up to age seven, children tend to take at face value what they see in ads and on television; they often cannot distinguish the ad from the program. As children grow older and begin to distinguish, advertising and television implicitly tell children that "grownups tell lies for money quite well."[28]

Effect of Advertising on Values

The effect that advertising has on our values should be of vital concern to all citizens and consumers. However, it is difficult to show a clear causal connection between advertising and values. Advertisers do try to convince us that if we are unattractive, ill, or unhappy, they have just the right product for us. Something we can purchase can solve our problems. In order to sell, advertisers often intentionally appeal to social status, fear of ridicule, and materialism.

Advertisers have been accused of being "creators of dissatisfaction." They present the handsome, immaculately dressed man or woman as an ideal to strive for; yet the ideal inaccurately reflects the actual world. It can create unattainable expectations and hence frustration, especially for the impressionable and the less affluent. To judge a person largely by his or her clothes and appearance is shallow and dehumanizing. Moreover, such an attitude sets one up to be disappointed later in life when one discovers that money, possessions, and power do not bring happiness.

Advertising encourages consumption. Advertising, in its promotion of an affluent life style, also presents an image of Americans as materialistic, shallow, and self-centered. Nevertheless, some argue that the United States is less materialistic than other societies:

> The more affluent a society is the less materialistic it tends to be, not because affluence makes for virtue but mainly because people have less to worry about

[27] For a fuller treatment of these ethical and value issues in advertising, see Chapter 5, "Advertising and Television," in Gerald F. Cavanagh and Arthur F. McGovern, *Ethical Dilemmas in the Modern Corporation* (Englewood Cliffs, N.J.: Prentice Hall, 1988); see also Kam-Hon Lee, "The Informative and Persuasive Functions of Advertising," *Journal of Business Ethics* 6 (January 1987): 55–57.

[28] Robert Heilbroner, "Realities and Appearances in Capitalism," in *Corporations and the Common Good*, ed. Robert B. Dickie and Leroy S. Rouner (Notre Dame: University of Notre Dame Press, 1986), p. 38; "Double Standard for Kids' TV Ads," *Wall Street Journal*, June 10, 1988, p. 21.

to survive from one day to another, and therefore there is a somewhat greater chance for altruism.[29]

Hence, a paradox: Americans, because of their affluence, have the opportunity to be less materialistic. At the same time they are pressured by advertising and each other to be more fixated on consumer goods and status.

Advertising firms now sell not only products but political candidates as well.[30] For the past two decades, advertising firms have provided idealized images of political candidates on which to base our voting decisions. Instead of being shown a real person giving statesmanlike explanations of complex issues, we are now subjected to a carefully crafted thirty-second image—complete with film footage, sound overlays, and other trappings of advertising. We are not introduced to the person but rather presented with an idealized picture. In an election campaign, we are thus asked to make a choice between two fictitious images. A thirty-second ad does not provide the time for a discussion of difficult issues. Even worse, it often communicates that complex issues are simple and easy to resolve, given a certain ideology and a healthy image. Of course, this is not only false but it can undermine democracy. Being an actor helps in running for political office.

Advertisers tell us that, as in the case of engineers or accountants, what they do is value-free. They are professionals, and they offer their skills and knowledge without regard to the merits of a particular product or firm. Whether this is a legitimate moral position is questionable. It is true that products, firms, and advertising strategies differ widely. Some products are more worthwhile than others. Some firms are sensitive to customers and employees; others are not. Some advertising campaigns are informative and uplifting, whereas others are manipulative, trivial, and even deceptive.

Advertisers also tell us that they do not create values; they merely build on the values that they find already present. Nevertheless, advertising does reinforce and solidify those embryonic, self-centered, and materialistic values present in all people. It does this especially effectively among the young and less mature. Advertising thus encourages people to value Coke more than juices, Fritos more than vegetables, Porsches more than people, fashionable clothes more than art, and soap operas more than reading. It promotes shallowness, acquisitiveness, and egoism.

Multinationals: Corporate Citizens of the World

Multinational corporations such as IBM (U.S.), Toyota (Japan), and Shell (Netherlands) have operations in dozens of countries. They provide

[29] Peter Berger, "The Moral Crisis of Capitalism," in Dickie and Rouner, *Corporations and the Common Good*, p. 24.

[30] S. W. Dunn and A. M. Barban, *Advertising: Its Role in Modern Marketing* (Hinsdale: Dryden Press, 1978), pp. 92–93.

jobs, goods, and income to tens of thousands of people around the world. They have a vested interest in stability. Wars and revolutions disrupt business as well as bring anguish and death to people. Multinational firms hire local people as managers and often provide them with education and training.

The multinational firm bridges nations, cultures, and peoples. In an era when individual nations and even the United Nations are often caught up in nationalism and bureaucracy, the multinational corporation crosses boundaries and deals with people where they live. From the standpoint of values, the person-to-person contact that occurs and the necessity to understand and work with people of different cultures are advantages of the multinational firm.

The business firm with operations outside its home country is a generator of jobs and wealth and also an instrument of technology transfer. Less widely acknowledged are the values that are communicated. The multinational firm brings the values of developed countries to developing ones. Values of a regulated workday, individual responsibility, discipline, and rewards for work under direction of another often conflict with the simple values of family, tribe, and village. Multinational managers are confronted with many unique national values and are thus challenged to understand and build on these values.

People in developing countries seek a better life. This most often means increased income and more goods and services. The multinational company can be a major actor in aiding the economic development of poor countries. In particular, the multinational firm

1. brings technology, management, and capital to poor nations
2. develops leadership and provides training for local people
3. reinvests at least some of its profits in the local economy
4. provides business and jobs for local firms, both through purchasing from local suppliers and through workers' purchases
5. provides mechanization, fertilizers, and other aids to local agriculture
6. produces foreign exchange by exporting goods
7. aids the host nation's development plans
8. encourages the development of engineering and other professional skills among local people
9. contributes to local and shared ownership projects

However, there is a negative side to the multinational corporation. Critics claim that it exploits poorer nations and peoples. According to these critics, the multinational firm

1. sends profits from operations in poorer countries back to richer home nations
2. supports right-wing dictatorships over democracies, because they are stable, predictable, probusiness regimes

3. widens the gap between the rich and the masses of the poor in the host country and encourages urbanization
4. intrudes on and threatens the sovereignty of host countries
5. closes plants abruptly when wage rates rise or regulations become burdensome
6. uses local capital for its own purposes
7. undermines local business initiative and leadership
8. encourages the use of expensive, unnecessary, and sometimes dangerous consumer goods (e.g., cigarettes, alcohol, perfume)
9. promotes inappropriate technology transfer and capital-intensive operations where jobs are scarce

Free Enterprise and Military Dictatorships

Private investors and multinational firms that seek to begin operations in another country look for political stability, local banks willing to lend, and a potential work force that is willing and trainable. They prefer a society in which the government can guarantee law and order and a sympathetic environment.

The Philippines offers a lesson. The United States supported Philippine dictator Ferdinand Marcos for decades, long after he had declared martial law, put major businesses in the hands of relatives and friends, stole billions for himself, dragged his nation into poverty, and ran up a national debt of $26 billion.[31] A U.S. Embassy officer said, "Democracy is not the most important issue for U.S. foreign policy in the Philippines, ... more important was the U.S. national interest, our security interest, and our economic interest."[32]

Thus some of the disparity of income in developing countries can be attributed to the narrow self-interestedness of U.S. foreign policy—and some is also due to multinational corporations. Let us consider the data in Table 1–4 on the average income of individuals in various nations. There is a considerable disparity of income between developing countries and industrial countries. Note especially how average personal income has actually declined in Latin America and Africa since 1980.

Multinational corporations are not the major cause of this gap. Nevertheless, a case can be made that it would be desirable for world stability if both multinational corporations and U.S. foreign policy could contribute to closing the gap—both between nations and between the rich and poor within nations. On the other hand, the rise in income in Asian countries from 1980 to 1984 is the result of successful development in Korea, Taiwan, Hong Kong, and Singapore, development that multinational corporations contributed to significantly.

---

[31] Raymond Bonner, *Waltzing with a Dictator: The Marcoses and the Making of American Policy* (New York: Times Books, 1987).

[32] Ibid.

TABLE 1-4   Income Gap Between Rich and Poor Nations

	PER CAPITA INCOME IN 1981 U.S. DOLLARS			
	1960	1970	1980	1984
Industrial countries				
U.S. & Canada	$7,891	$10,222	$12,386	$13,150
Europe	4,378	6,327	7,922	8,108
Japan	2,820	6,884	9,623	10,907
Developing countries				
Latin America	1,400	1,838	2,488	2,276
Africa	580	730	784	709
Asia	257	368	521	571

Source: "Third World Income Just Can't Catch UP". Reprinted from *Business Week*, Feb. 9, 1987, p. 21, by special permission, copyright © 1987 by McGraw-Hill, Inc.

Let us examine the effect of large foreign investments in Brazil. Brazil received billions in foreign investment over the last few decades, and its per capita income went up considerably. But that increased income has gone largely to the already wealthy, who are a small minority, and the very poor have benefited hardly at all. While the Brazilian gross national product increased by 25 percent, the wealthiest 20 percent of the people received 50 percent of that increase whereas the poorest 20 percent received but 5 percent.[33] Brazilians who have jobs receive wages that are a fraction of those in the United States, and Brazilian law forbids workers to strike. Brazil was ruled by a right-wing military dictatorship that had the express goal of bringing in more foreign investment and of keeping the country stable, even if it required sacrificing citizen's rights.

In another case, Litton Industries had been unable to negotiate a contract with Greece concerning certain development projects. Then came a military coup, and the right-wing military dictators *invited* the company to do business there.[34] Litton then helped the new government gain legitimacy in Washington, and the firm also worked well with that government, which was run much like its primary customer, the Pentagon. The military government of Greece had a clear chain of command, and there were no conflicting interests to be considered. In a military dictatorship, it is obvious where the power lies. It is not surprising that a corporation prefers to operate in a country with a stable, law and order, right-wing dictatorship, precisely the

[33] Lecture given by a World Bank officer, Wayne State University, Detroit, November 1973.

[34] David Harowitz and Reese Erlich, "Litton Industries: Proving Poverty Pays," in *The Radical Attack on Business*, ed. Charles Perrow (New York: Harcourt Brace Jovanovich, 1972), pp. 48–54.

kind of political system American citizens would find intolerable if it existed in their own country.

Working cooperatively with private business interests, the American government itself has for decades been helping to "stabilize" most of the Latin American countries by means of the aid, loans, and support it has given right-wing military regimes that deny individual freedoms. Chile, when it had a freely elected government, was denied American aid and loans because it was left leaning. After the right-wing military dictatorship took over, aid flowed freely. Chile, Uruguay, Guatamala, and a number of other Latin American countries had freely elected governments not long ago. With the encouragement from the American government and from some American business executives, right-wing dictatorships now rule. Argentina, Peru, and Costa Rica are currently democracies, although fragile ones.

Latin American police and military officers were brought to the United States and given the latest in weapons, hardware, and training in what Pentagon officers call "antisubversion and interrogation techniques." When they went back home, they were skilled in their work and, perhaps more importantly, had established ties with influential Americans in the State Department and the Defense Department. When they perceived a leftist threat to their government, they contacted their American friends to determine if the United States would support a coup and recognize a new right-wing government. With U.S. approval, the military then moved in with tanks and guns and placed themselves in power.

Two interpretations can be made of the actions of the United States. The first is more benign: The United States inadvertently provided the means whereby democracy fell in these Latin American countries; the results of U.S. aid were unforeseen. Another view, more commonly held among Latin Americans themselves, is that the United States supported the right-wing coup so as to make their country a more cooperative setting in which U.S. firms could do business.

Many of the problems discussed above can be effectively dealt with as the host country gains bargaining power.[35] After the firm has been in the host country a long time and its investment has grown, the host country gains increased bargaining power. Thus the host country can make legal demands on the firm with less fear that the firm will simply leave and move to another developing country. Another source of protection for the host country stems from the firm's own responsibility to monitor its overseas operations. Whether the issue is product safety, working conditions, salaries, pollution, or cooperation with a repressive dictatorship, managers have the responsibil-

---

[35] For a more complete discussion of this and other issues, see Cavanagh and McGovern, *Ethical Dilemmas in the Modern Corporation*, chap. 8. On the increased bargaining power model, see Theodore H. Moran, ed., *Multinational Corporations* (Lexington: Lexington Books, 1985), chap. 5.

ity to make conscientious decisions that are in the long-term interest of both the firm and the local people.

Thus the values and ethics of managers have a profound influence not only on domestic workers, suppliers, customers, and other stakeholders but also on stakeholders in many countries around the world. The very fact that a given person in a third world country has a job has a dramatic influence on that person and on his or her values and life style. In addition, the safety standards a firm sets, how it deals with its own pollution, the participative role it encourages local workers to have, the quality of the products it produces and markets locally—all are heavily influenced by the values and ethics of managers.

VALUES OF FREE ENTERPRISE

Let us return to the values of free enterprise. We have sketched above the short-term, materialistic, self-interest orientation of Americans. Moreover, many lament a decline in personal initiative in American society. Businesspeople point to a lack of the entrepreneurial spirit. Control Data founder William Norris calls the United States a "risk-avoiding, selfish society." He says that our emphasis on immediate payoffs has led to the spread of bureaucratic attitudes and thinking.

> But big business is not alone [in this]. It shares its apathetic, risk-avoiding, selfish, and reactionary profile with other sectors, including academia, organized labor, private foundations, the churches, and government.[36]

The intrusion of government bureaucracy and the growth of a sense of entitlement are blamed by many for this new frame of mind according to which one should try to do the least amount of work for the best possible pay.[37]

Michael Novak has also examined the roots of the entrepreneural spirit.[38] According to him, the distinguishing feature of democratic capitalism is that it encourages individuals to be the main source of social and economic energy. In fact, its past success in the United States puts it in a vulnerable position: Democratic capitalism is envied by poorer nations and criticized as

---

[36]William Norris, "A Risk-avoiding, Selfish Society," *Business Week*, January 28, 1980, p. 20.

[37]Dow Votaw, "The New Equality: Bureaucracy's Trojan Horse," *California Management Review*, 20 (Summer 1978): 5–17.

[38]Michael Novak, "Toward a Theology of the Corporation," in *Business and Society: Dimensions of Conflict and Cooperation*, ed. P. Sethi and C. Falbe (Lexington: Lexington Books, 1987), pp. 1–20; idem., *The Spirit of Capitalism* (New York: Simon & Schuster, 1982).

exploitative. Moreover, parents who grew up in poverty do not know how to bring up their children under affluence. Both of these factors blunt the spirit of innovation and the attitudes that encourage the entrepreneur.

Self-Interest as a Goal

The predominant business ideology in the United States holds that when firms and individuals pursue their own self-interest, market forces and the "invisible hand" bring about the most efficient use of resources and result in the greatest satisfaction of people's needs. According to the ideology of self-interest, the best that IBM can do for society is to provide quality computers at a reasonable price and, in so doing, provide a good return to shareholders. This is IBM's contribution to society. If IBM fails in this, it is a failure as a business firm.

The ideology of self-interest has worked well for generations in the United States. It is justified by economic theory and blessed by the Protestant ethic. (The Protestant ethic will be discussed in the next chapter.) Individuals and businesses pursuing their own self-interest have taken the United States and much of the industrialized world fast and far in economic development. Acquisitiveness, coupled with creativity, has made our economic system successful. The ideology of self-interest acknowledges that people tend to be selfish. Capitalism (or free enterprise) builds on this and directs it to work for the benefit of the entire society. Nobel prize–winning economist Milton Friedman is the intellectual spokesperson for the ideology of self-interest.[39]

Economic goals—increasing productivity, personal income, gross national product, and the availability of more and better goods—are even said to be the most important goals of our society. As president Calvin Coolidge stated it, "The business of America is business."

However, challenges to this ideology arose early in the Industrial Revolution, when there were sweatshops, for example, that employed ten-year-olds for seventy-hour work weeks. Similar challenges have arisen with respect to more current issues, such as pollution. Although it was in the interest of firms—because it maximized profits—to use cheap child labor and to not pay for the safe disposal of pollutants, it was not good for the rest of society. The pursuit of self-interest partly caused these problems in the first instance, and one can hardly expect that same motive to bring a solution.

To narrow the purpose of firms to the making of profit for shareholders is shortsighted. Kenneth Mason, when president of Quaker Oats, said, "Making a profit is no more the purpose of a corporation than getting enough to eat is the purpose of life. Getting enough to eat is a requirement of life; life's

---

[39] Milton Friedman and Rose Friedman, *Free to Choose: A Personal Statement* (New York: Harcourt Brace Jovanovich, 1980); see also Milton Friedman's earlier and better reasoned *Capitalism and Freedom* (Chicago: University of Chicago Press, 1962).

purpose, one would hope, is somewhat broader and more challenging. Likewise with business and profit."[40]

Moreover, an exclusive focus on self-interest can breed an arrogance in pursuing narrow goals, a self-righteousness resulting in indifference to consequences. These attitudes are described flippantly as "creative greed." Consider the values and tactics of raiders James Goldsmith and T. Boone Pickens. Critics note that the system thus honors those who are most aggressive in their greed; rewards them with money, power, and status; and thus reinforces selfishness and narrowness of vision.

The successes of Master of Business Administration graduates indicate their values and ethics. As one executive graphically puts it, "In my business I'd as soon take a python to bed with me as hire [a Harvard MBA]. He'd suck my brains, memorize my Rolodex, and use my telephone to find some other guy who'd pay him twice the money."[41]

Chief executive officer of Johnson & Johnson, James Burke, a Harvard MBA graduate himself, explains why his firm rarely hires such graduates:

> The problem begins with the selection process. If you lean heavily on test scores, you necessarily end up with people who are very adept at quantification. And human nature being what it is, people who are good at numbers tend to put a lot of faith in numbers. Which means that kids are coming out of business schools with less and less language skills, less and less people skills, and more and more to unlearn. The really important decisions don't have anything to do with quantification, as everyone figures out—eventually.[42]

Defenders of the ideology of self-interest have responded by maintaining that they speak of "enlightened" self-interest, that is, self-interest taken over the long-term. It is in the long-term self-interest of a manager and a firm to produce high-quality goods in order to maintain the loyalty of customers. So, too, with safe and attractive working conditions that help to hold able employees. Contributions to universities are justified because graduates will benefit the firm's community and the firm itself. Indeed, recent research indicates that a firm that is more socially responsible, obeys the law, and contributes more to charities does have a better financial performance.[43]

When reflecting on the purpose of the economy and society, some conclude that money and wealth are instruments of bringing work and goods

[40] Kenneth W. Mason, "Responsibility for What's on the Tube," *Business Week*, August 13, 1979, p. 14.

[41] Laurence Shames, *The Big Time: The Harvard Business School's Most Successful Class and How It Shaped America* (New York: Mentor, 1986), pp. 181–82.

[42] Ibid., p. 182.

[43] Richard E. Wokutch and Barbara A. Spencer, "Corporate Saints and Sinners: Philanthropy, Crime and Organizational Performance," *California Management Review* 29 (Winter 1987): 62–77.

to people and are not ends in themselves.[44] When money and wealth become ends in themselves, values, priorities, and ethics are altered as a result. Spelling out the cost of this skewing of purpose, Oliver Williams says, "Capitalism without a context in a humane community would seem to inevitably shape people into greedy and insensitive human beings."[45]

Individualism, Commitment, and Community

Many Americans believe that the emphasis on self-interest and freedom of the individual contributes to a lessening of cooperation, commitment, and community. Consider the eloquent words of Robert Bellah and his coauthors:

> Freedom is perhaps the most resonant, deeply held American value. In some ways, it defines the good in both personal and political life. Yet freedom turns out to mean being left alone by others, not having other people's values, ideas, or styles of life forced upon one, being free of arbitrary authority in work, family, and political life. What it is that one might do with that freedom is much more difficult for Americans to define. And if the entire social world is made up of individuals, each endowed with the right to be free of others' demands, it becomes hard to forge bonds of attachment to, or cooperation with, other people, since such bonds would imply obligations that necessarily impinge on one's freedom.[46]

One of the most basic human needs is to share joys, problems, and aspirations with others. Our deep-rooted values of individualism and self-interest, which support a free enterprise system, can nevertheless fracture community and turn the individual in on himself or herself. Our social system, responding to people's material wants and the resulting demands of the economic system, values the person who is mobile, energetic, creative, and ambitious. People of this type were attracted to the New World and have thrived here in succeeding generations. We as a society, however, have rarely acknowledged the negative qualities of people of this type. Granted, the New World gained and encouraged the energetic and the daring; it also drew more than its share of "the rootless, the unscrupulous, those who value money over relationships, and those who put self-aggrandizement ahead of love and loyalty." More critically, we gained and encouraged people who,

---

[44] Charles C. West, "The Common Good and the Participation of the Poor," in *The Common Good and U.S. Capitalism*, ed. Oliver F. Williams and John W. Houck (Lanham, Md.: University Press of America, 1987), pp. 20–21; see also Amitai Etzioni, *The Moral Dimension: Toward A New Economics* (New York: The Free Press, 1988).

[45] Oliver F. Williams, "To Enhance the Common Good: An Introduction," in *The Common Good and U.S. Capitalism*, ed. Oliver F. Williams and John W. Houck (Lanham, Md.: University Press of America, 1987), p. 5.

[46] Robert N. Bellah et al., *Habits of the Heart: Individualism and Commitment in American Life* (New York: Harper & Row, 1985), p. 23.

"when faced with a difficult situation, tended to chuck the whole thing and flee to a new environment."[47] The same qualities that we value so highly— mobility and willingness to take risks—encourage us to flee the difficult situation in the hope of leaving our problems behind when we begin again. We have all seen the lives and careers that have been shattered when a person walks out, whether it be on a firm, a group of friends, or a marriage. It is easy to escape long-term responsibility in the tolerant, freedom-loving United States if one has a mind to do so.

Two current trends in political life accelerate the loss of community in the Unites States: Narrow special interests are now stronger and more vocal, and there is a paralyzing lack of consensus regarding national priorities and direction. The confrontational mode of dealing with others has long been a part of the American way. Not only do we use the adversary system in the law courts, but we have institutionalized conflict generally (e.g., labor versus management, business versus government). The rhetoric is one of "battle" and "struggle," "win or lose," as if a loss for one group is a win for another. Special interest groups have gathered in the political arena to push for their narrow objectives, including the American Medical Association (physicians), National Educational Association (public school teachers), auto dealers, anti-abortionists, and the New Right, who target members of Congress who are not to their liking. A lack of communication and trust grows at a time when cooperation is badly needed.

When Americans are able to agree on an issue, the consensus always involves opposition to something: taxes, big government, bureaucrats. But we Americans find it hard to tell others what we stand *for*—what kind of a society we *favor*. We are not at ease in expressing social ideals and we lack the vocabulary. We have not been aided by our national political discussions, which appeal to simplistic ideologies and fail to aid us in sorting out priorities and balancing the resulting tradeoffs, which we must do if we are to decide what sort of society we want. These failures of the political forum tend to encourage Americans to be deaf to others' views and distrustful of one another. Finding a common bond and developing a sense of community become both more important and more difficult.

SUMMARY AND CONCLUSIONS

The United States economy has been successful over the past generation in providing both goods and jobs for hundreds of millions of people. Free markets, competition, flexibility, and innovation are all strongly held values

---

[47] Philip Slater, *The Pursuit of Loneliness* (Boston: Beacon Press, 1970), p. 14.

of U.S. society. On the other hand, increasing debt, lessened productivity, hostile takeovers, and advertising also stem from those same values.

Capital markets are designed to provide funds for new projects, which in turn provide jobs and products. Speculation is secondary, and unnecessarily injuring stakeholders is unethical. Self-interest motivates business and our society. Advertising and the media encourage self-interest. Excessive self-interest undermines loyalty, family, community, and obligations to others. The following chapters will examine the historical roots and the effects of American business values.

DISCUSSION QUESTIONS

1. Why do Americans choose to consume more and save less than people in other countries? How does this affect (a) productivity and (b) values?
2. Outline the reasons why management bears prime responsibility for poor productivity in the Unites States.
3. What is the evidence for a loss of confidence in American business?
4. What analogy does Kenneth Mason, former president of Quaker Oats, use in rejecting Milton Friedman's position that the purpose of a corporation is to maximize returns to shareholders?
5. Is self-interest as a personal motivation a correct description of most business activities as we find them?
6. Is self-interest an adequate motivation for businesspeople? When is it most effective? When is it least adequate?
7. Does self-interest as a goal for businesspeople necessarily cast government in the role of a regulator? How so?
8. What causes most of the cases of cancer in men and women? What are the implications of this for private sector planning? For public policy?
9. In what way does advertising influence values? Does advertising present a false and deceptive image to citizens?

CASES

College Test

Joe Fontana and Kathy Blakenship, Lincoln University Business School juniors, are both taking a basic finance course taught by Hugh Pleasant. Kathy is an honor student. Joe is not a top student but is a friendly young man. On the first exam, Kathy scored the second highest grade in the class and Joe failed. The next exam, more heavily weighted, was given the following month. During the exam Hugh noticed Joe glancing in the direction of Kathy's paper several times. When grading the papers, Pleasant noted all fifteen multiple choice items to be identical on Joe's and Kathy's papers, including four responses that were incorrect. 1. You are a student sitting behind Joe, and you see what he is doing. Do you have any responsibility to speak to Joe? To the instructor? 2. As the instructor, you notice Joe's activities during the exam. What should you do? Why? 3. As you grade the papers, you note the identical items on the exam. What should (or would) you do?

Latin American Plant

You are president of Cero Corp, which is planning to set up operations in a Latin American country. For the plant location you have a choice of two countries which are relatively equal in wage rates, resources, and marketing opportunities. The first is a democracy much like the United States, with elections, labor unions, and building and pollution control requirements. The second is a stable dictatorship which outlaws unions and labor disruptions, has but one strong central authority to deal with, and is very friendly to American business. Which country would you recommend to your board of directors for the plant site? Why?

EXERCISE: PERSONAL VALUES AND LIFE GOAL INVENTORY

This exercise is designed to help clarify your own personal values and to see how these values support or conflict with your life goals.

I. *Procedure:*
   A. Rank order the two sets of values on the *value survey* below (fifteen long-range values).
   B. Complete the *life goal inventory.*
      1. Write out your major goals for the next one to two years in each of the areas indicated.
   C. Write a paper (four to five double-spaced typed pages) examining and comparing your most important values and your life and career goals. It is not necessary to turn in the completed order of personal values or the completed life goal inventory.
II. *Criterion* for evaluating the paper: demonstration of the ability to analyze and articulate your own values and goals. Such demonstration includes the following.
   A. Clarity of analysis of goals and values.
   B. Ability to *recognize* and deal with the *implications of* conflicts in values and goals, and their significance for future career and life style decisions.
III. *Suggestions* for writing the paper.
   A. Write in the first, not the third, person.
   B. Include a paragraph or two of personal history to put your values and

goals in context. What events in your life have affected your values and goals?

   C. Discuss at least briefly each of the five goals but deal only with the most important values.

      1. What do these values imply about personal goals? Do your values support your goals? Or do they conflict?

      2. Compare present activities, job, etc., with these values.

      3. Any particular satisfaction or frustration that might be explained by support from or conflict between values and goals?

      4. Clarify points with specific personal experiences and examples.

   D. Write reflections honestly and straightforwardly. No one else will see your paper. It is confidential.

   E. The values and goals sheets are to help you in *your* analysis. Use them to help you in writing your paper.

   F. Use clear language and good grammar. Choose directness and clarity over elaboration.

IV. *Apologies* for intruding into your personal values. Experience indicates that most of us do not explicitly reflect on our goals and values unless (1) we are asked to do so or (2) a crisis arises in our lives. The paper will enable you to gain a better understanding of yourself.

Rank Ordering of Personal Values

Rank the following fifteen long-range personal values in order of importance to *you*, that is, insofar as they are guiding principles in your life. Study the list of possible goals carefully. Place a 1 in front of the value that is most important in your life, a 2 in front of the next most important, and so on. The least most important value for you should be ranked 15. If you change your mind, feel free to change the ranking.

When you are finished, the list should indicate as accurately as possible the importance of the various values in your life.

_____ Achievement (promotions at work)

_____ Beauty (natural and artistic beauty)

_____ Dollar rewards (money and salary)

_____ Equality (equal opportunity for all; everyone as equal)

_____ Family security (taking care of and being with loved ones)

_____ Freedom (independence)

_____ Love, friendship, and intimacy

_____ Physical health and well-being

_____ Pleasure (a sensually and sexually enjoyable personal life)

_____ Possessions (good car, clothes, home, many material goods)

_____ Recognition (respect, admiration from others)

_____ Self-respect (a good self-image, self-esteem)

_____ Sense of accomplishment (making a lasting contribution)

_____ Union with God (prayer, striving to be a good person)

_____ World at peace (lessening of war and conflict)

Life Goal Inventory

This inventory is designed to help you examine your life goals. Describe as fully as possible your aims and goals in all areas of your life. List all goals that are important to you, whether they are fairly easy or difficult to attain. Be honest in this assessment; only then will the inventory be useful to you. If your major goal is to recreate, indicate this so as to better understand and assess yourself. The categories are a guide; feel free to change them to suit your own life. It may be easier to indicate your goals for the next year or two. In your own words, describe two to five goals in each of the following areas.

Career Satisfaction

Goals for future job or career; specific positions aimed for.

1.

2.

3.

Personal Relationships

With friends, parents, spouse, colleagues, others.

1.

2.

3.

Leisure Satisfactions

Vacations, sports, hobbies, other interests.

1.

2.

3.

Learning and Education

New skills you would like to learn or areas of knowledge you would like to study.

1.

2.

3.

Spiritual Growth and Religion

Relation to God, prayer, giving self to others, larger questions.

1.

2.

3.

CHAPTER TWO
ESTABLISHING
AMERICAN VALUES

Probe the earth and see where your main roots are.

Henry David Thoreau

The lives of Americans are strongly influenced by their values. Some of these values are unique; others also occur in other cultures. Values can be better understood to the extent we know their origins. Our ancestors' experiences can help us understand current American values and ideologies.

This chapter examines the people, events, and commentators that have influenced American values. It then focuses on the origin, function of, and content of American business values and ideology.

Values and ideologies are not merely theoretical statements of purpose; they can also motivate people to act (see Figure 1–1 for definitions). They typically function as rationales for action. An ideology provides answers to such questions as these: What are my most important activities and values? How do I explain those actions and values to others? How do I defend my life and values when they are criticized from either inside or outside the group?

An ideology also embodies accepted ideals, the ultimate goals possessed by an individual or a society. Thus ideals can significantly influence values. Ideals are sometimes distant, whereas values affect actions. Unless ideals are integrated into an ideology, they do not have much influence on actions and choices. We can gain insight into our lives and values by examining the major ideologies and ideals that played a role in American history. Let us now learn from our forebears.

EARLY AMERICANS AND ENTERPRISE

The immigrants who came to the New World risked their lives and their fortunes in the hope of finding freedom and new opportunities. They came to a land that seemed to have limitless natural resources—timber, coal, much good farming land. Clearing the land was backbreaking, but the result was good, fertile acreage that could be handed on to one's children. The changing climate encouraged work—it was brisk and invigorating—and the winters, when there would be no fruits or crops, demanded that settlers plan ahead and save something from the harvest. Two wide oceans provided natural defenses that until recently allowed the New World to focus on its own needs and development without much fear of foreign intrusions.

All these natural characteristics affected the values and ideology of the people. But when the settlers came, they also brought with them their own values and ideals that heavily influenced their attitudes. Most of the early American immigrants were religious people. In fact, many of those who came to the colonies did so largely because of religious persecution in their native countries; they sought a land where they could live and pray as conscience dictated. The men and women who settled along the coasts came from Europe and so brought with them the religion that predominated there—Christianity. Of these groups, the Puritans, who came very early, probably had the most profound influence on early American values and ideology.

The Puritans fled Europe so that they might freely follow their anti-hierarchical religious faith and practices. To these men and women, who came well before the American Revolution, their work or their "calling" was an essential part of their total world view. To us today, the Puritan ideal is a delicate, even mysterious, paradox. Puritan preacher John Cotton (1584–1652) described it thus:

> There is another combination of virtues strangely mixed in every lively, holy Christian: and that is, diligence in worldly business, and yet deadness to the world. Such a mystery as none can read but they that know it.[1]

Puritans plunged into their work with a dedication that could come only because it was their calling. In John Cotton's words, "First, faith draws the heart of a Christian to live in some warrantable calling ... though it be of

---

[1] Perry Miller, *The American Puritans* (Garden City, N.Y.: Doubleday, 1956), p. 171.

an hired servant."[2] Worship of God was not shown in hymn singing, colorful religious services, or sterile monasticism; worship was a simple, reverent prayer. Moreover, the Puritans' prayer was not separated from work, for work was their most effective means of giving glory to God. So work was disciplined and clear-eyed, because "when he serves man, he serves the Lord; he doth the work set before him and he doth it sincerely and faithfully so as he may give account for it."[3] This early Puritan ideology strengthened the emerging social order by giving importance to every type of work. Again, in John Cotton's words, "[faith] encourageth a man in his calling to the most homeliest and difficultest and most dangerous things his calling can lead and expose himself to."[4] Self-discipline was also important, for Puritans were not to be caught up in their own success or failure. They were ascetics in the world; although in it, they were detached from it.

Two generations later, Cotton Mather (1663–1728) was born into the same family of erudition and clerical leadership. Like his grandfather, Mather held that "A Christian has two callings: (1) a general calling 'to serve the Lord Jesus Christ,' and (2) a particular calling which was his work or his business. Both of these callings are essential if the Christian is to achieve salvation. The Puritan divine says, 'Contemplation of the good means nothing without accomplishment of the good. A man must not only be pious; he must be useful.'"[5] The Puritan businessman fully integrated his work with his worship. Often he would mention God in his invoices, thanking him for a profit or accepting losses for his greater glory. Moreover, each individual determined his or her calling, and work was generally done individually. In the same fashion, people achieved salvation individually.

American Puritans did not invent this position; they took the theology of John Calvin and spelled out in some detail the implications for the businessman. The businessman in turn, eager for some justification of the efforts to which he devoted most of his waking hours, happily received the Puritan preacher's words. So there began the mutual understanding and support between preacher and businessman that became a hallmark of New World society.

Benjamin Franklin's Way to Wealth

In the prerevolutionary period, Benjamin Franklin accepted the work values of the Puritans, shifted them from a religious to a secular foundation, and restated them for Americans. Franklin, especially in *Poor Richard's Al-*

---

[2] Ibid., p. 173.

[3] John Cotton, quoted in Miller, *The American Puritans*, p. 176.

[4] Ibid., p. 177.

[5] A. Whitney Griswold, "Two Puritans on Prosperity," in *Benjamin Franklin and the American Character*, ed. Charles L. Sanford (Boston: D. C. Heath, 1955), p. 41.

manack, was prolific, mundane, incisive, and widely influential. Many of his homely bits of advice have become embedded in our language and now belong to us all. Looking back over twenty-five years of his *Almanack,* Franklin brought together his writings on the world of work and of business and published them in 1758 as the essay "The Way to Wealth."

> God helps them that help themselves.... Diligence is the mother of good luck, as Poor Richard says, and God gives all things to industry. Then plough deep, while sluggards sleep, and you shall have corn to sell and to keep, says Poor Dick. Work while it is called today, for you know not how much you may be hindered tomorrow.... Be ashamed to catch yourself idle.... When there is so much to be done for yourself, your family, your country, and your gracious king, be up at peep of day; ...'Tis true that much is to be done, and perhaps you are weak handed, but stick to it steadily, and you will see great effects, for constant dropping wears away stones ... and little strokes fell great Oaks.[6]

In his own simple way, Franklin focuses on the importance of saving and the need for capital when he notes that "a man may, if he knows not how to save as he gets, keep his nose all his life to the grindstone.... If you would be wealthy, think of saving as well as of getting."[7] It must have been immensely satisfying to Franklin's early American contemporaries to see him supporting the same values and justification for their work as did their ministers. He provided a rationale for work and a purpose for life; at the same time, he buttressed the existing social order.

Franklin's writings were best sellers in his day and have exerted a tremendous influence up to the present. In his *Almanack,* his *Autobiography,* and his own life, Franklin embodied the Puritan virtues. Here was a man who was eminently successful as an inventor, statesman, diplomat, and business-man and who espoused the same virtues as did the Puritan ministers. Although some aristocrats of his day, such as John Adams, resented Franklin's popular wisdom, he was held in esteem by the people. Harvard-educated John Adams was a New England patrician: brilliant and courageous but also haughty and stubborn. Adams conceded that Franklin was a genius, a wit, a politician, and a humorist, but he questioned his greatness as a philosopher, a moralist, or a statesman.[8] In spite of Adams's petty quarrels with Franklin, history shows Franklin to have had a greater influence on values. Thomas Jefferson agreed with the hard-working, individualistic ideals of Franklin, although Jefferson, who wrote the *Declaration of Independence,* was convinced that these virtues could best be fostered in, and the new nation grow best as,

---

[6]Benjamin Franklin, *The Autobiography and Other Writings* (New York: New American Library, 1961), p. 190.

[7]Ibid., p. 192.

[8]For this essay, see John Adams, "An Exaggerated Reputation," in Sanford, *Benjamin Franklin,* pp. 22–26.

an agricultural society.[9] Jefferson felt that as long as one had one's own land to till and crops to care for, the economy would thrive and people would be happier.

At this time more than 80 percent of the American work force were farmers, and if Jefferson had had his way, that is how it would have remained. Jefferson was opposed to the industrialization he had seen in England. He would rather import finished manufactured goods than undergo the undesirable changes manufacturing inevitably brings: urbanization, landless workers, banking. In an agricultural society, where work and initiative immediately pay off for the individual and for the society as a whole, government intervention could be kept to an absolute minimum. It could only retard the natural forces of growth and encumber society with additional overhead, regulations, and bureaucracy. In Jefferson's own oft-quoted words, "That government is best which governs least." The ambivalent feelings toward and even fear of industry appeared early, for industry spawns cities. An agrarian society is simpler; duties and rewards are more easily seen and measured. Early Americans were therefore not always favorably disposed toward industry or cities.

The American Frontier

The continuing westward expansion served to keep alive the simpler, measurable agrarian values. The effect of this westward movement and the frontier on the American character was spelled out by Fredrick Jackson Turner[10] just before the turn of the twentieth century. For successive waves of hunters, traders, ranchers, and finally farmers, there were always new lands to conquer. It seemed to be a world without limits. The Indians were nomadic, and there were few of them to offer resistance. For the brave and hearty immigrant, it was worth taking great risks, whether in moving or in building. Success meant wealth; failure, the chance to try again somewhere else.

The new territories demanded the strenuous labor of clearing the land. The first farmers faced the immense task of pulling out trees and building their homes and barns. Nevertheless, the rewards were also great: They would have homes and incomes and could pass on those farms to their children. The rewards were clear, tangible, and permanent, and they gave settlers incentive and zest. The land is measurable and unambiguous. It is open to human effort; if one works harder, one will be able to produce more.

---

[9] Arthur M. Schlesinger, "Ideas and Economic Development," in *Paths of American Thought*, ed. Arthur M. Schlesinger, Jr., and Morton White (Boston: Houghton Mifflin, 1963), pp. 108–9.

[10] Frederick Jackson Turner, *The Frontier in American History* (New York: Holt, 1920).

Turner himself sums up how the frontier has given the American intellect its striking characteristics:

> That coarseness and strength combined with acuteness and inquisitiveness; that practical, inventive turn of mind, quick to find expedients; that masterful grasp of material things, lacking in the artistic but powerful to effect great ends; that restless, nervous energy; that dominant individualism, working for good and for evil, and withal that buoyancy and exuberance which comes with freedom—these are traits of the frontier or traits called out elsewhere because of the existence of the frontier.[11]

Turner's thesis has been widely quoted and has had a great influence on thinkers and on men and women of affairs. Although there are few new physical lands to conquer, current challenges demand something of the same creativity, risk taking, energy, and sense of purpose.

Tocqueville's View of Americans

As anyone who has lived in another culture knows, the peculiar characteristics of that culture stand out in bold relief to the foreigner. In that same process, of course, one is also far better able to recognize the unique qualities of one's own culture. A people's characteristic values and ideology can best be understood in comparison with those of another culture. Thus a perceptive foreign visitor often is able to describe the values and characteristics of the host people with penetrating insight. As an example, Alexis de Tocqueville has remained one of the best commentators on the American character.

A young French lawyer, Alexis de Tocqueville came to the United States in 1831 to observe and learn from the people. His reflections, which he set down in his book *Democracy in America*, were intended for the French, but they attained instant success not only in France but in England and the United States as well. Published in English translation in 1838, *Democracy in America* was immediately praised for its insight and lack of bias, and it is still regarded, 150 years later, as one of the finest commentaries on American life. Tocqueville tried to understand Americans on their own terms. The well-known leader of English liberalism, John Stuart Mill, reviewed Tocqueville's work and was deeply impressed with it.[12]

On arriving, Tocqueville noted the physical expanse of the new country: "The inhabitants of the U.S. constitute a great civilized people, which fortune has placed in the midst of an uncivilized country."[13] It was this same

---

[11] Ibid., p. 37.

[12] For the substance of the review, see the introduction to *Democracy in America*, trans. Henry Reeve, vol. 1 (New York: Knopf, 1946), pp. xxix-xl.

[13] Ibid., vol. 1, p. 422.

combination, of course, which was to help give rise to the independence, resourcefulness, and frontier spirit of which Fredrick Jackson Turner was later to write. Tocqueville noticed that, preoccupied by the great task to be accomplished, Americans tended to value facts more than consistent ideals, that which works more than the beauty of a comprehensive ideological system. He characterized the American "philosophical method," the American method of reflection and learning, as "to evade the bondage of system and habit, of family maxims, class opinions, and, in some degree, of national prejudices." Americans accepted tradition only as a starting point, the existing situation only "as a lesson to be used in doing otherwise and in doing better."[14] Each individual seeks to understand for him- or herself. All these characteristics Tocqueville summed up as an individualism of thought: "Each American appeals only to the individual effort of his own understanding." This mentality shows that what we today call the generation gap is no new thing: "Every man there readily loses all traces of the ideas of his forefathers or takes no care about them."[15]

Tocqueville saw Americans as hardworking and individualistic. The only rationale they might have for their actions and attitudes is enlightened self-interest. They are not inclined to reverence tradition, to philosophize, or even to engage in much reflection. He focused on the same favorable attitude toward work that has been attributed to the Puritan, the immigrant, and the frontier settler. Americans see work "as the necessary, natural, and honest condition of human existence."[16] Labor is not only not dishonorable, it is held in honor among the people. Even the rich person feels the obligation to take up some sort of worthwhile work, whether this work be private or public.

When Americans were asked *why* they work, act, and think as they do, Tocqueville reported that they gave a rather consistent response:

> The Americans…are fond of explaining almost all the actions of their lives by the principle of self-interest rightly understood; they show with complacency how an enlightened regard for themselves constantly prompts them to assist one another and inclines them willingly to sacrifice a portion of their time and property to the welfare of the state.[17]

Although not unique to America, by the time of Tocqueville's visit enlightened self-interest had taken firm root here. In the generation following the publication of *Democracy in America*, social Darwinism was to make even more popular the doctrine that acting self-interestedly contributes to the common good, as we shall see later.

[14] Ibid., vol. 2, p. 3.
[15] Ibid., vol. 2, p. 4.
[16] Ibid., vol. 2, p. 152.
[17] Ibid., vol. 2, p. 122.

Enlightened self-interest: Norm for assessing self-interest used by a person who is mature and enlightened and who takes the long view.

Individualism: A view that all values, rights, and duties originate in the individual and that the community or social whole has no value or ethical significance not derived from the individual constitutents.

Norm: Criterion for distinguishing right from wrong.

Self-interest: Norm for thinking and acting that focuses on the benefits and advantages accruing to oneself.

Selfishness: Concern for oneself without regard for others.

FIGURE 2-1   Definitions of Self-Interest Terms

With remarkable insight, Tocqueville underscored both the strengths and the weaknesses of this philosophy. The principle of self-interest does not entail lofty goals, but it is clear and certain. It does not demand much of a person, yet acting in accordance with it does produce results. It is not difficult to understand for all sorts and classes of people. As a principle of human life, self-interest builds on peoples' infirmities:

> By its admirable conformity to human weaknesses it easily obtains great dominion; nor is that dominion precarious, since the principle checks one personal interest by another, and uses, to direct the passions, the very same instrument that excites them.[18]

The principle of enlightened self-interest produces no great acts of self-sacrifice, but it encourages a daily discipline of self-denial. By itself self-interest cannot make people good and virtuous and hence can hardly serve as a cornerstone of morality. Nevertheless, said Tocqueville, "it disciplines large numbers of people in habits of regularity, temperance, moderation, foresight, self-command."

Enlightened self-interest (see Figure 2–1) is closely related to individualism. Tocqueville's work was the first to discuss individualism and, in fact, the first to bring the word into the English language. It is characteristic of Americans that individualism was not a common word among them, even though it so well described some of their salient attitudes and values. People develop a vocabulary for those things of concern to them, those things they therefore want to discuss. Americans were not then, nor are they now, a very reflective people. Tocqueville suggested that there was probably no other civilized country in which less attention was paid to reflection and philosophy than the United States.

[18] Ibid., vol 2, pp. 122–23.

Tocqueville described individualism as a mature and calm feeling which disposes each member of the community "to sever himself from the mass of his fellows and to draw apart with his family and his friends." Each individual retreats to his or her own familiar turf and thus "leaves society at large to itself." The Frenchman contrasted individualism and selfishness, and he found both seriously deficient:

> Selfishness originates in blind instinct; individualism proceeds from erroneous judgment more than from depraved feelings; it originates as much in deficiencies of the mind as in perversity of heart.
> Selfishness blights the germ of all virtue; individualism, at first, only saps the virtues of public life; but in the long run it attacks and destroys all others and is at length absorbed in downright selfishness.[19]

Tocqueville pinpointed possibly the most serious weakness of the American character. Enlightened self-interest and individualism narrow one's perspective. They encourage one to think less of public responsibilities, and they lead eventually, and almost inevitably, to selfishness. He almost sounded like a contemporary critic reflecting on the weaknesses of the corporate executive or the bureaucrat. Tocqueville's sensitive assessment of the American character—its impatience with tradition, reflection, and abstract ideals; its task-orientation and individualism; its self-interest leading to selfishness—still stands as one of the great social commentaries. Later observers often used Tocqueville as a starting point, but few have done a better overall appraisal than he.

Social Darwinism and Herbert Spencer

Herbert Spencer (1820–1903) proposed a harsh "survival of the fittest" philosophy. Spencer's thesis was that the bright and able contribute most to society and so are to be encouraged and rewarded. The poor, the weak, and the handicapped demand more than they contribute and so should not be supported but rather be allowed to die a natural death. Contact with harsh and demanding reality is a maturing experience that should not be diluted by well-intentioned but in reality destructive charities and handouts. If "natural" principles were followed, evolution and the survival of the fittest in the competition of human life would be the result. Spencer did not set out to examine any particular society and its values; rather, his critique was proposed as "culture-free." According to Spencer, it applied to all people, for it was derived from basic, organic principles of growth and development. Spencer applied to society the same principles that Charles Darwin saw in biological life—hence the name *social Darwinism*.

[19] Ibid., vol. 2, p. 98.

The events of the latter half of the nineteenth century had a profound impact on attitudes. The Industrial Revolution, the growth of cities, and the beginning of the concept of evolution shook the foundations of life and thought. Speaking of evolution, the contemporary American historian Richard Hofstadter has said, "Many scientific discoveries affect ways of living more profoundly than evolution did; but none have had a greater impact on ways of thinking and believing."[20]

Spencer, William Graham Sumner, and others who became prophets of the new evolutionary social ideology were impressed by the suffering of the poor, but they nevertheless felt that progress in an industrial society could come only through long hours of work, saving, self-discipline, and even the death of the less able. Rather than considering this a tragedy, they were convinced that through this process of natural selection, those of greater talent, intelligence, and ability would survive and be successful. The physically and mentally handicapped, unable to compete successfully, are less apt to survive. It would be a mistake for the government to provide assistance to these handicapped and deficient persons. That would allow them to stay alive, and worse, to reproduce and so transmit their deficiencies to future generations.

Any attempt to minister to the needs of the poor or needy is misguided on several counts. It keeps alive those who are less able. It diverts the attention and abilities of able people who would be better off pursuing more profitable careers. And, finally, it insulates the less able from a sobering contact with harsh reality and poverty, an opportunity that might have jarred them from their complacency and encouraged them to work harder to better themselves. Although it might be painful to the weak in the short run, the overall good of society in the long run demands that these less fit individuals not be supported or encouraged. According to Spencer, society improves because of the survival of the fittest:

> The poverty of the incapable, the distresses that come upon the imprudent, the starvation of the idle, and those shoulderings aside of the weak by the strong, which leave so many "in shallows and in miseries," are the decrees of a large, farseeing benevolence.... Under the natural order of things society is constantly excreting its unhealthy, imbecile, slow, vacillating, faithless members.[21]

It is especially clear in primitive societies that the strongest and cleverest survive best. But this is a natural process, and so it occurs in civilized societies, too. People would be wise to prepare themselves and their children for this struggle.

[20] Richard Hofstadter, *Social Darwinism in American Thought* (New York: Braziller, 1959), p. 3.

[21] Herbert Spencer, *Social Statics* (London: Appleton, 1850), pp. 323–26, 353.

Society as a whole will benefit from this struggle for survival. Since the most intellectually and physically fit survive, the race will improve. Given a difficult and demanding environment, over several generations the ideal man and woman will develop. There should therefore be little state interference in this natural selection process. The state must not regulate industry, impose tariffs, give subsidies, establish a church, regulate entry into the professions, operate schools, or run the mail service. Most especially, the government must not provide for the poor, improve sanitation, or look to the health needs of the less able.[22]

Herbert Spencer's philosophy was far more popular in the United States than in his native England. His praise of the strong, clever, and aggressive individual was in keeping with the spirit of the times. Further, his theory of inevitable progress was received enthusiastically in a country already marked by general optimism. Spencer's thinking provided both a rational foundation for existing attitudes and a justification for many public and private practices. In the last third of the nineteenth century, Spencer was an influential leader of thought and a hero to many in the United States.

The personal attributes Spencer extolled are those that many hold to be necessary for a free enterprise system. The focus is on the hearty, adaptable individual in a hostile climate. Survival requires careful planning ahead, hard work, loyalty and responsibility to family, and individual self-sufficiency. And as radical as they may have seemed to his contemporaries, Spencer's theories were actually quite conservative in overtone. Spencer saw great good in the way things were; paradoxically, there was no need to change or to plan ahead on a national or local level. Since natural processes will inevitably produce the best people and the best society, any sort of government or even private intervention in the process will only hurt society in the long run. Citizens must repress their feelings of pity for the poor and allow natural processes to work themselves out. Although Spencer's theories challenged all the established theologies of the time and were thus opposed by most clergy, to others his position seemed a natural extension of the traditional Puritan ethic, especially its secularized counterpart as expressed by Benjamin Franklin. It is thus no surprise that Spencer's theories were enthusiastically received by the business community of his day.

Struggle for Survival

The businessperson, and especially the entrepreneur, has always found the world to be nothing less than a struggle for survival. One may want to be humane and conscientious, but one cannot afford to be. Herbert Spencer's

---

[22]See Donald Fleming, "Social Darwinism," in Schlesinger and White, *Paths of American Thought*, pp. 124–25.

theories of the survival of the fittest and what has come to be known as social Darwinism had an immense influence on the America of the late nineteenth century. In fact, it described the American experience.

William Graham Sumner (1840–1910) was a social science professor at Yale and a proponent of Spencerism. Sumner's father was an immigrant English workingman who taught his children the Puritan virtues of thrift, self-reliance, hard work, and discipline.[23] His son was convinced that egalitarianism, made fashionable by the French Revolution and the freeing of the slaves, would undermine the initiative and independent spirit that encourage the best people to develop their talents fully. According to Sumner, the less able and adept are jealous of the successes of the more talented and through the political process they will require the latter to support them. This perversion undermines the creativity and motivation of the better and more talented people. Sumner applauded the era in which people would work and live, not because of inherited position and status, but because they themselves chose to do so through the new democratic device of contract. He clashed with Yale president Noah Porter when the latter objected to Sumner's assigning Herbert Spencer's book to students, but he won the long-term battle with one of the first clear statements of academic freedom.

Sumner and Spencer urged a tight-fisted, unemotional aloofness. Both one self and one's wealth must be saved and not spent without chance of a good return on investment. Free emotions and spontaneity were suspect; a person could lose all in a lighthearted or thoughtless moment. In the same vein, Sumner urged that government should not intervene in social and economic affairs. The environment should be kept clear of restrictions, taxes, restraints, and other needless and even harmful laws and regulations.

The opposition was led by Lester F. Ward (1841–1913). Ward's view, expressed in his *Dynamic Sociology*, is that people should control their environment, not allow it to control them. Evolution and natural selection as outlined by Darwin led to change without direction and without goals. According to Ward, the great value of evolution and natural selection was that they had brought people to the position in which they found themselves now. Moreover, it was precisely in Ward's era that individuals became able to take over and control their own future and not leave it to blind chance. For him, it would have been the supreme paradox for men and women, now that they had discovered these natural laws and forces, to retreat and allow themselves to become victims of them. Ward labeled Spencerism a do-nothing philosophy. Let us now turn our attention to the fresh views of America by visitors to the United States.

---

[23] Donald Fleming, "Social Darwinism," in Schlesinger and White, *Paths of American Thought*, p. 128.

Americans as Seen from Abroad

One who has visited another country finds sharp contrasts with one's own culture. An outsider viewing a culture is sensitive to elements to which members of that culture are often blind. While Alexis de Tocqueville is a superb example of a foreigner who had insights about America, other visitors expressed important insights as well.

A century after Tocqueville another French observer, the Jesuit paleontologist Pierre Teilhard de Chardin, lived and worked in the United States for many years and noted many of the same qualities as did Tocqueville. Teilhard had a sympathetic view of the American character in spite of his own inclination for reflection and asceticism. Writing while on an expedition in the Gobi desert that included Americans, Teilhard said,

> People here are inclined to treat the Americans as a joke, but the more I see of them the more I admire their ability to work and get things done, and the kinder and more approachable I find them.... In my own branch of science it's the Americans who are showing us how we must set to work on the earth if we are to read its secret and make ourselves its masters.[24]

Granting the ability of Americans to get a job done, their orientation to action is also the source of much criticism. Many foreign observers see Americans as shallow and materialistic—more wedded to things than to people, more inclined to do than to reflect.

Let us examine some comments on the United States made by other foreign observers. Israeli writer Amos Oz says,

> America has promoted and spread all over the world the simple ideal of individual happiness. Various religions, civilizations and ideologies throughout history regarded happiness as a collective rather than an individual experience. Almost all of them are losing ground to that triumphant American vision of private happiness. Hundreds of millions of people, from Tokyo to Leningrad, from Cairo to Buenos Aires, dream of being happy in the American way.... But is the new global America, this international happiness-oriented village, a happy place? ... The popular American dream of living happily ever after, while dazzling the world, reminds me of the American landscape itself: plentiful, elusive, and forlorn.[25]

The chairman and cofounder of Sony Corporation of Japan, Akio Morita, is more positive:

[24] Pierre Teilhard de Chardin, *Letters from a Traveller*, trans. Rene Hague et al. (New York: Harper & Row, 1962), p. 106.

[25] Quoted in "To See Ourselves as Others See Us," *Time*, June 16, 1986, p. 52–53. Quoted with permission.

What I like about the Americans is their frankness, their openness. In America, I feel I can openly express whatever opinion I have, and it is welcomed, even if it conflicts with other opinions. In Japan, even among friends we can't have a difference of opinion—disagreement destroys friendship. But in America, a difference of opinion can make friends, bring people closer together. That open-mindedness and frontier spirit is why I am so comfortable in the U.S.[26]

The president of the African nation of Zambia, Kenneth Kaunda, has yet another assessment:

You have developed your science and technology in an admirable way, but I am not sure that you use the wonderful achievements in this particular field in the interest of men and women as God wants us to. This part of your culture could lead, if not corrected in good time, to the collapse not only of American but of the entire world civilization as we know it today. If this set of cultural values were to become the order of the day in our world, sooner rather than later, we would have a third world war in which no one would survive.[27]

The well-known French writer and expert on technology, Jean-Jacques Servan-Schreiber, examines education:

From my first days in the U.S., I have been a regular student and admirer of America. But today the U.S. faces a crisis in education. The level of primary and secondary education is well below the worldwide average. Young Americans entering college can hardly write a decent one-page text. They take little time and no pleasure in reading. They also ignore that there is a world of human beings outside the borders of the U.S. and they are confident that the U.S. remains No. 1 and unchallengeable.[28]

Foreign social commentators have felt the pulse of America and pointed to the strengths and weaknesses of the American character. They underscore our openness, flexibility, pragmaticism, and respect for individuals. But they also acknowledge our parochialism, lack of interest in other cultures and languages, materialism, and self-centeredness. It is essential that we be aware of our national character lest we uncritically be victims of our biases. Such awareness is even more important if we are to have any influence on our own values and the values of our nation. The necessity for rapid changes that must occur if we are to live and compete in the wider world adds urgency to this task.

The events of history and social commentators provide us with considerable insight into our origins and character. Examining these foundation values helps us to get a better grasp of our current business values. In the

[26] Quoted in "To See Ourselves."
[27] Quoted in "To See Ourselves."
[28] Quoted in "To See Ourselves."

past, the geography of the United States, combined with the attitudes and values of the people who settled it, gave our country a unique world position. It had rich and abundant farmland, protected east and west borders, a slowly retreating frontier, and a people imbued with the Puritan ethic. This ethic will be discussed in the next chapter, which also contains more on the history of attitudes toward business.

THE FUNCTION OF IDEOLOGIES

An ideology is a coherent, systematic, and moving statement of basic values and purpose. It is a constellation of values generally held by a group, and members of the group tend to support one another in that ideology. An ideology provides systematic answers to these questions: What are we about? Why are we doing this? How can I explain my life and my society to myself and to others?

An ideology is an explication of values. It is a spelling out of attitudes, feelings, and goals. Without an explicit ideology, a nation or group is left without clearly stated purposes and hence without a consensus or the drive that comes from purpose. When an ideology is spelled out, it can be examined, challenged, and altered as conditions change and new needs arise. It is then in the open for all to accept or reject as they see fit. When an ideology is not explicit, it is sometimes claimed that there is no ideology; but this is hardly true. The ideology is merely implicit, unspoken, and hence unexamined. This is a precarious position for any society, since questions which arise can thus cause confusion and chaos.

Ideologies possess certain common features. They are selective in the issues they treat and in the supporting evidence and arguments they use. They are straightforward and uncomplicated, even when the actual material is quite complicated. Their content is limited to what is publicly acceptable. Finally, although ideologies are answers to questions and hence address the intellect, they nevertheless do so in a manner that also engages the emotions. They can inspire and motivate men and women to cooperate and even undergo great hardship for the sake of a compelling goal.

The positive effect of an ideology is that it gives a people direction, coherence, norms, criteria, and motivation. It can bring clarity and assurance to the mind and hence vigor and enthusiasm to life and work. These are great advantages, especially to a society troubled by doubts and by lessened confidence in institutions and inadequate leadership. A group possessing an ideology is thus given meaning, direction, and drive. Nations and peoples have left their mark on history, whether for good or ill, almost to the extent to which they have fashioned for themselves a comprehensive and compelling ideology—for example, ancient Rome, Victorian England, and Nazi Germany.

Most of what we do of any substance flows from an often implicit ideology, everything from raising children to going to work, from conducting foreign policy to meeting neighbors. Even the position that ideologies are unnecessary or demeaning or oppressive is itself an ideology. Subgroups within a society, even the Rotary Club, possess some sort of constellation of values, however limited or narrow. Generally the more embracing a group, a movement, or a state, the more complete will be its ideology.

On the other hand, ideologies have some disadvantages. They can rigidify. They tend to lock persons and systems into classes, roles, and expectations. A doctrinaire ideology can cause fanaticism, intransigence, and uncompromising attitudes. It can impede progress and cause problems for those in the group who find difficulties with the ideology, often those who are the most innovative and talented. The group as a whole then tends to expend a great deal of effort on defending its position instead of looking to the future.

For Marxists, a society's ideology is the rationalization of privilege by the upper classes. These classes use this ideology to justify the arrangements that protect their own positions and interests by claiming that they are essential for the good of the country and for humanity. Marx calls this "collective illusion," another tool of oppression by the ruling classes. He makes the excellent point that this sort of ideology mistakes the contingent and historical situation for a permanent and natural one.

Today many people are suggesting that we examine our current place in history and spell out our national values and the ideology in which they are embedded. There is a similar need for a rationale for our business activities, and that is the subject of this book. Demands for an exposition of our ideology come from a variety of sources:

1. Many Americans are increasingly asking themselves, their peers, and their national leaders, What are we about? What are our goals? What is worth living for? Why?
2. Any successful effort to lessen government intervention demands that individuals nand organizations have their own clear sense of goals, ethics, and self-discipline—all of which takes into account the public interest and the common good.
3. As the population increases and we live closer together, we find that what one person does often infringes on others. For example, building new houses on farmlands, driving a fuel-inefficient and smog-producing automobile, or moving a plant to the water-scarce sunbelt—all these actions place burdens on other people. As managers, citizens, or government officials, we need criteria for making decisions that will affect others.
4. Disagreements over public policy—for example, pollution control, tax cuts, nuclear weapons and armaments—come back to the earlier questions as to what kind of society we want, what our collective priorities are, and the tradeoffs we are willing to bear. Special interest groups plead their own cause but do not address the common good. Americans often find it easier to agree on what they dislike than on the far more important question of what they like: their positive values, goals, and policies.

There is a need for answering these questions and clarifying personal and corporate values and goals. Each person is challenged to work out his or her own answers to basic value questions, to formulate his or her own constellation of values. Some consensus is necessary on these values and on public issues in order to have an effective and consistent national policy. Without an agreed upon ideology, decisions are often made using crass, unexamined, and immediate criteria or on the basis of a currently popular myth or shallow set of values. The agreed-upon values, especially those that touch on public life and issues, can be called an ideology. As such, they can provide direction and verve. And an awareness of the dangers of any ideology—for example, that it may be a mask for privilege or that it may rigidify—should better enable us to avoid them.

Origin and Impact of Ideology

An ideology that is a rationalization of the existing order obviously tends to defend the status quo. An ideology based on ideals that aim to change that status quo into something that is viewed as better is often called utopian. To Americans, *utopian* has an idealistic, pie-in-the-sky, pejorative connotation. Here we will use it as a descriptive term only.

Karl Mannheim, in his classic *Ideology and Utopia*, says that a state of mind is utopian if it has some elements that transcend reality as it exists. In addition, when these elements pass over into conduct, they "tend to shatter, either partially or wholly, the order of things prevailing at the time."[29] In other words, ideas and ideals that tend to change reality can be called utopian. According to Mannheim, ideologies become utopian when groups begin to act on them and to challenge the existing order.

Many utopias of today become the realities of tomorrow. Indeed, one definition of utopia is that it is merely a premature truth. The principles of democracy and freedom were utopian in the minds of those who founded the United States. Their notions of representation and individual rights were ideals which, when they were written into documents and acted on, challenged the status quo, shattered the existing order, and even caused a revolution. The utopian ideology of freedom and equality became translated into the civil rights movement of the 1960s. Looking back over the period of rising aspirations, especially in the Western world, Mannheim calls the prevailing ideology of freedom a utopia:

> The utopia of the ascendant bourgeoisie was the idea of "freedom." It was in part a real utopia, i.e., it contained elements oriented towards the realization of a new social order and which were instrumental in disintegrating the pre-

---

[29] Karl Mannheim, *Ideology and Utopia*, trans. Louis Wirth and Edward Shils (New York: Harcourt, Brace & World, 1936), p. 192. Quoted with permission.

viously existing social order and which, after their realization, did in part become translated into reality. Freedom in the sense of bursting asunder the bonds of the static, guild, and caste order, in the sense of freedom of thought and opinion, in the sense of political freedom and freedom of the unhampered development of the personality became ... a realizable possibility.[30]

Generalizing, Mannheim points out that any nation or group which wants to translate its ideals into reality must formulate an ideology that builds on the existing values, needs, and aspirations of the people. This utopian ideology may then catch the imagination of the people and be the inspiration for change. For every utopian ideology that eventually becomes reality, there are dozens that never get beyond the state of ideas. Nonetheless, they may have caused some upset and discord in society, and their adherents are often considered fanatical.

There are a number of dangers inherent in any ideology in addition to those pointed out earlier. The dangers of being closed to facts and of fanaticism are highlighted by Mannheim: "Nothing is more removed from actual events than the closed rational system. Under certain circumstances, nothing contains more irrational drive than a fully self-contained intellectualistic world view."[31] Those who feel they are well adjusted to the current state of affairs have little incentive to theorize, according to Mannheim.[32] These "conservatives" are happy with their situation, and so they defend the status quo. He points out that as long as people are content, they do little theorizing about situations in which they find themselves. They then tend to regard their current situation as part of the natural order of things; the way things are is the way they ought to be. For those whose position is unchallenged, there is little impetus to reflect on the situation. Rather, they tend to emphasize practical "how to do it" concerns—the means of coping within existing structures. It is only in the face of challenges to the status quo that conservatives do much reflecting. So the reflection and therefore the ideology of conservatives are generally not as profound or comprehensive as those of the challengers. It thus happens that the "most recent antagonist dictates the tempo and the form of the battle."[33]

Challenge Brings Understanding

A valuable by-product of this type of challenge and reformulation of goals and ideologies is that the society is compelled to examine itself. This sort of unmasking and examining of ideology can result in self-clarification

[30] Ibid., p. 203.
[31] Ibid., p. 219.
[32] Ibid., p. 229.
[33] Ibid., p. 231.

for society as a whole. A society with a weak ideology, or one in which ideology is unimportant, can generally be characterized as stable, complacent, and content with its inherited laws, customs, and ideals. At the very end of his chapter on the utopian mentality, Mannheim paints a sad, even desperate, picture of a society or a people without a utopian ideology:

> The disappearance of utopia brings about a static state of affairs in which man himself becomes no more than a thing. We would be faced then with the greatest paradox imaginable, namely, that man, who has achieved the highest degree of rational mastery of existence, left without any ideals, becomes a mere creature of impulses. Thus, after a long, tortuous, but heroic development, just at the highest stage of awareness, when history is ceasing to be blind fate, and is becoming more and more man's own creation, with the relinquishment of utopias, man would lose his will to shape history and therewith his ability to understand it.[34]

Mannheim presents an impersonal, alienating, and frightening prospect of a world without utopias—without ideals or engaging goals.

On the other hand, injustices can also be perpetrated in the name of an irrational but compelling ideology. Any strong, moving ideology risks being gross, oversimplified, and even unjust. Mannheim's own Germany a few years later was to undergo a tragic revolution in the name of "Aryan superiority" and the "master race." In Iran today, Ayatollah Khomeini provides the leadership for his fanatical followers, who are spurred by a version of Muslim Shite ideology. Nevertheless, without ideals worked into some sort of ideology, little new can be accomplished on any significant scale. People cease to question themselves and their society. They lose their direction and their enthusiasm for life. Hitler's ideology was a reaction to such a vacuum.

Suspicion of Ideology

Probably a majority of Americans share with Arthur Schlesinger, Jr., an abiding distrust of ideology. In an attempt to outline what has caused the rapid economic development of the United States, Schlesinger acknowledges the physical advantages of the continent. But he points out that the fertile lands and natural resources were there for the native Americans, too, but were never exploited.[35] Schlesinger maintains that the most important element in the success story of the United States was the spirit of the settlers. He contends that this spirit manifested itself in three important ways. The first was a faith in education. Investment in people through education results in increases in productivity. A second factor encouraging development was the

---

[34] Ibid., pp. 262–63.

[35] See "Epilogue: The One Against the Many," in Schlesinger and White, *Paths of American Thought*, pp. 531–38.

commitment to self-government and representative institutions. Democracy was important for releasing people's talents and energies.

The third uniquely favorable element in the American spirit, and probably the most important one according to Schlesinger, was a rejection of ideology: "America has had the good fortune not to be an ideological society."[36] Schlesinger defines ideology as "a body of systematic and rigid dogma by which people seek to understand the world—and to preserve or transform it." Many Americans agree with Schlesinger that ideology constricts us and distracts us from reality. They would not allow ideology to "falsify reality, imprison experience, or narrow the spectrum of choice."[37] This is part of an attitude that encourages innovation and experiment, part of the dominant empirical and pragmatic American approach.

The principal difficulty with an ideology is that it is a partial depiction of reality. Certain elements are emphasized and others neglected. When decisions are made, they can thus be biased or even wrong. Communist states, for example, often do not tolerate positions that depart from the official ideology. The dominant American philosophy, pragmatism, is not heavily theoretical. It stays close to the facts; to simplify, it holds "that which works is true." Schlesinger rightly rejects rigid dogma that would subjugate people and facts to an ideology. Americans have achieved much success in being flexible, open, and risk taking in a pluralistic society.

Schlesinger may not like ideology, but his own position is itself an ideology. It is an ideology that values freedom, laissez-faire, and selective nonintervention. Moreover, that freedom is especially for me and mine. It does not apply to the American Indians, who, in spite of the fact that they did not "exploit" their lands as Schlesinger would have liked, were pushed off those lands. The Indians did not have the freedom to decide how they would use their lands. This double standard calls for government intervention to preserve *my* freedom and prerogatives; it calls for nonintervention when government regulations restrict *my* freedom or the freedom of *my* organization.

Most Americans hold that if each person or group uses its talents and intelligence to pursue its own long-term self-interest, it will work out most favorably for all. By any definition, this is an ideology. Its long-run effectiveness is questioned by many in the United States and around the world whose freedom and best interests have not automatically been served.

Values in American Life

Individualism and enlightened self-interest are still basic to the value systems of most Americans. Moreover, these values affect entire life styles,

[36] Ibid., p. 532.
[37] Ibid., p. 533.

not merely work attitudes. Indeed, whenever predominant American values are listed, it is remarkable how many of them support work attitudes and are directly related to individualism and enlightened self-interest. The current serious challenge to some of these values will be discussed in later chapters. Here, let us attempt to indicate what these prevalent traditional American values are.

Achievement and success. American culture has been and still is characterized by a stress on individual achievement. Horatio Alger, who rose from rags to riches, has become a legend. The American myth says that anyone who works hard enough can succeed in what he or she sets out to do. Moreover, if we meet a successful person, we are more impressed if he or she did not inherit wealth. Someone who was born poor and then worked hard to obtain what he or she has is an idol for the young. In fact, it is a bit embarrassing to us to be reminded that several of our recent presidents were born into wealthy families. This achievement and success ideal is, of course, manifested most extensively in business. The drive to achieve is especially strong among executives and managers.[38]

Money and wealth are valued for the comforts they can bring but even more because they are the symbols of having "made it." It is a measure to the person and to the world of one's own personal worth. Because these values developed in the westward expansion and the building of railroads and industry, there comes a correlative respect for size. Large homes, automobiles, and businesses are respected; they are signs of success.

Activity and work. A devotion to work on the part of both the unskilled worker and the executive has provided most of the wealth we now enjoy in the United States. Work is respected not only because it results in wealth but also for its own sake—"The devil finds idle hands." In the United States a person's self-respect is severely undermined when he or she is without work. Americans have traditionally not valued leisure for its own sake; it is valued if afterward a person can work better. It is *re*-creation, and it, too, has a purpose. Task orientation has become a compulsion for which Americans are frequently criticized.

Workers know that even though the job is well in hand, or ahead of schedule, they had best appear busy. "Busyness" is a virtue in its own right. To call a person lazy is a serious criticism, especially because the amount of activity is something over which a person seems to have control. Americans

---

[38] There is, of course a great amount of literature on this, and the issue will be discussed in greater detail in chapter 5. For now, see the insightful and synthetic work of Michael Maccoby, *The Gamesman: The New Corporate Leaders* (New York: Simon & Schuster, 1976).

value the active virtues; they set out to shape and control their own lives and their world. They heed the biblical injunction "to subdue the world."

Efficiency and practicality.   Closely related to the foregoing cultural values are efficiency and practicality, which are concerned more with methods of working and acting. We have seen how Tocqueville was much impressed with American ingenuity and ability to "get the job done." Americans are often criticized for an overemphasis on technique, with little reference to goals.[39] Critics say that engineers and accountants run our society and that their values are at best instrumental and thus means. They may know how to accomplish a specific task but rarely consider whether it is a good thing to do. A practical person, focusing on efficiency, assumes the basic worth of the task and of the social order itself. A practical orientation demands only short-range adjustments to immediate situations.

Americans are known as people who can quickly and effectively search out the best way to accomplish the task. They are active in the search for solutions and are rarely contemplative. To call an American "impractical" is a severe criticism. Characteristically, the best-known American philosophers, such as Dewey, Peirce, and William James, are not idealists or absolutists but rather relativists and pragmatists.

Moral orientation and humanitarianism.   Although Americans are eminently practical, they still see the world in moral terms. Conduct of self and of others is constantly judged: honest, impractical, "a comer," lazy. Even our foreign policy is filled with righteous terms, such as "manifest destiny" and "protecting the world for freedom."

Basic honesty and frankness are also part of our moral and humanitarian value orientation. Foreign commentators are often surprised at how open and straightforward they find Americans to be. However, a highly moral person can quickly become quite cynical when his or her moral code is found to be superficial, inapplicable, or too idealistic. American charities, along with our social legislation since the 1930s, are evidence of humanitarian attitudes. Social security, the minimum wage, and medical coverage are examples of our attempt to take care of the less fortunate.

Freedom.   Freedom is a prime value in American life. It is also the most discussed American value. The individual has freedom to operate in the social Darwinian world in which the fittest survive best, as we have seen earlier. He or she may freely move; change jobs; choose a home, friends, or a marriage partner. Freedom is the bedrock value not only of our laissez-faire, free

---

[39] For a classic statement of this position, see Jacques Ellul, *The Technological Society* (New York: Knopf, 1964).

enterprise economic system but for most of the rest of American life. Freedom has been touted alike by the Founding Fathers and the members of the local Rotary. American individualism, of course, is possible only when freedom is the foundation value.

The value of freedom has inspired the women's movement and other liberation movements. Cultural norms that tie certain persons to predetermined roles and expectations can be oppressive. Freedom urges the elimination of these one-sided and unjust bonds. Defense of freedom is a foundation of American foreign policy, and freedom is the cornerstone of the American business system—*free* enterprise. As we have pointed out earlier, this freedom is primarily for me and mine, foreign policy protestations notwithstanding. Freedom as a value so permeates business ideology that it will frequently come up as a topic in subsequent chapters.

Equality. The American emphasis on equality goes back to early constitutional statements: *All men* are created equal. Citizens of the new world witnessed the elimination of indentured servitude, imprisonment for debt, primogeniture, slavery, and property requirements for voting and public office. New immigrants were able to acquire land and a free public education, and women and minorities have gained many important human rights.

New arrivals and observers have often remarked on the unusual informality, frankness, and lack of status consciousness in our interpersonal relations. Such open and direct relations can endure over a long period only if they are supported by basic notions of the equality and importance of individual persons. But it became clear quite early that the value of freedom often ran counter to that of equality. When people pursued freedom in the rugged individualist climate in which the fittest survive, it resulted in some becoming rich and others remaining poor. In an attempt to resolve this conflict, some claim that our ideals call for equality of opportunity but not equality of result. Varying talents will also influence what a person can achieve.

Of all the government and corporate policies that have been developed to bring about better equality of opportunity in the workplace, none meets more opposition than "preferential treatment." In order to compensate for past practices that were clearly discriminatory, many contend that when equally qualified minority and white persons are presented for promotion, the minority should be chosen. Ironically, both the reason for the practice (to compensate for past discrimination) and the major objections to it (reverse discrimination) stem from the American ideal of equality, especially equality of opportunity.[40]

---

[40]See the detailed discussion of this complex question in Theodore V. Purcell and Gerald F. Cavanagh, *Blacks in the Industrial World: Issues for the Manager* (New York: Free Press, 1972), especially chap. 10, "Equal Versus Preferential Treatment," pp. 275–93.

Patriotism.   Every society has a sense of the greater value of its own people. Anthropologists tell us how in tribal societies the ordinary rules of respect for another's person and property do not apply to "outsiders." They apply only to the members of one's own tribe. This mentality emerges when, during warfare, we sometimes rate successes on the basis of how many of the enemy are killed. Racism, too, stems from these same parochial values.

In the United States our loyalties in the early days of the republic were with local cities (Boston, Philadelphia) and then with the states; finally, after several national efforts (especially the two world wars), our loyalties now lie primarily with the nation-state. Our attitudes toward Communist states and "un-American" activities find their roots largely in nationalism and loyalty to America.

Material comfort.   Americans generally place a high value on the luxurious automobile, the ample home in the suburbs, and a good meal. The fact that these things are material comforts and that they are clearly highly valued does not in itself indicate *why* they are valued. For each item of comfort or pleasure, the underlying reasons for valuing it may range from its being a symbol of achievement and success (moving to a larger home is a visible mark that one is moving up in the firm) to its providing hedonistic gratification in its own right.

The rise in popularity of spectator sports, packaged tours, film, television, and alcohol indicates a greater passivity on the part of people. There seems to be less active participation and more watching and being entertained. The drug culture and chemically induced pleasure take this tendency one more step. Seeking pleasure coincides with a decline in the Puritan values of self-denial and asceticism.

External conformity.   Probably the most common criticism Europeans have leveled at Americans is in the United States there is vast uniformity in speech, housing, dress, recreation, and general attitudes. Observers point to a certain flatness, to homogeneity, to lack of dissent and challenge. Witness the importance given to fashion, and "dressing for success."

To American rugged individualists, these criticisms may seem harsh and untrue. Yet, on closer examination, our individualism consists largely in the rejection of government interference and objecting to restrictions on personal and business activity. American society today lacks, and desperately needs, sufficient numbers of creative, risk-taking individuals and firms.

Rationality and measurement.   This value is probably best exemplified in approaching a problem. A person is to be objective, is to gather the facts first, and is not to be unduly influenced by bias or emotions. The "scientific method," which embodies this approach, is the model for problem solving. If elements of the solution can be measured, that will make the solution more rational and objective.

The value of science is demonstrated in its intelligent use in mastering the external environment. This value orientation is compatible with a culture that does not value emotion, tends to deny frustration, and looks on the world as open to effort and eventual control.

Optimism and the inevitability of progress.   The combination of an immigrant people willing to work hard with what seemed like unlimited natural resources and the existence of the frontier created an atmosphere in which optimism was able to thrive. Any job could be accomplished if only one put one's mind to it. The result of the tendency to work hard was the growth of jobs, products, and cities. Growth has been so characteristic of the last two centuries that for most Americans growth and progress seem inevitable.

The optimistic euphoria that had enveloped the American people has recently begun to dissipate. In the last decade the possibility of continued growth has been challenged and we are now reexamining what we mean by progress. We had defined progress largely in economic terms. As long as sales and the gross national product were increasing, progress was occurring. The problems of a slower-growing economy, the danger of wastefully using finite resources, the necessity of rethinking what "progress" is, and the impact these issues will have on business and business values will be discussed in greater detail in Chapters 8 and 9.

THE NECESSITY OF AN IDEOLOGY FOR BUSINESS

Let us now examine the importance of an ideology for business.[41] An ideology and a statement of goals and values are essential for any social system. Within a business firm, a mission statement, an ideology, and shared values make cooperation, decisions, and implementation much easier.[42]

---

[41] Richard M. Weiss, in *Managerial Ideology and the Social Control of Deviance in Organizations* (New York: Praeger, 1986), presents ideology as a social control mechanism in the rehabilitation of alcoholics and other "troubled" employees. Roger L. M. Dunbar, John M. Dutton, and William R. Torbert, in "Crossing Mother: Ideological Constraints on Organizational Improvements," *Journal of Management Studies* 19 (1982): 91–108, show how preexisting organizational ideologies are used to halt attempts at improvement. William H. Starbuck, in "Congealing Oil: Inventing Ideologies to Justify Acting Ideologies Out," *Journal of Management Studies*, 19 (1982): 1–27, shows how ideologies forcefully and universally affect organizations that are in crisis.

[42] Janice M. Beyer, "Ideologies, Values, and Decision Making in Organizations," in *Handbook of Organizational Design*, ed. Paul C. Nystrom and William H. Starbuck, vol. 2 (New York: Oxford University Press, 1981), pp. 166–202. This comprehensive article provides an overview of social science research on values and ideologies in organizations, along with several varying definitions. See also Richard M. Weiss and Lynn E. Miller, "The Concept of Ideology in Organizational Analysis: The Sociology of Knowledge or the Social Psychology of Beliefs," *The Academy of Management Review* 12 (January 1987): 104–16.

An ideology is especially important for business in our complex international society, because it can provide a useful response to several problems:

1. Global markets demand that a firm be flexible and able to quickly assess new needs and the firm's own capabilities. An ideology provides goals but does not constitute a straitjacket.
2. For decades scholars and citizens have questioned the legitimacy of the corporation. Where resides the ultimate power and authority in the corporation and where resides the responsibility that goes with them? An ideology responds to this question.
3. Managers are widely criticized for being too focused on themselves and their own careers. They thus manage for short-term returns and neglect long-term planning and investment for the firm. An ideology and mission helps managers to focus on benefits to the *firm*.
4. A few critics even question whether the free enterprise system, because of its inequities and inefficiencies, can survive in its present form. An ideology clarifies goals and beneficiaries of free enterprise.

Without some rationale, it is impossible for businesspeople and others to evaluate these challenges, intelligently defend themselves against unfair attacks, and establish new policies to rectify abuses. In the future, as in the past, an ideology will undergird the actions of business and whatever stature and power it possesses.

Without an ideology, the corporation risks losing its privileged position in the United States, perhaps even its legitimacy. Several decades ago Adolph A. Berle said of the corporation,

> Whenever there is a question of power there is also a question of legitimacy. As things stand now, these instrumentalities of tremendous power have the slenderest claim of legitimacy. This is probably a transitory period. They must find some claim of legitimacy, which also means finding a field of responsibility and a field of accountability. Legitimacy, responsibility and accountability are essential to any power system if it is to endure.[43]

This unstable period of which he spoke is still with us.

Notice how Berle links the issues of legitimacy, responsibility, and accountability. In clarifying these basic issues, the corporation is on weak ground. Without reviewing the classic position of Berle and Means,[44] suffice it to say that the corporation is responsible to no one. Management, often with little ownership or legitimacy, unilaterally makes decisions. Stockhold-

---

[43] Adolph A. Berle, *Economic Power and the Free Society* (New York: Fund for the Republic, 1958), p. 16.

[44] Adolf A. Berle and Gardiner C. Means, *The Modern Corporation and Private Property* (New York: Macmillan, 1932). David Cowan Bayne, a disciple of Berle, maintains that trust is the essential controlling element of corporate power. See his *Philosophy of Corporate Control* (Chicago: Loyola University Press, 1986).

ers have little control over the corporation. The board of directors is elected from a slate chosen by the board itself.[45] Elections are like those in the Soviet Union: If there are three directors to be elected, only three candidates are nominated. The shareholders have no choice. The annual meeting of stockholders is a public relations event, and stockholders exercise no real power. If a stockholder does not vote, the abstention is often counted as support for management.

Questioning the corporation's power and legitimacy raises serious questions about the role, purpose, and responsibilities of the corporation. The role and responsibilities of the chief executive officer and the board of directors will be discussed in more detail in Chapter 8. As we will see, assessment of these issues requires having a clear idea of the purpose, rationale, and responsibilities of the corporation, its very reason for existence—its ideology.

Without an ideology that is clear, consistent, and moving, these gnawing questions will continue to arise but will be unanswerable. In a social system, such a situation is not stable. The recent probusiness Reagan era masked a deep lingering distrust of big business and businesspeople. Some of the current loss of respect for corporations stems from their inability to articulate their purpose and the purpose of business as a whole. Without accountability and a clear statement of purpose, business risks losing its respected position in American society. An individual firm's statement of purpose must be understandable to its many stakeholders and the firm must be held accountable to act in accordance with it. If this does not occur generally, the rebuilding of trust in business will not succeed. The following chapters are intended to aid that rebuilding.

SUMMARY AND CONCLUSIONS

This chapter examined major values and ideals in American life and the geography and personal characteristics that contributed to the development of those values. The vast expanse of virgin land was a challenge to the righteous, task-oriented Puritans. Their theology supported their work ethic: self-denial, hard work, thrift, early rising. Furthermore, the favorable results of working hard showed that the individual was saved. Though not a Puritan, Benjamin Franklin found the work ethic attractive, and he presented a secularized version of it.

Perceptive visitors during the last century and a half noted an honesty, frankness, and directness in Americans. They found us a pragmatic people

---

[45] Harold S. Geneen, "Why Directors Can't Protect the Shareholders," *Fortune*, September 17, 1984, pp. 28–32.

with little time for unproductive theorizing. Freedom is a bedrock value that has been institutionalized in our laws, Constitution, and attitudes.

With this information as background, we then reflected on ideologies, including their function and some of their effects. The main values in American life were assessed. This examination of American values and ideology provides a framework for considering business values. Business values exist in society, and we see remarkably well how U.S. society's ideals support the ideology of its business community. Nevertheless, the very legitimacy of the corporation and of business itself is being questioned. An adequate response to these questions is possible only by spelling out a purpose and an ideology for business firms that are in better harmony with what society expects of them.

The values of American Puritans—hard work, saving, regular habits, diligence, self-control, and sobriety—still somewhat characterize the American work ethic. These values constitute what is known as the Protestant ethic, which will be discussed in the next chapter.

DISCUSSION QUESTIONS

1. Distinguish among values, goals, ideals, and ideologies. How do values relate to an ideology?
2. According to the Puritans, what constitutes a person's calling? How did Benjamin Franklin alter the Puritan ethic?
3. Compare and contrast Benjamin Franklin's attitudes toward work and efficiency with those of Thomas Jefferson.
4. Outline Alexis de Tocqueville's appraisal of enlightened self-interest. According to Tocqueville, what are the strengths and weaknesses of enlightened self-interest as a basic motive for Americans? To what extent are his assessments still valid today?
5. What is social Darwinism? Why does Herbert Spencer maintain that evolution and the "survival of the fittest" are not to be thwarted?
6. Describe the effect of the frontier on American values. Compare the effect of the frontier with the effect of social Darwinism on American values.
7. What is an ideology? What does it do for a society? What are the advantages and disadvantages to a society of having a well-articulated ideology? What happens to a society without such an ideology?
8. Are the American values outlined in this chapter predominant for the average American? For people in your environment? For you?
9. Does business today possess a consistent ideology? What are the disadvantages of not having a business ideology?

CASE: EDUCATIONAL REIMBURSEMENT

Rob Stewart, an assistant professor of marketing, is teaching the introductory marketing course for the fall term at Southwestern State University; there will be about 600 in the course. Stewart can select from among six basic marketing texts, and he negotiates with various publishers to determine which will provide the best "educational reimbursement" (i.e., gifts to a person or department of computers, films, or dollars). The publishing house of Smith and Luster agrees to $600 worth of reimbursement, and Stewart decides on its text even though it is not quite as well done as another text. How do you judge the ethics of Stewart's decision? Who benefits? Is there a conflict of interest here? Explain. Make any necessary distinctions.

CHAPTER THREE
HISTORICAL ROOTS
OF BUSINESS VALUES

In the past the man has been first; in the future the system must
be first.

Frederick Winslow Taylor

Knowledge of history benefits the businessperson and the business student.
Knowing history, the manager recognizes elements in current problems that
were earlier solved by others. The manager is thus better able to recognize
situations that are new and hence demand new solutions. History encom-
passes such diverse elements as the growth of our cities and the energetic,
entrepreneurial attitudes of earlier generations.[1]

We are products of our past. No matter how rapidly society changes,
current attitudes have their roots in history. Where we go and what we do are
very much influenced by past values and attitudes.[2] Whether we view the
present as part of an organic development from earlier events or as breaking
new ground, the past has great influence. For example, an inherited pragmatic faith in technology undergirds the conviction of many that we can
readily overcome current productivity, trade deficit, and budget deficit problems. On the other hand, concern for the quality of work life and for a clean
environment stems partly from a disenchantment with attitudes of earlier

---

[1] "Why History Matters to Managers," a roundtable discussion with Alfred D. Chandler
et al., ed. Alan M. Kantrow, *Harvard Business Review*, January-February 1986, pp. 81–88.
[2] Ibid., p. 84.

generations that were autocratic and wasteful. It is impossible to understand current values and what the future will bring without knowing the path that has led us to where we are.

QUESTIONING THE PAST

People in industrialized and developing societies have a strong need to assess their values for several reasons. First, change takes place so rapidly that people need explanations for their current activities and behavior. Some values are basic, provide a sense of stability, and perdure through major changes; other values are no longer helpful. It is essential to examine our values so as to determine which are which.

Second, the many more choices that people face in industrialized societies—choosing a career, a style of life, whether or not to marry and have children—encourage them to examine the values on which they base their decisions.

Third, formal education encourages people to be more questioning and reflective.

Fourth, an understanding of basic values and goals is necessary in industrialized societies because actions, goals, and rights are often in conflict. For example, the goal of increased productivity conflicts with the right to work. The goal of producing at lowest cost conflicts with the goal of reducing air and water pollution. The resolution of these conflicts requires clarification of goals, principles, and values. Moreover, the inquiry that is part of the clarification process will be the foundation for future public policy and legislation and will greatly affect society and styles of life.

Some ask the fundamental question, Why work? What is the value of work? Further, what is the value of business? Granted, if I want a car or a refrigerator, it must be designed and produced and I must have some means of obtaining it. But if I can obtain it in a lawful fashion without working, why not? If I have a spouse and two children, why not earn just enough to keep us happy? Does work have any greater value to a person or to society than as a means to individual happiness? People ask such basic questions with increasing frequency. Also, people in other nations inquire into the value of work and the goals of free enterprise. An intelligent response is essential for a mature, happy people and a successful society.

These questions are not new, but now they are asked by more people and with greater urgency. In earlier and more traditional societies, they were theoretical questions and were asked by the educated people, not by ordinary citizens. The ordinary worker's life was largely determined at birth. If a man's father was a shoemaker or a baker, he would become one too and would use the tools, workshop, and home that had belonged to the family for generations. Rarely was there any question of whether a person *would* work, or at what occupation. There was little choice. There was also little regret or frustration, because there was no alternative. Heredity, custom, and geography determined a person's life. To ask people in economically undeveloped, traditional societies why they work is like asking them why they try to stay alive. They have little reason to question the value of work.

The growth and success of business depends on people's attitudes toward work. The early American Puritan ethic supported tireless work and thus economic growth. Current business behavior also depends on people's assessment of the place and importance of work in their lives. Let us examine our own roots.

LISTENING TO OUR FOREBEARS

Change took place rapidly in the United States from its beginning. Almost all its people immigrated from other lands, mostly from Europe. All the Founding Fathers were influenced by European thinkers, such as John Locke, Jean-Jacques Rousseau, and Adam Smith, on such issues as the value of work, business, and private property. Although there were alternate strains of thought in the East, until recently these values had little impact on the West. Hence we will limit ourselves largely to Western attitudes and philosophies on these practical issues.

Throughout most of recorded history, work has been an integrating force for the individual. It was a basic binding strand for the fabric of the social system, the family, and the city. It gave stability and meaning to people and their relationships. A clear change, however, emerged with industrialization. Changes in work, such as division of labor, mass production, and "scientific management," were introduced. And the individual worker had increasing choice as to the type and location of the work he or she might do. It is ironic that just when individuals began to be able to choose work and thus expect greater satisfaction from their jobs, that work became more fragmented, repetitive, and less able to provide pride of accomplishment and workmanship.

The Ancient Greek Attitude Toward Business and Work

The ancient Greeks thought of work and commerce as demeaning to a citizen. At best, it was a burden required for survival. The meager legitimacy and value accorded to work was given to it, not because it had any value in itself, but because it was a necessary evil. There are two limitations to our knowledge of ancient attitudes toward work. First, most of our information comes from written sources whose authors were generally not from the working class; they were citizens and hence persons of leisure. Second, most of the work was done by slaves under grueling, dirty, and difficult conditions. These slaves were uneducated and often prisoners of war from other cultures.

Plato speaks of work as if it were a temptation to be avoided because it hinders a person's ability to live and to contemplate. In his *Laws*, Plato speaks for himself and his fellow citizens when he urges, "If a native stray from the pursuit of goodness into some trade or craft, they shall correct him by reproach and degradation until he be brought back again into the straight course."[3] Citizens of ancient Athens thought of work as something not worthy of a citizen. Plato, however, reveals the extent to which his contemporaries' attitudes were based on the accidental conditions under which work was done as he cuts to the heart of their disenchantment and even revulsion with work:

> Suppose the very best of men could be compelled—the fancy will sound ludicrous, I know, but I must give it utterance—suppose they could be compelled to take for a time to inn-keeping, or retail trade or some such calling; or suppose, for that matter, that some unavoidable destiny were to drive the best women into such professions: then we should discover that all are humane and beneficent occupations; if they were only conducted on the principles of strict integrity, we should respect them as we do the vocation of mother and nurse.[4]

Even under conditions of general disapproval, Plato recognizes that most of the objections to work are not basic to work itself. In fact, these occupations are in themselves "humane and beneficent."

Plato's pupil Aristotle is more severe in his condemnation of the life of the worker or tradesperson. To him, such a life is irksome and beneath the dignity of a citizen:

> The citizens must not lead the life of mechanics or tradesmen, for such a life is ignoble, and inimical to virtue. Neither must they be husbandmen, since leisure is necessary both for the development of virtue and the performance of political duties.[5]

From his observations, Aristotle found crafts, trade, and business detrimental to health and character. Much of the work was done in cramped and unhealthy surroundings, and it was necessary to have daily dealings with the rude, the unprincipled, and the unethical. So industrial and commercial life was thought to begin by robbing the body of its health and to end by degrading the character. Moreover, whether those who followed a trade or

---

[3] Plato, *The Laws of Plato*, trans. A. E. Taylor (London: Dent, 1934), 847B.

[4] Ibid., 918B–E.

[5] Aristotle, *Politics*, in *Basic Works of Aristotle*, ed. Richard McKeon (New York: Random House, 1941), p. 1141.

craft should even be admitted to citizenship was a problem for Aristotle. This sort of work was generally done by slaves, and many contemporary states did not admit the laborer and the skilled worker to citizenship. "Even in states which admitted the industrial and commercial classes to power, popular sentiment held trade and industry cheap."[6]

Aristotle speaks of two types of business and trade activity, and his distinction goes to the root of a difficulty that perplexes many to the present day: the difference between the careful management of goods and what often seems to be a merely selfish profit orientation. He approves of the first but disapproves of the second. *Oeconomia*, from which our word *economics* derives, is literally "household management." It includes careful and intelligent use not only of the household but of all one's property and resources. On the other hand, *chrematistike* means the use of skill and goods to achieve a profit. This term described the city traders, who were few in number compared with the farmers and skilled workers. These traders often resorted to deceptive practices, and it seemed to Aristotle, and scores of generations that followed him, that they really contributed little or nothing to society. Aristotle's objections are not unlike those of Marx: The trader adds no value to a good; his service as a middleman does not enhance the good in question. Not surprisingly, then, Aristotle approved of *oeconomia* but disapproved of *chrematistike*.

Plato and Aristotle generally agree in their objections to the pursuit of a career in trade or a craft, although Aristotle raises these objections more strongly: (1) The practice of business or a craft deprives a person of the leisure necessary to contemplate the good, the true, and the beautiful. (2) It hinders proper physical, intellectual, and moral development. (3) It is "illiberal" because it is done for pay. (4) It is less perfect because its end is outside of itself.

Work in Biblical Times

Unlike the Greeks, who had slaves, the ancient Hebrews could not remain aloof from work; it was an integral part of their lives. They saw work as necessary but also as a hardship. Even the painful aspect of work had its self-inflicted cause in original sin. This gave reason, integrity, and even verve to what for most other cultures was only something to be endured. On the positive side, the Hebrews pointed to the commands of God in Genesis that men and women were to cultivate the world and subdue it (Gen. 2:15). Work was still drudgery for the Hebrews, but it was better integrated into their lives and had greater meaning for them. The God of the Hebrews is close to them. God is often pictured as one who labors: a vine dresser (Ezek. 15:6), a pottery maker (Gen. 2:7), a soldier (Isa. 27:1).

[6]W. L. Newman, *Politics of Aristotle*, vol. 1 (Oxford: Clarendon Press, 1887), p. 98.

Christianity built on the Hebraic tradition with regard to work, trade, and commerce. The new religion itself had working-class origins. Jesus was a carpenter (Mark 6:3) and Paul, a tentmaker (Acts 18:2). The apostles, all working men, were mostly fishermen. They were not from the priestly class. The Gospels caution against an excessive and exclusive concern with work and the things of this world (Matt. 6:24–34), but they also make clear that work is a serious responsibility for the Christian (Luke 12:41–49). Furthermore, in the often-quoted parable of the talents (Matt. 25:14–30), the servant who has intelligently and profitably invested his money and his efforts is the one who is given additional rewards.

But the unique contribution of Christianity with regard to the value of work is its view that work is done also out of love and concern for one's brothers and sisters. Work is necessary "not only to earn one's living, asking alms of no man, but above all so that the goods of fortune may be shared with one's needy brothers."[7] In investigating the foundations of industrial civilization, John U. Nef points to this new concept of love preached by Jesus Christ and presented in the New Testament. He finds it "a peculiarly generous concept of charity, of the opportunity we have to give ourselves to others here and now, insofar as we love our neighbors for God."[8] Throughout the ages, including our own time, Christians most often have fallen short of these ideals. Nevertheless, Nef is convinced that as a foundation for work and business values, especially in its emphasis on love of neighbor, Christianity was an important step forward.

In the early centuries of the Christian era, the most important commentator was Augustine. He approved of handicraft, farming, and commerce on a small scale. But in any selling, no more than a "just price" can be asked; asking interest on the use of money is immoral. Those who have wealth should prize it as a trust from God. After their own modest needs are met, they should give the rest to the poor.[9] As early as the fifth century, Augustine held that work was obligatory for monks. During later centuries in the monasteries, especially among the Benedictines, a new work ethic developed.

Monks as Capitalists

Benedictine monasteries have been credited as being "perhaps the original founders of capitalism."[10] The Benedictine Rule, as embodied in tens of

---

[7] Adriano Tilgher, "Work Through the Ages," in Sigmund Nosow and William Form, *Man, Work and Society*, (New York: Basic Books, 1962), p. 13.

[8] John U. Nef, *Cultural Foundations of Industrial Civilization* (Cambridge: Cambridge University Press, 1958), p. 89.

[9] Tilgher, "Work Through the Ages," pp. 14–15.

[10] Lewis Mumford, *Techniques and Civilizations* (New York: Harcourt, Brace, 1934), p. 14.

thousands of monasteries throughout Europe, brought a much more positive attitude toward production and work. For the monks, work was not merely a curse and manual work not merely degradation. These men looked on work as an opportunity to build and to grow and develop individually and as a community. They chose to work together, and they were among the first to cooperate voluntarily in all tasks. Since the monks often worked in groups and varied their occupations, they found it helpful to work by the clock. They would begin and end their work together. They standardized tasks so that anyone could handle the work.

Living and working as a cooperative community helped to stimulate the use of various labor-saving devices. When, in 1115, Bernard of Clairvaux led a band of monks to found a new monastery, one of his prime requisites for a new site was that it have a rapidly moving stream that could be harnessed by the monks to help them do their work. Bernard himself provides us with a description of his famous abbey at Clairvaux, and he provides considerable detail on the mechanical devices that are geared to waterwheels to make the work of the brothers easier.[11]

The monastery is built at the base of a mountain and extends over a fast-moving stream to make best use of the waterpower. The river is guided by "works laboriously constructed" by the monks so that the water may be of the greatest help to their efforts. The water thus "passes and repasses the many workshops of the abbey." The water is channeled so that it "passes on at once to drive the wheels of a mill." In moving these wheels, "it grinds the meal under the weight of the mill-stones, and separates the fine from the coarse by a sieve." The river's waters are also harnessed to raise and drop hammers for the traditional fulling of cloth and to help the shoemaker in his chores. The waters are then split into smaller streams where they help "to cook the food, sift the grain, to drive the wheels and hammers, to damp, wash, soak and so to soften, objects; everywhere it stands ready to offer its help." The monks also constructed an elaborate irrigation apparatus to water the fields. Recall that all this happened in the 1100s, six centuries before the Industrial Revolution.

A century later the great Christian theologian of the Middle Ages, Thomas Aquinas, provided a rationale for work. He spelled out clearly and in some detail the reasons why it seemed to him that manual labor was necessary for all: to obtain food, to remove idleness, to curb concupiscence, and to provide for alms-giving.[12] Although Aquinas saw clearly that work was not

---

[11] Bernard of Clairvaux, *Patrologiae Latinae*, ed. Migne, vol. 185 (Paris: Garnier, 1879), pp. 570–74. A translation of much of this is in Samuel J. Eales, *Life and Works of St. Bernard*, vol. 2 (London: Burns & Oakes, n.d.), pp. 460–67. The quoted words that follow are those of Bernard himself.

[12] Thomas Aquinas, *Summa Theologica*, II-II, qu. 87, art. 3.

only necessary but also of considerable value, there was still a remnant of the view that work was a burden, something to endure for the sake of leisure.

Work, however, was not a burden for the monks; it was a vehicle of love and service. When setting up a new monastery, the monks would deliberately choose a site far from existing towns. They did this both because it would be a better locale for prayer and because they deliberately set out to communicate their new view of the value of work as rooted in charity. Benedict and Bernard expected their monks to work in the fields and the shops whether they were sons of aristocrats or of serfs. According to Lynn White, Jr., historian of technology and industry, this provision

> marks a revolutionary reversal of the traditional attitude toward labor; it is a high peak along the watershed separating the modern from the ancient world. The Benedictine monks regarded manual labor not as a mere regrettable necessity of their corporate life but rather as an integral and spiritually valuable part of their discipline. During the Middle Ages the general reverence for the laboring monks did much to increase the prestige of labor and the self-respect of the laborer. Moreover, since the days of St. Benedict every major form of Western asceticism has held that "to labor is to pray," until in its final development under the Puritans, work in one's "calling" became not only the prime moral necessity but also the chief means of serving and praising God.[13]

The monks lived together and lived thriftily, and that enabled them to invest in productive machinery like that described above to aid them in their work. This is why some call the monks the first capitalists. Their resources and inventiveness combined and resulted in division of labor, interchangeable work, a clock-regulated workday, and ingenious labor-saving equipment—all of which added up to considerably greater productivity. They used the additional time that was then available for their common life and prayer. A few hundred years later, this same love-centered ethic was brought to the cities and marketplaces of seventeenth-century France by an eminent group of saints, artists, poets, and theologians. John Nef maintains that it was this unique emphasis on the centrality of love for one's brothers and sisters, especially as embodied in women, that made industrial society and its requirement of cooperation and hard work possible.[14] More specifically, he shows that the law of love and its vision as carried out by women were two of the greatest impetuses to the sort of civilization that makes industrialized society possible.

By 1700, Christianity, with its central love ethic, had helped to provide many of the elements necessary for the development of business and com-

---

[13] Lynn White, Jr., "Dynamo and Virgin Reconsidered," *American Scholar* 27 (Spring 1958): 188. Quoted with permission.

[14] See Nef, *Cultural Foundations;* see also his briefer *Civilization, Industrial Society and Love* (Santa Barbara, Calif.: Fund for the Republic, 1961).

merce. Work began to be looked on as something of value; it provided self-discipline and an integrating force in a person's life. Christianity helped the individual to focus on the value of the product of work; if the same thing could be produced more easily, this was good—especially when it enabled one to help one's family and neighbors. The importance of quantity and a new consciousness of time developed first in the monasteries and then spread to the larger society. Furthermore, the Catholic church urged all to attend mass side by side: worker and artisan, rich and poor, peasant, scholar, and duke. This fostered communication and cooperation.

In its otherworldly theology, however, Catholicism thwarted the coming of capitalism. Material goods, wealth, and success were not the measures of holiness. According to this theology, the purpose of life on earth was not merely to build up material goods. This attitude led to suspicion of those who would lend money to others and charge them for the use of it. Even as late as the sixteenth century, theologians condemned the opening of state banks.[15] Lending money at interest in the Christian tradition was the sin of usury.

In Christian society, work and industry were much more respected than they had been in aristocratic Greece or Rome. The average citizen had many reasons to do tasks well, and there were no slaves to do them instead. In addition, a person's trade or craft gave meaning and integrity to life. But it was the Protestant Reformation that provided the impetus for the development of attitudes that would propel Western society toward rapid economic growth.

From Luther and Calvin to the Protestant Ethic

It was Protestantism that eventually established hard work and the making of profits as central to a Christian life. Ironically, Martin Luther (1483–1546), the initiator of this new movement, intensely disliked the commerce and economic individualism of his day. Luther was appalled at the regal high living of the popes, local merchants, and princes. The sharp contrast between the ideals of Christianity and what he actually found around him motivated Luther to push for reform. He called for a return to a simple, hardworking peasant life; this would bring sufficient prosperity for all. A person should earn a living and not make an excessive profit.

Luther saw a number of Christian institutions as actually encouraging idleness: the mendicant friars glorifying begging, the many religious holidays, and the monasteries' support of some who did not work. Idleness is unnatural, according to Luther, and charity should be given only to those who cannot work. His original contribution was in emphasizing the importance of one's profession. The best way to serve God was to do the work of

---

[15] Lewis Mumford, *The Myth of the Machine* (New York: Harcourt, Brace & World, 1966), p. 279.

one's profession as well as one could. Thus Luther healed what had been a breach between worship and work. As long as work was done in obedience to God and in service to one's brothers and sisters, every type of work had equal value in God's eyes.

Luther held that a person's salvation is achieved solely through faith in God; good works do not affect salvation. Moreover, all legitimate human activities are acts of worship, no one more than another. Since formal prayer and worship, and especially the monastic life of prayer, are no more valuable than tilling the fields, Protestantism released all human energies for the world of work. The farmer, the smith, and the baker all do work that is quite as honorable as that of the priest. Although the life of the simple worker is better, Luther concedes that

> trade is permissible, provided that it is confined to the exchange of necessaries, and that the seller demands no more than will compensate him for his labor and risk. The unforgivable sins are idleness and covetousness, for they destroy the unity of the body of which Christians are members.[16]

Luther was vehement in preaching against lending at interest, yet paradoxically his denial of all religious authority eventually set economic life free from strictures on usury. This denial left business and commerce to develop their own life and laws independent of existing moral authorities. Capitalism thus set up its own norms of right and wrong, and capitalist activity was carried on beyond the influence of the church.

Luther's insistence on investing everyday life with the same value as worship and on breaking the system of canon law and religious authority eventually resulted in profound changes in economic and social life. The elaborate prescribed relationships with neighbor, family, and church were swept away. Although they were encumbering and limiting, they also provided roots, personal relationships, and a meaning for life. Secular interests, work, and business now formed another world, one little connected with the religious and moral values that had until this time governed all aspects of life.

The most important influence on what we now call the Protestant ethic was the theology of John Calvin (1509–1564), who followed Luther as a reformer of Christianity. Calvin and his followers did not idealize the peasant, as did Luther, but accepted urban life as they found it. As R. H. Tawney puts it, "Like early Christianity and modern socialism, Calvinism was largely an urban movement."[17] Calvin's central theological notion, which distinguishes his position from that of Luther and of Catholicism, is predestination. According to Calvin, God is infinite, absolute, supreme and totally above and beyond human beings. There is no way of grasping or under-

---

[16] R. H. Tawney, *Religion and the Rise of Capitalism* (New York: Mentor, 1947), p. 83.
[17] Ibid., p. 92.

standing God and God's ways. In God's infinite power and wisdom, God has determined that it is fitting for his glory if only a small number of men and women be saved. Moreover, Calvin maintains that there is absolutely nothing a person can do to influence his or her own salvation; from all eternity God has freely predetermined it. A person lives to glorify God, and the major way a person glorifies God is in his or her life. If a person bends every talent and expends every energy in work and achieves success, this may be an indication that he or she is one of the saved. Although these individual efforts cannot directly affect or ensure salvation, if successful they do glorify God and may thus be a sign that the person is numbered among the elect. Probably even more motivating was the conviction that if a person was idle, disliked work, or was not successful, these were most likely signs that that individual was not among the saved.

Calvin taught that all must work and must never cease working. Profits earned must not be hoarded but must be invested in new works. Investment and resulting profit and wealth were thus encouraged: "With the new creed comes a new man, strong-willed, active, austere, hard-working from religious conviction. Idleness, luxury, prodigality, everything which softens the soul, is shunned as a deadly sin."[18] Calvin proposed a unique paradox: Deny the world; live as an ascetic in the world, because it cannot guarantee your salvation. Yet remember that your one duty is to glorify God, and the best way of doing that is by being a success at your chosen work, your calling. It is a precarious balance, difficult to achieve and even more difficult to maintain.

The Protestant ethic, therefore, stems directly from Calvin's teachings. He stressed the importance of hard work and the necessity to reinvest one's earnings in new works. Moreover, Calvin did not condemn interest and urban trade, as did Luther and Catholic leaders. Calvin not only urged working hard at one's occupation but also held that successful trade and commerce was but another way of glorifying God.

Weber's Analysis of the Protestant Ethic

Before leaving the influence of the Reformation on business ideology, let us look at the summary of that influence drawn up some two hundred years later by the sociologist Max Weber in *The Protestant Ethic and the Spirit of Capitalism*. It is ironic that Max Weber, a German, cites no other person more often as an example of the Protestant ethic than Benjamin Franklin, an American (we have examined Franklin's attitudes in Chapter 2).

Weber begins his analysis by noting that "business leaders and owners of Capital, as well as the higher grades of skilled labor, and even more the higher technically and commercially trained personnel of modern enter-

[18] Tilgher, "Work Through the Ages," p. 19.

prises, are overwhelmingly Protestant." He goes on to compare the Catholic and the Protestant: "The Catholic is quieter, having less of the acquisitive impulse; he prefers a life of the greatest possible security, even with a smaller income, to a life of risk and excitement, even though it may bring the chance of gaining honor and riches."[19] In trying to determine the reason why Protestants seem to be more successful, Weber examines the roots of the theology of Luther and Calvin, as we have done above. He notes that Reformation theology encouraged individuals to look on their work more seriously. Life demanded sobriety, self-discipline, diligence, and, above all, planning ahead and saving. A person's attention to the life of this world was serious in the extreme. In addition to having its own rewards, success was a reflection of God's glory and hence a hint as to whether that person was saved or not. It was therefore incumbent on all to be successful. Moreover, they had the means to achieve that success: "In practice this means that God helps those who help themselves. Thus the Calvinist ... himself creates his own salvation, or, as would be more correct, the conviction of it."[20]

An asceticism adequate to achieve the goal flowed from the Calvinistic ethic: "Waste of time is thus the first and in principle the deadliest of sins." On the same theme, the Calvinist asceticism "turned with all its force against one thing: the spontaneous enjoyment of life and all it had to offer." On the positive side, in the Calvinist and Puritan churches Weber finds "the continually repeated, often almost passionate preaching of hard, continuous bodily or mental labor."[21] But Weber observes that even in his day "the people filled with the spirit of capitalism today tend to be indifferent, if not hostile, to the Church." Then it most often happens that the pursuit of business and a career takes on the vehemence and all-embracing aspects of active religion: "Business with its necessary work becomes a necessary part of their lives." But this is what is "so irrational about this sort of life, where a man exists for the sake of his business, instead of the reverse." The Protestant ethic changed history. Contrary to the ethical convictions of centuries, "money-making became an end in itself to which people were bound, as a calling."[22]

In his last chapter Weber quotes both John Wesley and John Calvin when they point out a paradox. It is religion that makes people careful, hardworking, frugal; and this, in turn, enables them to build up wealth. "But as riches increase, so will pride, anger, and love of the world," in Wesley's words. Speaking of those on the lower end of that same economic ladder, Weber quotes Calvin: "Only when the people, i.e., the mass of laborers and

---

[19] Max Weber, *The Protestant Ethic and the Spirit of Capitalism*, trans. Talcott Parsons (New York: Scribner, 1958), pp. 35–41. Quoted with permission.

[20] Ibid., p. 145.

[21] Ibid., pp. 157–66.

[22] Ibid., pp. 70–73.

THE PROTESTANT ETHIC URGES
Hard work Self-control and sobriety (that is, humorlessness) Self-reliance Perseverance Saving and planning ahead Honesty and observing the "rules of the game"

FIGURE 3-1   The Protestant Ethic

craftsmen, were poor did they remain obedient to God."[23] Therein lies a paradox; the men who themselves are most responsible for the Protestant ethic foresee its collapse. Their religion demands hard work and saving, and this provides wealth. But wealth brings pride, luxury, and lack of will. It is therefore a highly unstable ethic, in part because its religious foundations tend to dissolve. But as we have seen in the case of Benjamin Franklin and many others, the ethic can take on a secular life of its own. It can perhaps continue with other, though no less vital, sources of vision and motivation. It remains for us to ascertain precisely what this new secular vision and new motivation will be.

The Protestant ethic (see Figure 3–1) derives from the Calvinist vision of how people should act in order to be successful in this life and also in the next. With the help of its tenets, Americans achieved success and developed the values described in the last chapter in the section "Values in American Life."

The Protestant ethic urges planning ahead, sobriety, diligence, and self-control for the individual. It promises a material reward and, in its religious strand, a good chance of salvation. Moreover, the Protestant ethic serves an additional and psychologically perhaps more important purpose. It assures the successful and wealthy that their wealth is deserved. They have property because they have worked for it and so have a right to it. As Weber himself observed, the wealthy man is not satisfied in knowing that he is fortunate:

> Beyond this, he needs to know that he has a *right* to his good fortune. He wants to be convinced that he "deserves" it, and above all, that he deserves it in

---

[23] Ibid., pp. 175–77. Some reject the attempt to link economic success with religious faith. They maintain that there are more plausible explanations for commercial success, such as "special education, family relationships and alien status." See Kurt Samuelson, *Religion and Economic Action*, trans. E. G. French (New York: Basic Books, 1961), p. 154. Nevertheless, the fact that Weber's theses are so widely accepted makes it a theory to be reckoned with. Whatever the causal relationships, religious values and economic development are there to be observed, and they have had a marked influence on one another.

comparison with others. He wishes to be allowed the belief that the less fortunate also merely experience their due.[24]

Thus the Protestant ethic not only provides a set of directions on how to
succeed and a motivation for doing so but also attempts to legitimate the
wealth that is acquired. The successful person says, "Anyone who was willing to work as hard as I did could have done as well, so it is clear that I
deserve the wealth I have." This attitude was also in accord with the acceptance of social Darwinism or survival of the fittest.

John Locke and the Right to Private Property

John Locke (1632–1704) had a considerable influence on the Founding
Fathers and through them on the American Constitution. He and Jean-Jacques
Rousseau also influenced the French Revolution and most of the subsequent
efforts to move toward more democratic governments. The Oxford-educated
Locke was both a philosopher and a politician. He was a practical man, having
served various government figures of his day, and his philosophy showed a
great concern for political and social questions.

Locke was concerned with various natural rights, but the right to which
he devoted most of his energy was the right to private property.[25] Locke held
that an individual has a right to self-preservation and so has a right to those
things that are required for this purpose. Individuals require property so that
they may feed and clothe their families and themselves. A person's labor is
what confers primary title to property. If individuals settle on land and work
it, they therefore deserve title to it. Locke's ideal was America, where there
was unlimited property available for anyone who was willing to clear and
work it.

Locke has been criticized for overemphasizing the rights of private
property and thus catering to the interests of his landowning patrons, and
this criticism may be justified. But he did not allow for a person's amassing
wealth without limit. Whatever is beyond what the individual can use is not
by right his or hers; it belongs to others and should be shared with them.

Rousseau's Social Contract

Jean-Jacques Rousseau (1712–1778) shared with other members of the
French Enlightenment a distrust of contemporary society and its institutions.
He believed that society, and even Enlightenment ideals such as reason,

---

[24] Max Weber, "The Social Psychology of World Religions," in *Max Weber: Essays in
Sociology*, ed. H. H. Gerth and C. Wright Mills (New York: Oxford University Press, 1946), p. 271.

[25] John Locke, *An Essay Concerning the True Original Extent and End of Civil Government*,
especially chap. 5, "Of Property," and chap. 9, "Of the Ends of Political Society and Government." See also the summary in Frederick Copleston, *A History of Philosophy*, vol. 5 (London:
Burns and Oates, 1964), pp. 129–31.

culture, and progress, had created unhealthy competition, self-interest, pseudosophistication, and a destruction of the "simple society" he valued. He believed it was unjust, effete, and dominated by the rich and by civil and church authorities. According to Rousseau, "Man was born free and everywhere he is in chains." Man's original state in nature is free, and although some form of society is necessary, freedom, reverence, family life, and the ordinary person must be central to it.

The *Social Contract* is an attempt to achieve the necessary activities, associations, and governments required in a civilized society without losing basic individual rights. A citizen's duty of obedience cannot be founded simply on the possession of power by those in authority. To be legitimate, it must rest on some sort of freely given consensus.[26] Rousseau's distrust of society's institutions also included private property. According to him, when private property is introduced into a society, equality disappears. Private property marks a departure from primitive simplicity and leads to numerous injustices and evils such as selfishness, domination, and servitude. In the state he proposes, Rousseau supports a sharply increased tax on any property that is not necessary for a man to modestly support himself and his family. For property that is necessary for that, there should be no tax at all. With regard to the illegitimacy of excessive wealth, Rousseau agrees with Locke.

Adam Smith's Capitalist Manifesto

The Scot Adam Smith (1723–1790) is the grandfather of capitalism and of free enterprise economics. As a political economist and moral philosopher, he was among the first to emphasize free exchange and to present economics as an independent branch of knowledge. His classic work *Wealth of Nations* was published in 1776 and so supported independence for economics and business in the same year that the American colonies declared their political independence from England.

In explaining economics Smith says, "Nobody ever saw a dog make a fair and deliberate exchange of one bone for another with another dog." A bit later he spells out the implications of this inability to exchange by showing that each animal is obliged "to support and defend itself, separately and independently, and derives no sort of advantage from that variety of talents with which nature has distinguished its fellows." Human beings, says Smith, are quite different in that they can take advantage of one another's unique genius. What a man is good at he does in abundance, sells to others, and thus "may purchase whatever part of the produce of other men's talents he has

---

[26] Jean-Jacques Rousseau, *The Social Contract and Discourse on the Origin and Foundation of Inequality Among Mankind* (New York: Washington Square Press, 1967). See also the summary of Rousseau in Copleston, *History of Philosophy*, vol. 6, especially pp. 68–69 and 80–100.

occasion for."[27] Smith's first and most familiar example is of the division of labor in pinmaking. One man, working alone and forming the entire pin, could perhaps "make one pin in a day, and certainly not make twenty." But when the operation is divided up into a number of separate operations so that "one man draws out the wire, another straights it, a third cuts it, a fourth points it, a fifth grinds it at the top for receiving the head," and so on, a group of pinmakers are able to make pins at a daily average of 4,800 pins per pinmaker, as Smith himself has observed.[28]

In addition to the value of exchange and the division of labor, Smith also examines the value of the free market, competition, and profit maximization. Smith was among the first to make a clear and plausible case that when individuals follow their own self-interest, it automatically works to the benefit of society as a whole. As individual competitors pursue their own maximum profit, they are all thus forced to be more efficient. This results in cheaper goods in the long run. Free competition in all markets and with all goods and services is thus to be encouraged; government intervention serves only to make operations less efficient and is thus to be avoided. The same principles apply to international trade. There should be a minimum of government interference in the form of duties, quotas, and tariffs. Smith's is the classical argument in support of free trade.

Smith takes some of his basic inspiration from the English philosopher Thomas Hobbes (1588–1679). Hobbes had maintained that individuals act simply to gain that which gives them pleasure or to avoid that which causes displeasure. Since this may differ for each individual, there is no objective good or value in reality itself. Hobbes's view of human motivation is that of "egoistic hedonism." Since Hobbes's view is that human nature is largely self-seeking and that there is no objective morality, it is not surprising that he held that might makes right. It is important to have power to protect one's person and goods. Whatever a person has the power to take belongs to that person. Hobbes acknowledges that this leads to insecurity and even war but maintains that they are an inescapable part of the human condition. On the theme of trade and economic activity, Smith quotes Hobbes's claim that "wealth is power." Wealth enables its possessor to purchase what he or she wants, and this in itself gives that person considerable control over others. So it is in the interest of individuals to increase their wealth.

To explain profit maximization, Smith uses the example of rent. Even though the owner of the land contributes nothing to production beyond the fact of ownership, nevertheless the owner will strive for a contract stipulating the highest rent the tenant can possibly afford to pay. The landlord will try to leave the tenant as little as possible of what he or she earns. Smith contends

---

[27] Adam Smith, *Wealth of Nations*, ed. J. C. Bullock (New York: Collier, 1909), pp. 19–23.
[28] Ibid., pp. 9–10.

that this is as it should be. On some occasions the landlord may leave the tenant a bit more for him- or herself, but this is and should be exceptional; it is due to "the liberality, more frequently the ignorance, of the landlord."[29]

As the grandfather of modern economics, Smith spells out clearly and graphically most of the current major principles operating in economic and business theory. He illustrates the great advantages of the division of labor, the free competitive market, and profit maximization and how they contribute to more efficient production. As individuals pursue self-interested goals, Smith's famous "invisible hand" guides economic and business activities so that they are more productive and cheaper and thus benefit society as a whole. Industry and commerce in the two centuries following Adam Smith have been extraordinarily successful. Moreover, business activities closely followed the model Smith described. The free market encouraged rapid economic growth. Economic motivation for most people up to Smith's time had been based more on obligations to a lord, proprietor, or one's family and on threats, fears, and sanctions. The free market and potentially unlimited monetary rewards shifted the entire basis of economic activity.

The free market and the possibility of unlimited profits are at the heart of the system's greatest strength: It taps positive motivation and rewards. It draws a man or woman into greater activity and creativity and quickly rewards those efforts. Furthermore, the rewards are tangible and measurable; by these standards there is little doubt as to who is a success. On the other hand, this new model for economic activity also includes the system's greatest weakness. It insulates a person from obligations to friends, family, fellow citizens, and the larger community, and replaces these obligations with an easily broken contract whose purpose is to obtain individual profit. Hence, individuals can much more readily come to feel that they are alone, that they are isolated, and that they are easily replaceable. Literature on the attitudes of managers and blue-collar workers alike shows that most experience this feeling of isolation and alienation.[30]

Put another way, Adam Smith and the Industrial Revolution that followed shifted people's view of society in such a way that they tended to compare it to a machine instead of to an organism, as formerly. In earlier times, men and women knew they were part of something larger than themselves. Families worked together, and they cared for their neighbors. They were dependent upon one another—like parts of an organism. They had a stake in their community and they belonged. This was replaced by a situation in which one's own work was sold. One no longer belonged, and one's very self became just another commodity in the market system. Every individual

---

[29] Ibid., pp. 153–71. See also Harold L. Johnson, "Adam Smith and Business Education," *AACSB Bulletin*, October 1976, pp. 1–4.

[30] See, for example, evidence of this dissatisfaction in Purcell and Cavanagh, *Blacks in the Industrial World*, pp. 72–75, 236–38.

can and will be replaced when he or she becomes obsolete, old, and inefficient, just as is the case with parts of a machine.[31]

Adam Smith provided a remarkably accurate and integrated picture of
developing business activities. He clearly detailed the advantages of free
exchange and the free market. As such, he was to people of the nineteenth
century a father of "liberal economics." Smith is still widely quoted and,
although challenged and criticized, remains to this day a principal spokesperson for capitalism and free enterprise.

THE PROTESTANT ETHIC AND THE GROWTH OF A NATION

The year 1776, when a new nation was born on an unspoiled continent, is an
appropriate point at which to shift our attention back to the United States. In
Chapter 1 we surveyed the early values that developed in the American
colonies, with an examination of the Puritans and the work of Benjamin
Franklin. After independence, those values and attitudes had an unprecedented opportunity to be realized. The nation provided an ideal testing
ground for enterprising farmers, traders, prospectors, entrepreneurs, and
theorists. Business and commerce grew at an extraordinary pace. It is important to examine that growth briefly and, more to our purpose, the attitudes
that undergirded it.

The early days of the new republic were dominated by the farmer. The
colonial merchant provided the trading link between the early Americans,
responding to needs and transporting food and goods. From 1800 to 1850,
wholesalers took the place of merchants. They "were responsible for directing the flow of cotton, wheat and lumber from the West to the East and to
Europe."[32] The rapid growth of the American industrial system that was to
make the United States the most productive nation in the world had begun
by the middle of the nineteenth century. "In 1849 the United States had only
6,000 miles of railroad and even fewer miles of canals, but by 1884 its railroad
corporations operated 202,000 miles of track, or 43 percent of the total mileage in the world."[33] The number of those working in factories also grew very
rapidly during this period. In terms of manufactured goods, "By 1894 the
value of the output of American industry equalled that of the combined
output of the United Kingdom, France and Germany."[34] Growth continued to
accelerate, until within twenty years the United States was producing more
than a third of the industrial goods of the world.

---

[31] For this and many other insights, the author thanks Otto Bremmer.

[32] Alfred D. Chandler, "The Role of Business in the United States: A Historical Survey,"
Daedelus 98, no. 1 (1969): 26.

[33] Ibid., p. 27.

[34] Ibid.

Mining in the mountains of the far West provides a paradigm of the strengths and weaknesses of the American character: energetic, flexible, and enterprising, but also self-centered and with little concern for long-term consequences. Tales of silver, gold, and other minerals in the mountains thrilled imaginations across the continent. Mining called for strong, resourceful people. Hundreds of thousands took the challenge, risking their fortunes, their lives, and often their families to try to find the ore. Vast amounts of capital and superhuman energies were expended. The "get rich quick" spirit of these prospectors was a prelude to that of the entrepreneurs who came later. Virginia City, Nevada, was built over the famed Comstock Lode. What was bare desert and mountains in 1860 became within five years one of the most rapidly growing and thriving cities of the new West. The energies and genius of thousands sank dozens of shafts into the rock, supported them with timbers, built flumes—and an entire city. Between 1859 and 1880 more than $306 million worth of silver was taken from the mountains.[35] The magnitude of the effort and the accomplishment can be gathered from this description:

> In the winter of 1866 the towns and mills along the Comstock Lode were using two hundred thousand cords of wood for fuel, while the time soon came when eighty million feet of lumber a year went down into the chambers and drifts. Since the mountains were naked rock, flumes had to be built from the forested slopes of the Sierras, and by 1880, there were ten of them with an aggregate length of eighty miles.[36]

Adolph Sutro owned a quartz mill on the other side of the mountains on the Carlson River, and he saw an easier way to get the ore out of the mountains. He envisioned a three-mile-long tunnel that would extend through the mountains from the river valley and intersect the Comstock mines 1,600 feet below the surface. The tunnel would drain the series of mines to that level and also enable the ore to be taken out through the tunnel for processing where fuel and water were plentiful. By 1866, Sutro had obtained contracts from twenty-three of the largest mining companies to use the tunnel when it was completed:

> After incessant effort, in which any man of less marvelous pluck and energy would have failed, he raised sufficient capital to begin the project. In 1869 he broke ground for the tunnel and set a corps of drillers upon the task that was to occupy them for eight weary years. It was the labor of a giant.[37]

Sutro finished his tunnel and put it in use in 1877. But within three years, the boom collapsed. The value of the silver mining stock sank from a high of $393

---

[35] Allan Nevins, *The Emergence of Modern America*, vol. 8 (New York: Macmillan, 1927), p. 137. For a discussion of these and other issues raised in this chapter, see Daniel T. Rodgers, *The Work Ethic in Industrial America, 1850–1920* (Chicago: University of Chicago Press, 1978).

[36] Nevins, *Emergence of Modern America*, p. 136.

[37] Ibid., p. 137.

million in 1875 to less than $7 million in 1880. People slowly began to leave Virginia City, and today it is literally a ghost town, with only remnants of roads, homes, and a few of the more substantial large buildings left to remind us of what it once was.

Virginia City illustrates how the great talents and wealth of a society can be quickly channeled to accomplish tremendous feats; it also shows how such accomplishments are often short-lived and not designed to encourage stability. This sort of activity appeals to the energetic and fast-moving entrepreneur; it does not appeal to family people, who look to their own and their children's future. Virginia City illustrates both the strengths and the weaknesses of the American entrepreneurial spirit. The gold rush a decade earlier in California left a more permanent mark, since the new inhabitants did not leave when the gold ran out. The prospectors, miners, and fortune seekers converged from all parts of the country, disrupting communities and families. Before their coming, California had had a unique style. "To these California imperatives of simple, gracious, and abundant living, Americans had come in disrespect and violence."[38] Exploitation of the land kept people moving, and California chronicler Kevin Starr focuses on some of the problems they left in their wake:

> Leaving the mountains of the Mother Lode gashed and scarred like a deserted battlefield, Californians sought easy strikes elsewhere. Most noticeably in the areas of hydraulic mining, logging, the destruction of wildlife, and the depletion of the soil Americans continued to rifle California all through the nineteenth century.
>
> The state remained, after all, a land of adventuring strangers, a land characterized by an essential selfishness and an underlying instability, a fixation upon the quick acquisition of wealth, an impatience with the more subtle premises of human happiness. These were American traits, to be sure, but the Gold Rush intensified and consolidated them as part of a regional experience.[39]

Throughout these years of rapid economic change, the role of the entrepreneurs was central. Their brains, ingenuity, and willingness to risk gave us most of our economic success and growth. At the same time, their myopic desire for short-term gain caused many failures and much personal anguish. With this as background, let us return to the leaders of thought who have had a profound influence on American business values.

American Individualism Ralph Waldo Emerson Style

To this day, the American businessperson is characterized as an individualist. One articulate, persuasive, and most influential champion of freedom and the importance of the individual was Ralph Waldo Emerson (1803–

---

[38] Kevin Starr, *Americans and the California Dream* (New York: Oxford University Press, 1973), p. 33.

[39] Ibid., pp. 65–66.

1882). Coming soon after the French Enlightenment and Rousseau, Emerson is the best-known American proponent of individualism. He sees human nature as having natural resources within itself. Societal structures and supports tend only to limit the immense potential of the individual. Given freedom, individuals can act, grow, and benefit themselves and others. But they require an absence of restraints imposed by people, cultures, and governments. Emerson's friend Henry David Thoreau acted on this ideology and built himself a hut at Walden Pond, outside Boston, where he reflected and wrote alone in the unimpeded, open atmosphere of trees, grass, and water.

In Emerson's book of essays *The Conduct of Life*, there is one entitled "Wealth."[40] Here Emerson applies his philosophy of individualism to economics and the marketplace. A person should contribute and not just receive. If an individual follows his or her own nature, he or she will not only become a producer but will also become wealthy in the process. Individuals contribute little if they only pay their debts and do not add to the wealth available. Meeting only one's own needs is expensive; it is better to be rich and thus be able to meet one's needs and add to wealth as well. And doing both coincides with one's own natural inclinations. Emerson insists that getting rich is something any person with a little ingenuity can achieve. It depends on factors the person has totally under his or her own control:

> Wealth is in applications of mind to nature, and the art of getting rich consists not in industry, much less in saving, but in a better order, in timeliness, in being at the right spot. One man has stronger arms, or longer legs; another sees by the course of streams, and growth of markets, where land will be wanted, makes a clearing to the river, goes to sleep, and wakes up rich.[41]

Emerson's heroes are the independent Anglo-Saxons. They are a strong race who, by means of their personal independence, have become the merchants of the world. They do not look to government "for bread and games." They do not look to clans, relatives, friends, or aristocracy to take care of them or to help them get ahead; they rely on their own initiative and abilities. Emerson's optimistic view of the potential of the free and strong individual released from the fetters of government and custom remains an important support of American values. While much of the Protestant Ethic has changed, Emerson's view of the individual is still with us.

Children and Immigrants in Nineteenth-Century Factories

Before 1840, factory workers in the United States labored 12–14 hours a day, six or seven days a week. An 84-hour workweek was common. By 1860,

---

[40] Ralph W. Emerson, *The Conduct of Life and Other Essays* (London: Dent, 1908), pp. 190–213.

[41] Ibid., p. 192.

the average workday dropped to 10.6 hours a day, six days a week, but the 12–14 hour workday was still typical in many industries, including the textile mills of New England.[42]

In 1890, steelworkers worked 12 hours a day, seven days a week; most made $1.25 a day. Those wages went for rent, and there was little left to buy food or anything else for a family. Even if a steelworker worked 12 hours a day every day of the year, it was still not sufficient to support a family.[43] Therefore, many of these poor immigrants were single, and others left their families in Europe. Someone working in the steel mills could not readily support a family.

When the immigrants came, they knew that the work would be difficult and dangerous. They were at the bottom of the status ladder and therefore had to accept the hardest and most poorly paid work. A Hungarian churchman examined the conditions in Pittsburgh steel mills and said, "Wherever the heat is most insupportable, the flames most scorching, the smoke and soot most choking, there we are certain to find compatriots bent and wasted with toil."[44]

Many young children also worked under some of these same conditions. In 1910 two million boys and girls, one-fifth of all American children ten to fifteen years old, worked ten to fourteen hours a day. In Syracuse, New York, factories would not hire children unless they were at least eight years old.[45] Those who worked were the children of the immigrants and the poor, since their families needed the additional income. Child labor was a bargain for employers, since children's wages were less than those for adults. Further underscoring contemporary values and the acceptance of such factory conditions is the fact that before 1920 two laws passed by the U.S. Congress to restrict child labor were declared unconstitutional by the Supreme Court.

Working conditions were most often miserable and dangerous. Textile workers suffered brown lung disease, quarry workers breathed stone dust, coal miners suffered black lung disease and many deaths due to cave-ins, and many other workers inhaled toxic chemical fumes. The annual toll of those killed or injured in industry was roughly one million at the turn of the century.

At U.S. Steel's South Works in the Pittsburgh area in 1910, "almost one-quarter of the recent immigrants in the works each year—3,273 in five years—were injured or killed."[46] Working on the railroads was also very

---

[42] Gary M. Walton and Ross Robertson, *History of the American Economy* (New York: Harcourt Brace Jovanovich, 1983), pp. 280, 437.

[43] David Brody, *Steelworkers in America: The Nonunion Era* (Cambridge, Mass.: Harvard University Press, 1980), p. 98.

[44] Ibid., p. 99.

[45] Walton and Robertson, *History of the American Economy*, p. 439.

[46] Brody, *Steelworkers in America*, p. 101.

dangerous. In 1890, 2,451 railroad workers were killed, and this figure does not include many more civilians killed by trains.[47]

Companies often provided housing for their workers. Steel companies built good housing for better paid men and "shanties" (their own word) for the unskilled. Four men slept, ate, and washed in a ten-by-fourteen-foot shanty. The annual rent charged was more than twice the cost of building the pine board shanty.[48] Steel owners and executives had ready responses to criticisms: The immigrants were eager for work, they made much more than they would have made in Europe, and their living conditions were poor because they used their salaries on beer and whiskey.

Given such low wages and poor treatment, it is not surprising that in the United States during this period the rich became richer and the poor became poorer. One percent of the population owned as much as the remaining 99 percent combined.[49]

Establishment Churches and Business

Churches have two sometimes conflicting roles to play in society: (1) to help people worship God and (2) to help them understand and deal with the moral issues of their everyday lives. The second role involves sensitizing people to the moral problems that exist. Before 1920 this required calling attention to the abuses indicated above: child labor, dangerous working conditions, and working hours so long that decent family life was impossible. Yet as a church and its leaders become recognized and respected in society, they are easily lulled into blindness concerning the evils of the society that gives them increased status; they are thus deterred from acting as prophets and prodders of the public conscience.

A church has a responsibility to help all, yet it can be so influenced by its affluent members that its ministers oppose change, "rabble rousers," and social justice and it becomes part of the Establishment. The church and its members would risk losing too much if change occurred. A lesson for today can be learned by examining the actions of the more respected churches in the United States in the last century.

The dominant American Protestant churches in the nineteenth century, while preaching charity and concern for the poor, nevertheless vehemently defended the economic system that had grown up with the Protestant ethic. In this period, churches and schools had much more influence over American life and morals than is true today. The prestigious private colleges of the eastern Establishment taught the values of private property, free trade, and

[47] Otto L. Bettmann, *The Good Old Days: They Were Terrible!* (New York: Random House, 1974), p. 70.

[48] Brody, *Steelworkers in America*, p. 110.

[49] Bettmann, *The Good Old Days*, p. 67.

individualism. These religiously oriented schools (both Harvard and Yale were still Congregationalist at this time) generally taught conservative economic and business values along with their moral philosophy.

To many of the clergy, since God had clearly established economic laws, it would be dangerous to tamper with them. Francis Wayland, president of Brown University and author of the most popular economics text then used, intertwines economics and theology in stating his basic position: "God has made labor necessary to our well being." We must work both because idleness brings punishment and because work brings great riches; these are two essential, powerful, and immutable motives for work.[50] Wayland concluded from this simple principle that all property should be private and held by individuals. Charity should not be given except to those who absolutely cannot work, and the government should not impose tariffs or quotas or otherwise interfere.

In the last twenty-five years of the nineteenth century, the major Protestant Churches went through an agonizing reexamination. Up to this time, the churches had wholeheartedly accepted Adam Smith's economics and canonized it as part of the "divine plan." They defended private property, business, the need to work, and even wealth. Then two severe, bloody labor disturbances occurred that forced the churches to reconsider their traditional survival-of-the-fittest theories.

The first of these conflicts followed a severe economic depression in 1877. Wages of train workers were cut by 10 percent, and they protested. They picketed and halted trains. Army troops were called to defend railroad property, and they fought with desperate mobs of workers. In the confusion, scores of workers were shot. The churches generally sided with the Establishment and self-righteously preached to the workers on the divine wisdom of the American economy. Hear the *Christian Union:*

> If the trainmen knew a little more of political economy they would not fall so easy a prey to men who never earn a dollar of wages by good solid work. ... What a sorry set of ignoramuses they must be who imagine that they are fighting for the rights of labor in combining together to prevent other men from working for low wages because, forsooth, they are discontented with them.[51]

The religious press, reflecting the attitudes of its patrons, took a hard line against what it saw as anarchy, riots, and support of weak and lazy men.

A decade later another serious confrontation occurred. On the occasion of a labor meeting at the Haymarket in Chicago, the police shot several of a group of strikers. A few days later, a bomb was thrown at the police. As is

---

[50] Henry F. May, *Protestant Churches and Industrial America* (New York: Harper & Row, 1949), p. 15.

[51] Ibid., p. 93.

often the case in such situations, facts and circumstances were forgotten as near hysteria swept the religious press. The Protestant *Independent* was typical: "A mob should be crushed by knocking down or shooting down the men engaged in it; and the more promptly this is done the better."[52] Only when these strikingly un-Christian outbursts had ended did the clergy have the opportunity to reflect on what had happened and how they themselves had reacted. It then became clear how biased, inflexible, and violent had been their stance—hardly what one would expect of churches. During this period the clergy were anxious to accommodate their churches' position to the new industrial movements. They changed no creeds or confessions but "progressively identified [themselves] with competitive individualism at the expense of community."[53] From the rubble of these mistakes and later recognized biases came the impetus toward a new social consciousness, specifically in the form of the social gospel.

Praise of Acquisitiveness and Wealth

Defense of free enterprise and praise of acquisitiveness and riches were not limited to the Establishment Congregational and Presbyterian churches. The Baptist preacher Russell Conwell traveled the country giving his famous speech "Acres of Diamonds." He delivered it more than five thousand times around the turn of the century to enraptured audiences eager to hear that to gather wealth was God's will.

Conwell's speech tells of a man who goes out to seek wealth; in the meantime his successor on the farm finds diamonds in the yard he had left behind. His message: Any man has it within his grasp to make himself wealthy if he is willing to work at it:

> I say that you ought to get rich, and it is your duty to get rich. How many of my pious brethren say to me, "Do you, a Christian minister, spend your time going up and down the country advising young people to get rich, to get money?" "Yes of course I do." They say, "Isn't that awful. Why don't you preach the gospel instead of preaching about man's making money?" "Because to make money honestly is to preach the gospel." That is the reason. The men who get rich may be the most honest men you will find in the community.[54]

Conwell here cites what to him was the happy confluence of deeply felt religious convictions and the life of the marketplace. Because of the more traditional religious values of poverty and humility, riches often brought qualms of conscience to contemporary believers. Conwell represents the

---

[52] Ibid., p. 101.

[53] Martin Marty, *Righteous Empire: The Protestant Experience in America* (New York: Dial, 1970), p. 110.

[54] Russell Conwell, *Acres of Diamonds* (New York: Harper, 1915), p. 18.

tradition that tries to wed faith and fortune: There can be no better demonstration of faith in God than to use one's abilities to their fullest, to be a success, and to accumulate the goods of the earth (to be used responsibly, of course). Conwell himself made a fortune from his lectures and, following his own advice on investment, used the money to found Temple University.

Praise of wealth not suprisingly also came from those who became wealthy. A handful of industrialists—called the robber barons—had an immense, enduring influence on America and American industry around the turn of the century. Among them, the immigrant Scot Andrew Carnegie enjoyed his role as industrial and "moral" leader. With the help of financier J. P. Morgan, Carnegie had put together United States Steel in 1901; he accumulated immense wealth in the process and loved to tell all who would listen why he deserved it. Furthermore, with millions at his disposal, Carnegie set out to establish libraries in every city and town in the United States, each proudly bearing the Carnegie name.

Carnegie had amassed a huge personal fortune, even though he was well aware that many of his own steelworkers were not well paid. He maintained that God gave him his wealth. Carnegie made no apology for the inequality and in fact defended it as the survival of the fittest. The millionaire's money would do no good if it were paid to the workers:

> Much of this sum, if distributed in small quantities among the people, would have been wasted in the indulgence of appetite, some of it in excess, and it may be doubted whether even the part put to the best use, that of adding to the comforts of the home, would have yielded results for the race at all comparable.[55]

According to Carnegie, it is only the wealthy who can endow libraries and universities and who can best look after the long-run good of society as a whole. The money is much better spent when the wealthy accumulate it in large amounts so that with it they can accomplish great things.

For this reason, Carnegie felt that the wealthy person should "set an example of modest, unostentatious living, shunning display or extravagance." He should hold his money in trust for society and be "strictly bound as a matter of duty to administer in the manner which, in his judgement, is best calculated to produce the most beneficial results for the community."[56] Inequality and the accumulation of great fortunes are good for society, along with "the concentration of business, industrial and commercial, in the hands

---

[55] Andrew Carnegie, "Wealth," in *Democracy and the Gospel of Wealth*, ed. Gail Kennedy (Boston: D. C. Heath, 1949), p. 6.

[56] Ibid., p. 7. David M. Potter, in *People of Plenty: Economic Abundance and the American Character* (Chicago: University of Chicago Press, 1954), maintains that in an even more fundamental sense, a democratic system depends on economic surplus (pp. 111f).

of a few." This concentration of wealth enables the most able to use the funds for the best interest of society.

Carnegie defended his fortune, his right to have it and dispose of it as he saw fit. He was not totally objective in his examination of the socioeconomic system; he was profiting too much from it. Thus, not surprisingly, he was able to overlook the injustices he and his company supported.

Manufacturing and Scientific Management

The growth of manufacturing did, in fact, provide a new and much faster means of attaining wealth and economic growth. With increases in productivity, higher wages could be paid and greater profits obtained for the owner at the same time. This was a considerable departure from past eras, when fortunes had been made by trade, transport, or lending (and, of course, wars and plunder). As a result, wealth had been considered more of a fixed quantity: What one person gained, another lost. The advent of manufacturing demonstrated clearly that the economy was not a zero-sum game—it was *possible* for each party in the exchange to benefit financially. Whether this occurred depended largely on productivity.

Frederick W. Taylor, founder of scientific management, focused on better methods in manufacturing as a way to increase productivity. Productivity is, of course, the amount of a product that is produced within a given period of time. Mechanization and careful planning would enable workers to produce more than they could without planning. This was Taylor's insight: Worker and management experience plus intuitive judgment are not enough. For the sake of greater productivity, which would benefit all concerned, the work setting and even the motions of the job itself ought to be carefully studied to discover the most efficient tools and techniques.

As factory work became more complex, Taylor gained greater support for his view. No single person, worker or supervisor, could be aware of all the mechanical, psychological, and technological factors involved in planning even one job. Efficiency required careful planning by a team with various competencies. Intuition, experience, and seat-of-the-pants judgments would no longer do. Scientific management unwittingly undermined Spencer's notions of survival of the fittest. Taylor pointed out that allowing the "best person" to surface naturally was inefficient. In the contemporary complex world, few people had the ability to achieve maximum productivity by themselves. Greater efficiency and productivity demanded the intervention of planners.[57]

---

[57] Frederick Winslow Taylor, *Scientific Management* (New York: Harper & Brothers, 1947), pp. 36, 98, 99; see also Daniel Nelson, *Frederick W. Taylor and the Rise of Scientific Management* (Madison: University of Wisconsin Press, 1980).

Taylor was in favor of higher wages and shorter hours for workers, but he saw no need for unions. If scientific management is implemented and the best and most efficient means of production achieved, there will be no grounds for petty quarrels and grievances. Policies and procedures will be set by scientific inquiry into what objectively is most efficient. And that which is most efficient will benefit worker and management alike, since both will share in the results of this greater productivity: greater profits. In Taylor's scheme, the personal exercise of authority would be eliminated. Managers would be subject to the same policies, rules, and methodology as the workers themselves.

Although he agreed with the traditional managerial ideology that workers pursue their own self-interest and try to maximize their own return, Taylor challenged the notion that each person worked out this struggle in isolation, apart from and even in competition with other human beings. In an industrial organization greater productivity can be achieved only when each worker, along with management, cooperates to find the best means of production. Taylor pointed out how the returns to all were diminished if a single worker is not working at his or her most efficient job and pace. Taylor set out to help both worker and manager achieve maximum efficiency, which can be done only in cooperation. Up to this time a lazy man or woman had been penalized; now Taylor proposed to reward workers by enabling them to work to their greatest capacity and receiver greater financial return.

Scientific management was not greeted happily by either workers or managers, because it tended to deprive each of a measure of freedom and judgment. Nevertheless, in the long run Taylor's methodology, and perhaps even more his ideology, have had an immense impact on industrial life. In a sharp break from earlier American individualism, Taylor demonstrated that productivity and the system, in this case manufacturing, were more important than the lone individual. The emerging corporation itself bore additional testimony to the new importance of planning, expertise, and cooperation. In subsequent decades the corporation was to provide even more individual benefits: vacations, retirement, and medical care. It was no longer the individual standing alone but rather the person working and cooperating with a larger group to achieve greater productivity that characterized American business. Today managers recognize the importance of cooperation and participation, but they also seek to encourage individual initiative and entrepreneurship—even within large firms.

Masculine Management

The world and the ideals we have been discussing in this chapter are those of the business*man*. For centuries, business, commerce, and trade have all been largely "for men only." Women did not even obtain the right to vote until the twentieth century. Fully half of the potential technical and managerial talent has been lost. Also, a glance at any firm's equal employment opportunity figures, especially at the "officials and managers" category, immediately spotlights the results of centuries of racial prejudice. Moreover, it has been only within the past generation or so that the religious prejudice in the executive suites of the largest corporations has broken down; the WASP (white Anglo-Saxon Protestant) clique is cracking. Blacks, Jews, Catholics, and women are only now climbing up the managerial ladder into the executive suites.

SUMMARY AND CONCLUSIONS

From ancient times to the Middle Ages, Western attitudes toward work lost their negative cast and became progressively more positive. Biblical injunctions and monastic practices helped to integrate work, labor-saving devices, and a planned day into the average person's life. Then, in the sixteenth century, the Protestant Reformation made the successful performance of an individual's "calling" or occupation one of the primary duties of life. Although a rather joyless vision, it encouraged a focusing of energies that made rapid economic growth possible. The central importance given to private property and the freedom of the individual further supported this growth.

The American business ideology as described in this chapter was ideal for a period of expansion, rapid growth, and exploitation of land and resources. It gave the poor an opportunity and exploited the immigrant's eagerness for work. It also gave a new nation its railroads, mines, industries, and cities.

It was an ideology that advocated hard work, competition, self-reliance and self-discipline, individualism, and saving and planning ahead. These were called forth by a vision preached in church, school, and town meeting alike, a vision of growth, superiority, and improvement of the world for the next generation.

Several elements converged to fashion this new and unique vision called the American business ideology:

1. The *frontier* provided opportunities to the immigrants who had come to the New World looking for a challenging new life in farming, mining, or manufacturing, where potential rewards were immense.
2. The *Protestant ethic*, which underscored the value of hard work in a person's occupation, was carried to the New World by the Puritans and translated into a secular vision by people like Benjamin Franklin.
3. *Faith in free enterprise* gave the individual confidence and vigor. The system worked well in encouraging economic growth and, moreover, was shown to be intellectually sound by the classical economists.
4. *Competition* became more explicit and central with the advent of the theory of evolution and the recognition of the principles of natural selection and the

survival of the fittest. Natural forces, if allowed to operate without constraint, would provide the best specimen of human being and, in a parallel fashion, the most efficient firm.

5. *The role of government* was to apply as few constraints as possible to business activity; its central purpose was to protect the private property of its citizens. On this Thomas Jefferson is often quoted: "That government is best which governs least."

It is an irony of history that emphasis on the rugged individualist peaked during the latter half of the nineteenth century, just at the time the business scene was dominated by oligopolies and trusts. A few firms in an industry virtually controlled production, prices, and even wages. It was difficult for an individual, no matter how rugged, to raise the capital necessary to compete. At that time and since then, it has become apparent that this American business ideology, although it may provide a motivation and a vision for the enterprising individual, does not really give an accurate description of the marketplace. For the market is not totally free.

The goal of the traditional American business ideology is expansion and growth; its focus is on material reward for the individual. But the assumption that an individual always wants more in the way of material goods leads to further questions. Is the goal of more material goods sufficient to motivate the individual to give most of his or her physical and psychic energy to the business enterprise? Are there other, more subtle values of the individual in an affluent society that must be tapped if we are to continue to be economically healthy? From another perspective, to what extent will one's "calling" continue to be central in one's life? Or consider a question that will have profound impact on national policy: Is a goal of material growth necessary for a business creed for the future? If so, what sort of growth? These and other, similar questions will be addressed in the following chapters.

DISCUSSION QUESTIONS

1. How does a knowledge of history help the manager? How does it help in understanding the development of business values?

2. What was the attitude of Plato and Aristotle toward work? What influence did Jesus and the Gospels have on the value of work?

3. What attitudes toward work did the early Benedictine monasteries contribute? What meaning might these attitudes have for work today?

4. Describe how John Locke's attitude toward private property influenced the Protestant ethic and early American attitudes? How does it influence current business values?

5. Did Martin Luther have a favorable attitude toward business and commerce? Did John Calvin? Why did Calvin think that the Protestant ethic would decay?

6. Why is Adam Smith called the grandfather of economics? Compare his attitudes on work and efficiency with those of Benjamin Franklin.

7. Citing historic events and attitudes, indicate what characteristic American values were illustrated during the silver-mining days at Virginia City, Nevada. Compare these values with those of the Establishment churches during the same period (i.e., roughly 1860–1890).

8. What are the similarities and dissimilarities between the Protestant ethic and American individualism? Outline how the Protestant ethic aided in the economic development of the New World.

9. Describe the hours, wages, and working conditions of poor people, immigrants, and children before 1920.

10. What are the two conflicting responsibilities of churches? How does your church meet each of these responsibilities?

11. Outline the arguments of Conwell and Carnegie on the goodness of acquisitiveness and wealth.

12. What was Andrew Carnegie's position on wages, wealth, and the responsibilities of the rich? Compare his attitudes on work with those of Frederick W. Taylor (scientific management). What do they have in common? How do they differ?

CASE: TAX-FREE CAMERA

Eric has a work-study position in the marketing department at Queenstown University. At a local camera shop Eric is about to purchase a $250 camera for his personal use. He realizes that if he tells the salesperson that he is purchasing it for university use, he will save $15 sales tax. Eric's friend Joan says, "Everyone does it. And the state has more money than they can use anyway." Eric agrees and tells the salesperson that it is for university use. What are the ethical issues in this case? Do you agree with Joan's statement? What should Eric do? Why?

EXERCISE: ETHICAL CLIMATE OF AN ORGANIZATION

The real goals, values, and ethics of an organization are vitally important yet rarely receive the attention they deserve. The purpose of this project is to enable you to examine and articulate the values, ethics, and commitments of an organization of your choice. To complete the exercise do the following:

1. Form teams of three people each by randomly counting off. Meet with your team and, through discussion, decide on the organization you wish to study (e.g., a firm you have access to information about).

2. On a single sheet of paper indicate (a) your team members, (b) your choice of firm, (c) sources of information, and (d) plan for the division of labor. Turn this in at the end of class today.

3. With your team, determine the *proclaimed* goals, values, and ethics of the organization and its *proclaimed* commitments to its key stakeholders—customers, employees, suppliers, the local community, the larger community (including the physical environment), and shareholders. For this purpose, study the mission or goal statement of the organization, its codes of ethics, the speeches of top managers, and relevant materials from annual reports or training manuals. Indicate any values missing from those proclaimed. Be explicit and comprehensive.

4. Determine the *real* goals, values, ethics, and commitments of the organization. Consult individuals who have direct contact (employees, customers, others), use personal observation, and study written materials evaluating the company.

5. Prepare a twelve- to twenty-page double-spaced typed report of your group's findings. This may include an appendix with supporting materials. Spell out the (a) proclaimed values and (b) actual values of the firm. See if the organization is doing what it says it does. Specify what it is doing to meet obligations to stakeholders. Indicate if it is meeting these obligations very well, satisfactorily, or not well and give suggestions for improvement. Be explicit and specific.

6. Finally, evaluate your own and each team member's contributions to the project and give feedback to each team member. This written evaluation is due with the report.

CHAPTER FOUR
CRITICS OF FREE ENTERPRISE

Capitalism has drowned the most heavenly ecstasies of religious fervor, of chivalrous enthusiasm, of philistine sentimentalism, in the icy water of egotistical calculation. It has resolved personal worth into exchange value.

Karl Marx and Frederick Engels*

No critique of free enterprise has proven as perceptive, trenchant, or appealing as Karl Marx's. Marxism raises serious questions about the moral and social consequences of the economic system we have adopted. It also offers an alternative set of values and indeed an entire alternative economic system. Marxism has given us not only intelligent critics of the free enterprise system but also a block of Communist nations whose people outnumber those of the capitalist nations of the world.

Marxism, along with the variety of attempts to organize people and production along communal lines, is an important movement in world history and deserves its own chapter. Its ideology and the presuppositions of that ideology stand in marked contrast to the ideology of Western nations. Moreover, nations which embrace Marxism separate themselves physically from their neighbors in order to develop their own value system. Marxist leaders regard Western self-oriented materialism as corrupting; for them, it is best to keep a distance from any value system that emphasizes self-interest.

There is indeed much that is good in the presuppositions and way of

---

*The principal author of the section on Marxism in this chapter is Arthur F. McGovern, S. J., professor of philosophy, University of Detroit. He is the author of *Marxism: An American Christian Perspective* (New York: Orbis, 1981).

living that Marxists advocate. We can learn from their valid criticisms of free enterprise and from the alternative models of living which they espouse and on which they base their own lives.

Free enterprise, or *capitalism* as it is called by its critics, is the socioeconomic system of most of the developed, industrialized countries of the northern hemisphere. The countries of North America and Western Europe, as well as Japan, constitute the powerful core of the so-called first world countries. Russia, China, Cuba, and the countries of Eastern Europe operate with a Marxist socioeconomic system; they make up the so-called second world. The poor nations of Asia, Africa, and South America are considered third world countries. The term *third world* originally referred to nations not belonging to either of the two main ideological camps. The rapidly developing Pacific rim nations (e.g., Korea, Taiwan, and Singapore) are essentially capitalist, yet they have large numbers of poor people.

Marxism is not the only social system built on cooperative, rather than competitive, ideals. Much earlier, Christians called for sharing one's goods with one's sisters and brothers (Acts 2:44–47). Monastic living, discussed in Chapter 3, is an enduring model of living and working together and sharing goods. However, Catholic orders of women and men, which depend on shared religious values and a lifelong commitment, were never intended for everyone; they are voluntary associations for those who choose them.

Medieval European communities were more cooperative than their contemporary counterparts. Guilds, stable populations, and extended families all living within walking distance gave these early communities cohesion. On the other hand, they also had a rigid hierarchical social system. If the father was a butcher, so too was the son.

Criticism of capitalism also did not begin with Marx. As the Industrial Revolution took hold of Europe in the nineteenth century, numerous critics and socialist theories emerged. Saint-Simon, Fourier, Cabet, Hess, Blanqui, Owen, and countless others attacked the capitalist system and proposed various ways of achieving socialism: state ownership, national workshops, voluntary communes, revolutionary overthrow by elitist conspiracy groups, revolutionary overthrow by the masses. (The communes advocated by Cabet [who first coined the term "communism" in the 1830s] and by Fourier inspired some of the ventures in communal ownership attempted in the United States. One was Brook Farm, which was located in West Roxbury, within the city limits of present-day Boston. We will consider American experiments in cooperative communal life later in the chapter.)

Before examining the criticisms of capitalism, let us step back for a moment to probe some of *our own* beliefs and presuppositions. Each of the following questions can be asked of any of the major leaders of thought discussed in this book. To obtain additional clarity on your own goals, beliefs, and value system, ponder these questions. What do *you* believe regarding the following fundamental issues:

1. Is humanity inevitably headed toward long-term progress and the better life or is it headed for the collapse of civilization and catastrophe?

2. If neither progress nor collapse is inevitable, do we have it in our power to affect future societies (e.g., societies existing one hundred years hence)? If so, in what way?

3. Is anything always wrong or always right (e.g., murder)? Is lying or stealing always, or generally, wrong, or is it all relative, a matter of social expectations and the law?

4. Does life end at death? Is there an afterlife? How does this influence my work, my life, and my attitudes?

5. Is human nature essentially good, needing only support and encouragement for its development, or is human nature essentially self-seeking, so that an economic system ought to build on this selfishness and make best use of it?

6. Is competition the most effective motivator for you? Is cooperation more effective, or do you respond to some combination?

7. Have you ever thought about the above questions or do you put them aside— either because you do not understand their relevance or because they are too difficult?

Your answers to these questions might well have exposed the framework you use in making daily and long-term decisions. Your answers also might be profoundly related to your goals, values, and ethics. On the other hand, it is possible that you have not thought much about these questions. You many have answered them implicitly or may have never faced these issues at all. Perhaps your values and ethics have been merely absorbed from television, other people, and superiors at work. In that case you are making daily decisions with far-reaching implications without having examined the presuppositions which mightily affect those decisions. Problems which stem from this posture, and how people cope or fail to cope, will be discussed in the next chapter.

It would be instructive to raise these questions with regard to the beliefs of Bernard of Clairvaux, John Calvin, Benjamin Franklin, Adam Smith, Karl Marx, and others. But let us now continue with our examination of the criticisms of capitalism.

THE MARXIST CRITIQUE

Although French and English utopian socialists anticipated the idea of public or communal ownership as an alternative to capitalism, it was Karl Marx (1818–1883) who first forged a theory of communism as we know it today. Marx's criticisms of the capitalist system were incisive and based on careful empirical studies. His language was intentionally polemic, and he and his followers used terms like *exploitation, imperialism,* and *alienation.*[1]

---

[1]John E. Elliott, "On the Possibility of Marx's Moral Critique of Capitalism," *Review of Social Economy* 44 (October 1986): 130–44.

The criticisms come from a viewpoint that is designedly quite foreign to that of the American business community. Marxist critics make little effort to be balanced or conciliatory. But despite the differences in language, values, and attitudes, the Marxist critique can provoke us to examine our own national priorities and the values that govern our economic, political, and social policies. If we are here attempting an objective examination of the goals and values of free enterprise, we must not neglect its harshest critics.

A man of real genius, Marx combined analytic and critical power with an ability to weld his ideas into an overall theory of history. According to his theory, economic forces are the primary determinant of history. Economic structures give rise to class differences; class conflicts provoke social and political struggles. Marx thought the capitalist class conflict between workers and owners would inevitably erupt in revolution and usher in a new socialist system of production. Our concern here, however, is not with the Marxist theory of history but with its criticisms of our economic system. Not every person cited in this section is a strict Marxist (many would certainly not advocate social revolution), but all are severe critics of our current system. One critic acknowledged to be a Marxist economist in Paul Sweezy. Sweezy contends that the essence of Marx's criticism can be found in the very method he used to analyze the economy.[2] Until Marx's time, according to Sweezy, economic theory viewed economic factors (capital, labor, prices) as things. Marx insisted that economics does not deal simply with things; it deals with *social relations*. Every commodity produced and sold, every wage paid, involves very definite relationships between human beings. In failing to recognize these social relations, capitalism and capitalist theory consequently ignore the real effects of the system on human society.

This basic critique can be divided into several accusations made by Marxists and other critics of the capitalist system. For some readers, these accusations may seem exaggerated, one-sided, and wearisome. But they are presented with the conviction that criticism can also lead to constructive change and a healthy reappraisal of views.

Exploitation of the Worker

The free enterprise system operates on the theory that when people work for their own self-interest, they will simultaneously contribute to the welfare of all. Everyone profits from economic growth, and presumably each person receives monetary rewards in proportion to his or her efforts and skill. Marxists challenge these assumptions. That economic growth has occurred since the beginning of the modern industrial age is evident. That all have profited from this growth in any degree proportionate to their work is quite

[2]Paul Sweezy, *The Theory of Capitalist Development* (New York: Oxford University Press, 1942), pp. 1–5, chap. 2 passim.

dubious. For Marx, who knew the Industrial Revolution during its grimmest stage, it was difficult to see how the working class benefited at all from their labors. Factory workers lived in hovels, worked exhausting fourteen-hour days, and died prematurely. Marx's classic work, *Capital*, chronicles in page after page the price paid in human suffering for industrial growth: workers suffering from pulmonary diseases caused by the dust and heat of factories, small children working fifteen-hour days, a young girl dying of exhaustion after twenty-six consecutive hours of work.[3] Workers were forced to live on bare subsistence wages while owners acquired fortunes and lived in luxury.

Today the extremes between impoverished workers and wealthy owners described by Marx no longer prevail, in the United States at least. Labor unions and government legislation forced better wages and working conditions, which have significantly raised the standard of living of most workers. But if one looks to the *distribution* of wealth and income in the United States, great disparities remain. Five percent of family units have 40 percent of all personal wealth, and the bottom half account for only 3 percent of the wealth of all Americans. The top 20 percent of family units have three times the wealth of the bottom 80 percent.[4] U.S. Census statistics show that wealthy families in the United States, with $60,000 or more in gross assets, hold $629 billion in corporate stocks. The wealthiest 1 percent accounted for one-fourth the value of all personal assets, worth $1 trillion. They hold 56 percent of all corporate stock, 60 percent of bonds, and nearly 90 percent of trusts.[5]

For a Marxist, the reason for this disparity is clear. At best, workers can only bargain for higher wages. But the capitalist class, the owners and executives, determine the whole productive process (what is produced, how it is produced, the selling prices of products) and payment for respective contributions (how much to wages, to executive salaries, and to stockholders). Through power of ownership the capitalists control the system, and the great disparities which develop are a consequence of their control. Workers are not paid the real value of their work contribution, according to Marx. The difference, the surplus value, between what they should receive and the actual wages they do receive is the real explanation of the owner's profit.

A Belgian Marxist explains this notion of surplus value and the exploitation it involves quite graphically.[6] As long as the productivity of labor remains at a level where one person produces only enough for his or her own

---

[3] Karl Marx, "The Working Day," *Capital*, vol. 1 (New York: International Publishers, 1967), pp. 244–54.

[4] Maurice Zeitlin, ed., *American Society, Inc., Studies of the Social Structure and Political Economy of the United States*, 2d ed. (Chicago: Rand McNally, 1977), p. 63.

[5] *Statistical Abstracts of the United States* (Washington, D.C.: U.S. Bureau of the Census, 1983), table 742, p. 449.

[6] Ernest Mandel, *An Introduction to Marxist Economic Theory* (New York: Pathfinder Press, 1970), pp. 7–9.

subsistence, no social division of owner and worker occurs. But once a surplus is available, the possibility of exploitation develops. Exploitation was blatantly clear in the slave plantations of the Roman Empire. On six days of the week the slave worked on the plantation and received nothing. Most often slaves had to produce their own food by working a tiny plot of land on Sundays. The great domains of the Middle Ages furnish another illustration. Serfs worked three days on land whose yield belonged to them; the other three days they worked on the lord's land without remuneration. The revenue of the capitalist class, according to Ernest Mandel, is simply a more subtle form of the same exploitation. It is the uncompensated labor the wage worker gives to the capitalist without receiving any value in exchange. Or, in Marx's own words, "Suppose the working day consists of 6 hours of necessary labor and 6 hours of surplus labor. Then the free laborer gives the capitalist every week 6 times 6 or 36 hours of surplus value. It is the same as if he worked 3 days in the week for himself and 3 days gratis for the capitalist.[7]

It is not sufficient to respond that executives also work and merit their salary or that costs of raw materials and maintenance must also be computed. Marx argues that profit is precisely the surplus over and above all costs and salaries. Marxists recognize the need for capital investment for expansion and new industry; their quarrel is with its private possession and control. If workers are the prime source of production, then they, not private owners, should be the prime beneficiaries, and they should also have a significant voice in the whole process of production. The fact that labor unions have reduced the inequities between wages and profits does not alter the basic fact of exploitation for a Marxist. The capitalist still seeks to pay as little as possible for workers' services. The resulting profits or "surplus" are not the rewards of the capitalist's hard work or enterprising spirit but result simply from ownership of property and control over the work of others.

The contemporary Marxist challenges the contention that wealth in the United States has really been the product of "free" enterprise. Can American business be said to have "earned" its total income in the past without reference to the takeover of native American territories, to slavery, or to the minimal wages paid immigrant workers? Or in the present, do even relatively well-paid blue-collar workers receive a share proportionate to their work when executives of the same company earn ten times or more their salary. Inequality shows itself first in the difference between worker and executive salaries. Leo Huberman and Paul M. Sweezy provided a graphic, if now dated, example:

> In 1946, the union of shipyard workers in the Bethlehem Steel Company fought for and won an increase of 15 percent which raised the minimum shipyard rate to $1.04 an hour. That's $41.60 a week or $2,163.20 a year. In 1946, the executives

[7]Marx, *Capital*, vol. 1. p. 236.

in Bethlehem were given a 46 percent salary boost. Mr. J. M. Larkin, vice-president of Bethlehem, who insisted that the incentive rates for workers had to be cut, was given a bonus of $38,764 to his salary of $138,416. That's $177,180 a year, $3,407.30 a week, $85.18 an hour.[8]

The income gap between top managers and others continues to increase. In 1986 the average chief executive's salary increased 29 percent in just that one year, compared with a 6 percent increase for other managers and 2 percent inflation. That year, of 634 executives surveyed, 220 made more than $1 million in total compensation.[9] These large salaries were bestowed at a time when these same executives were urging others in their firms to limit wage expectations in order to lower costs and thus enable the firm to be better able to compete in world markets.

Critics of free enterprise argue that wealth produces more income than work itself. Great wealth derives from investments, not work. C. Wright Mills graphically illustrated this. If in 1913 you had bought $9,900 worth of General Motors stock and had gone into a coma for forty years, you would have awakened in 1953 worth $7 million.[10] A study of people who reported incomes of $1 million or more showed that only 4 percent of their income came from salaries and partnerships; the rest came from dividends and capital gains.[11] Graduated income taxes are supposedly designed to redistribute wealth. In fact, they do not. The proportion of income of the top 20 percent of income earners remains unchanged after taxes.[12]

Alienation of the Worker

In his earliest writings, Marx used the term *alienation* to describe the effects the capitalist method of ownership and production had on the working class. Capitalism alienates the workers first of all because it takes from them the product and profit they produced. Their life energy is poured into their work, yet they have little to show for it. "The more the worker exerts himself, the more powerful the alien objective world he fashions against himself; the poorer he and his inner world become, the less there is that belongs to him."[13]

[8] Leo Huberman and Paul M. Sweezy, *The Introduction to Socialism* (New York: Monthly Review, 1968), p. 47.

[9] "Executive Pay: Who Got What in '86," *Business Week*, May 4, 1987, pp. 50–51.

[10] C. Wright Mills, *The Power Elite* (New York: Oxford University Press, 1969), p. 111.

[11] Ferdinand Lundberg, *The Rich and the Super-Rich* (New York: Bantam Books, 1968), pp. 43, 935–36.

[12] Richard C. Edwards, Michael Reich, and Thomas E. Weisskopf, eds., *The Capitalist System* (Englewood Cliffs, N.J.: Prentice-Hall, 1986), pp. 223–24.

[13] Loyd D. Easton and Kurt H. Guddat, trans. and eds., *Writings of the Young Marx* (Garden City, N.Y.: Anchor, 1967), p. 289.

But Marx was concerned not only about the distribution of wealth and fair return for work done. He felt an almost greater concern for the way people work. Under capitalism, he charged, work is forced and dehumanizing. The work is forced because the average worker, though theoretically free to accept a job or not, has little choice but to take a job or go unemployed. Nor do workers have much freedom in the way they carry out the work. They do the work assigned at the pace designated. The work is thus dehumanizing because it does nothing to develop the human potential of the workers (e.g., their potential to be inventive, to make decisions, to develop different skills). The worker is simply an appendage to a machine. He "does not affirm himself in his work but denies himself, feels miserable and unhappy, develops no free physical and mental energy but mortifies his flesh and ruins his mind."[14] The capitalist works him as he would "a horse that he has hired for a day."[15]

Many critics, Marxist and otherwise, believe that capitalism still sacrifices humanizing work to efficiency and profit maximization. Kenneth Keniston describes the impact of alienated work in terms that echo Marx's analysis a century before. In most traditional societies, he observes, one's work was one's life. Work, play, and social life flowed into each other. Work meant simply tasks to be done, and there was no division of life into work and nonwork. For most Americans, in contrast, work has unpleasant connotations. The reason for this lies in the characteristics of most jobs. With increasing specialization, each worker finds him- or herself assigned to a smaller and smaller portion of a task. The product is finished far down the line: out of sight and out of mind. There is little sense of satisfaction from work. Moreover, too few jobs challenge one's abilities, imagination, or spirit; most call simply for a capacity to follow exact routines in an orderly way. As a result, most Americans speak of "working for a living" and rarely of "living for their work." Many have stopped even expecting work to be meaningful.[16]

Harry Braverman's *Labor and Monopoly Capital* is an important Marxist study of "the degradation of work in the twentieth century." He begins by noting rising discontent in the labor movement today stemming from job dissatisfaction.[17] What distinguishes *human* work from animal instincts, Braverman argues, is the power of conceptual thought. True human labor unites mental and material action. The degradation of labor in capitalist society results from their separation.

[14] Ibid., p. 292.

[15] Marx, *Capital*, vol. 1, p. 185.

[16] Kenneth Keniston, "The Alienating Consequences of Capitalist Technology." in Edwards, Reich, and Weisskopf, *The Capitalist System*, pp. 269–73; see also Herbert Gintis's essay on alienation, which follows Keniston's.

[17] Harry Braverman, *Labor and Monopoly Capital: The Degradation of Work in the Twentieth Century* (New York: Monthly Review, 1974), pp. 31–39.

The "scientific management" which Frederick Taylor proposed in the late nineteenth century, and which greatly influenced the U.S. system of production, very deliberately divorced mental and material labor. Taylor wrote,

> The managers assume...the burden of gathering together all of the traditional knowledge which in the past has been possessed by the workmen and then of classifying, tabulating, and reducing this knowledge to rules, laws, and formula....All possible brain work should be removed from the shop and centered in the planning or laying-out department.[18]

The introduction of assembly lines carried this concept of mechanized labor to its fullest expression. Henry Ford's decision in 1914 to raise workers' pay to five dollars a day was hailed as an enlightened, progressive move done to enable workers to become more affluent customers. This view overlooks the fact, says Braverman, that Ford faced an angry revolt by workers against his new assembly lines. The turnover rate in 1913 had forced the Ford Motor Company to hire 963 workers in order to keep 100 jobs filled.[19]

If the separation of mental from manual work has been most obvious in factory work, it has increasingly characterized clerical work as well. The drive for speed and efficiency has reduced more and more work to simplified, routinized, and measured tasks.

Although work has been dehumanized, unemployment proves far more degrading still. To speak of *only* 6 percent unemployed—a figure once thought intolerable—does little to describe the powerlessness, frustration, and alienation of millions of unemployed people. Welfare may permit an income on which to live, but it can only be dehumanizing. From a Marxist perspective, worker exploitation and alienation are among the most serious failures of the free enterprise system.

Imperialism: Exploitation of Other Countries

In recent years, much of Marxist criticism of free enterprise has been directed against the influence of capitalism in poor countries. When Americans praise the achievements of free enterprise, they point to the overall affluence of the United States and the political democracy which accompanies it. But in Latin America and other parts of the third world, free enterprise often means desperate poverty, oppressive right-wing military rule, and exploitation by foreign companies. For example, in El Salvador free enterprise has for decades meant 2 percent of the population owning 60 percent of the land and 8 percent taking half of all income; the remaining 92 percent of the population live in poverty and three-fourths of the children suffer from

---

[18] Cited in Braverman, *Labor and Monopoly Capital*, pp. 112–18.

[19] Braverman, *Labor and Monopoly Capital*, p. 149.

malnutrition. Yet efforts at reform have been crushed by right-wing death squads.

Marxists argue that capitalist countries want to maintain the status quo in countries of the third world in order to exploit them. Profit always has exploitation as it source, according to Marxist critics. Underdeveloped countries of the world provide natural resources and cheap labor which make investment very profitable if the political regimes remain favorable. Moreover, economic development generally does not bring benefits to the poor. Studies of income distribution in Brazil, Colombia, and India, where development has taken place, show that inequality has increased. Industrialization benefits the wealthy and has little effect on the poor.[20]

The very beginnings of capitalism in Europe, Paul Sweezy contends, were made possible by the plunder and exploitation of foreign countries.[21] At first, European countries simply plundered the gold, silver, and minerals of countries in the southern hemisphere. Then colonial rule put complete control of resources in the hands of the colonizing countries. Specialized economies were developed by foreign investors. Today we associate certain products with certain countries—coffee in Brazil, tin in Bolivia, copper in Chile, sugar in Cuba. But the development of such commodities did not result from initiatives within those countries. They were developed by European and U.S. companies to meet needs in the "developed world." The concentration on one or two products often upset a natural balance of production and created "one-crop" economies very dependent on the fluctuating prices in the world market for that one crop. Brazil's northeast was once that country's richest area; now it is its poorest. Portugal granted lands to Brazil's first big landlords. Sugar production flourished for a time but left washed-out soil and eroded lands.[22] Barbados, in the West Indies, suffered the same fate. It once produced a variety of crops and livestock on small holdings: cotton, tobacco, oranges, cows, and pigs. Cane fields devoured all this; the soil was exhausted and unable to feed the population. The story is similar in Africa. Gambia once grew its own rice on land now used to grow peanuts. Northern Ghana grew yams and other foodstuffs on land now devoted to cocoa. Liberia was turned into a virtual rubber plantation. Seizures of land, taxation, the undercutting of domestic prices, and forced migrations were all employed by colonizers to gain control of the land.[23]

[20] Arne Bigsten, *Income Distribution and Development* (London: Heinemann, 1983), pp. 68–71, 84–87; see also Ozay Mehmet, *Economic Planning and Social Justice in Developing Countries* (New York: St. Martin's Press, 1978), pp. 37–57.

[21] Paul Sweezy, *Modern Capitalism and Other Essays* (new York: Monthly Review, 1972), pp. 18ff.

[22] Eduardo Galeano, *Open Veins of Latin America: Five Centuries of the Pillage of a Continent*, trans. Cedric Belfrage (New York: Monthly Review, 1973), pp. 72–75.

[23] Frances Moore Lappé and Joseph Collins, *Food First: Beyond the Myth of Scarcity* (Boston: Houghton Mifflin, 1977), pp. 78ff.

Thus the economies of most countries in the third world now depend on the one or two crops which foreign investors cultivated. Bananas accounted for 23 percent of Panama's export earning and 25 percent of Honduras's in the late 1970s. Until recently, coffee brought in 65 percent of Colombia's foreign exchange and 44 percent of Haiti's. Moreover, their export earnings on foodstuffs declined as the price of manufactured goods soared. In 1960, the equivalent of three tons of bananas could buy a tractor; in 1970, the same tractor cost the equivalent of eleven tons.[24]

Does not the presence of foreign mining firms, manufacturers, fruit growers, and banks bring needed capital, technology, and know-how to poor countries? To some extent, yes. However, the income that comes back to the United States from private investment in poor countries exceeds that going into initial investment by more that 80 percent.[25] In a typical recent year, only 30 percent of the earnings generated in developing countries was reinvested in those countries. The remainder was brought back to the United States. This compares with 63 percent of similar earnings reinvested in developed countries.[26] Putting the situation graphically, if a box of bananas retails at $5.93 in the United States, producers in Honduras receive roughly $0.66. Chain supermarkets in the United States gross $1.90 on that same box.[27]

"Let the market decide" and "consumer sovereignty" are bywords justifying the free enterprise system. But the consumer who decides is the consumer who has money, and profits are determined by this. The poor and hungry cannot buy food enough to match the profits that can be made on exports. Therefore, Central America sends its vegetables to the United States, where 65 percent are dumped or used as animal feed because their quality is not good enough or markets are oversupplied. Mexico grows strawberries, cantaloupes, and asparagus for Del Monte and other U.S. corporations to sell in the United States. Colombian private owners grow flowers for export because one hectare of flowers brings nine times the profit that wheat or corn could. Cocaine now brings even more profits, of course.[28]

When poor nations attempt to change internally, the United States has often intervened—sending Marines into Guatemala in 1954, supporting the military overthrow of Goulart in Brazil in 1964, and using the CIA to subvert the Allende government in Chile in 1973. For Marxists, the reason for such interventions is clear: protection of U.S. business investments. In Cuba, before Castro's revolution, U.S. companies controlled 80 percent of Cuba's

[24]Ibid., p. 182; see also *Economic Survey of Latin America, 1977* (Santiago, Chile: United Nations, 1978), pp. 136, 278, 292, 373; Harry Magdoff, *The Age of Imperialism: The Economics of U.S. Foreign Policy* (New York; Monthly Review, 1969), pp. 99–100.

[25]"U.S. Direct Investment Abroad," *Survey of Current Business*, August 1986, p. 70.

[26]Ibid., table 4, p. 42.

[27]Lappé and Collins, *Food First*, pp. 194–98.

[28]Ibid., pp. 255–56.

utilities, 90 percent of its mines, and almost 100 percent of its oil refineries. U.S. firms received 40 percent of the profits on sugar, a crop that represented 89 percent of all Cuban exports.[29]

Finally, if wars protect overseas markets, the massive defense industry is seen as essential to free enterprise. Defense contracts ensure new markets, new jobs, and new uses for capital. Without the artificial stimulus of defense spending, say Marxist critics, the United States would face crises of unemployment and severe recession.[30] Exploitation of other countries, war, and a giant defense industry—these alone, say Marxists, provide the outlets without which the free enterprise system would collapse.

Capitalist Domination of the State

Americans take pride in their democratic system: "Whatever its faults, it's the best in the world." Every citizen has a voice in the government. All can vote; all can aspire to political office. The two-party system offers choices in policies and candidates. The division of executive, legislature, and judiciary creates a balance of power. Opposition to Marxist communism most often expresses itself as a defense of democracy.

Marxists challenge this "pluralist" view of the state and its faith in U.S. democracy. Their quarrel is not with the principles and values of democracy as such but with claims that they have been realized in the United States and in other capitalist nations. Marx had argued, in his early writings, that political freedoms created only an "illusion" of true human freedom. People's lives are determined far more by the conditions in which they live in society than by abstract political rights. Political power, moreover, reflects economic power. When John Locke, the seventeenth-century English philosopher, stated that the great and chief end of persons uniting to form a government was "the preservation of property," he reflected all too clearly the goals of his social class. The democratic state in capitalist society claims to represent the common good of all its citizens, and indeed it must pass legislation needed to legitimize that claim. But it serves primarily to maintain the power and interests of the dominant class. As Marx expressed it in *The Communist Manifesto*, "The executive of the modern State is but a committee for managing the common affairs of the whole bourgeoisie."[31] Marxists may be exaggerating and using heavy rhetoric when they speak of "capitalist domination of the state," but it is important to consider the arguments for the Marxist position.

[29] Felix Greene, *The Enemy: What Every American Should Know About Imperialism* (New York: Vintage, 1971), p. 139.

[30] See Clemens Dutt, ed., *Fundamentals of Marxism-Leninism* (Moscow: Foreign Language Publishing House, 1961), p. 330.

[31] "The Communist Manifesto", in *The Marx-Engels Reader*, ed. Robert C. Tucker (New York: Norton, 1972), p. 337.

First, the most obvious evidence for the Marxist position is the disproportionate representation of the rich in high office. In theory anyone can be president of the United States. But in fact millionaires and multimillionaires, though they constitute a miniscule fraction of the population, have consistently been elected over the last fifty years—Franklin D. Roosevelt, John F. Kennedy, Lyndon Johnson, Richard Nixon, Jimmy Carter, Ronald Reagan, George Bush. Cabinet posts as well usually go to the "wealthy elite." G. William Domhoff, in *Who Rules America?*, noted that five of eight secretaries of state and eight of thirteen secretaries of defense over the thirty-six-year period he studied were listed in the elite Social Register.[32]

Congress has a broader composition, but the power of wealth is quite evident there also. Representative Torbert H. MacDonald, a Democrat from Massachusetts, noted that "in the nation's seven largest states in 1970, 11 of the major senatorial candidates were millionaires. The four who were not lost their bids for election.[33] A Ralph Nader study in 1975 revealed that twenty senators were millionaires; well over half of those who responded to Nader's inquiry had assets of $250,000 or more; only five had assets under $50,000. The average American that same year had assets of $4,000.[34] One would very likely look in vain for even one member of Congress who is representative of the average American. Legislators come from the ranks of business and the professions, law in particular. The main work force of the United States—factory workers, truckers, secretaries, etc.—goes virtually without any direct representation from its ranks.

The presence of wealthy capitalists in high office is not the only argument used by Marxist critics. Michael Harrington, James O'Connor, and many neo-Marxists stress far more the "function" played by the state in behalf of free enterprise. Corporations may complain of government regulations and taxes, but these Marxist critics point to the many ways in which government subsidizes big business.

James O'Connor, in *The Fiscal Crisis of the State*, argues that the state assists big business both by creating a climate for its accumulation of capital and by bearing much of the burden of social expenses (e.g., education and health care), which would otherwise have to come from higher workers' wages. He illustrates government subsidy of private industry by reference to the automobile industry. Cars need roads, but private industry does not bear the full cost of building them. The entire transportation budget from 1944 to 1961 was given to the construction of roads and highways. The federal

---

[32] G. William Domhoff, *Who Rules America?* (Englewood Cliffs, N.J.: Prentice-Hall, 1967), pp. 97–99, 105–7.

[33] Cited in *Detroit Free Press*, May 23, 1976, Parade sect., p. 4.

[34] Ibid; see also Richard Zweigenhaft, *"Who Represents America?"* a study of the Ninety-second Congress, *The Insurgent Sociologist* 5, no. 3 (1975): 119ff.

government assumes 90 percent of the cost of interstate freeways and 50 percent of the cost of all other primary roads. Eighty percent of the funds earmarked for the redevelopment of Appalachia went into roads.[35]

The state subsidizes private industry, and hence private profits, in a variety of ways: through loans (as in the case of Lockheed and Chrysler), through helping to finance land development and building, through tax exemptions for building depreciation and oil exploration, and through funding research. By providing welfare it tempers the discontent created by unemployment. By assuming much of the cost of medical care it frees industry from paying higher salaries to cover these costs. It bears much of the expense for industrial pollution as well. The discontent of citizens demanding more benefits gets directed at the state, because it picks up expenses and responsibilities that private corporations escape.

Michael Harrington makes a similar case against "state management of the economy on behalf of the capitalists":

> Over the past three decades, the government has helped to build ten million units for the better-off and 650,000 units of low-cost housing for the poor. In 1969, the *Wall Street Journal* reported that there were $2.5 billion in subsidies for the urban freeways, which facilitated the commuting of the privileged, and only $175 million for mass transit. All of this made good commercial sense even though it helped to perpetuate the social disaster of the disintegration of the central cities, the consequent isolation of the racial and ethnic minorities, the subversion of the passenger-rail system, and so forth.[36]

Government policies regarding farming reveal the same priorities. From 1940 to 1985, the number of farms in the United States decreased by 60 percent and the size of the average farm increased by 160 percent. The "farmers" included ITT, Gulf + Western, Boeing, and other large corporations. But it was these giant agribusinesses which were the prime recipients of federal subsidy. In 1985, large farms with more than $100,000 in sales a year received $5,295,000, 69 percent of the total federal subsidy of $7,704,000. Payments to the very largest farms, with sales of over $500,000 a year, went from 7 percent of the total subsidy in 1975 to 13 percent of a subsidy nine times larger in 1985. During this same period, subsidies to smaller farms (less than $20,000 total sales) went from 26 percent to less than 3.5 percent of the total.[37]

[35] James O'Connor, *The Fiscal Crisis of the State* (New York: St. Martin's Press, 1973), pp. 105–6.

[36] Michael Harrington, *The Twilight of Capitalism* (New York: Simon & Schuster, 1976), p. 224.

[37] *Statistical Abstract of the United States, 1986*, p. 632; see also Douglas F. Dowd, *The Twisted Dream: Capitalist Development in the United States Since 1776* (Cambridge, Mass.: Winthrop, 1977), pp. 177–78.

Charles Lindbloom, in *Politics and Markets*, presents a third argument, one that focuses on the influence of big business on the state. Though a defender of a "market" economy and not a Marxist, Lindbloom believes that giant corporations are inconsistent with democracy. Business executives and not government officials, he argues, make most of the public policy decisions that affect the economic life of the nation. Their decisions, in turn, affect almost every aspect of life—jobs, homes, consumer goods, leisure. These executives determine income distribution, allocation of resources, plant locations, the pattern of work, the technologies to be used, what goods should be produced, the quality of goods and services, and of course executive compensation and status.[38] These major decisions are turned over to business leaders and taken off the agenda of government. Thus citizens have no vote at all on policies that affect every sphere of their welfare.

But these major decisions only begin to indicate the public role of business leaders. Their influence on government is quite different than that of any other group in society. Public functions in the market system rest in their hands. For example, jobs, prices, production, growth, the standard of living, and the economic security of everyone are under their influence. Government officials cannot, consequently, be indifferent to how business performs its functions. Business leaders are not just representatives of one or more special interest groups; the whole welfare of society depends on what they do. They never get all they ask for or want, it is true. But whether they ask for subsidies for transportation and research, for aid in overseas promotion of business, for troops to protect investments in foreign countries, for tax reductions to stimulate investment, or for similar advantages, the state must respond.[39]

All citizen groups can compete in politics, but they depend on the use of their members' own incomes and energies. Business corporations can draw on extraordinary sources of corporate funds, organizations, and personnel and can use their special access to government. Business has myriad avenues by which to do its own "consciousness forming or raising." Through lobbying, through entertainment, through litigation, business uses its resources to confirm its position and gain approval. Roughly $60 billion a year is spent on advertising and other sales promotion. Some of this is institutional advertising with a political content, such as Exxon's "Energy for a Strong America." This matches all the funds spent on education or health in the country.[40] Few radical or dissenting journals even exist to compete with dominant business views. The large private corporation, Lindbloom concludes, is not consistent with democratic theory and vision.

[38] Charles Lindbloom, *Politics and Markets: The World's Political-Economic Systems* (New York: Basic Books, 1977), p. 171.

[39] Ibid., pp. 172ff.

[40] Ibid., pp. 195, 214.

Social Consequences of Capitalism

To these major issues might be added a host of problems the Marxist considers directly related to the capitalist economic system. The inequality of women and their subservient role in society were for Marx consequences of private property and the division of labor. He viewed the family itself, with the husband dominating his wife and children, as the first form of property and as a "latent slavery."[41] Engels argued that

> to emancipate woman and make her the equal of man is and remains an impossibility so long as woman is shut out from social productive labor and restricted to private domestic labor. The emancipation of woman will only be possible when woman can take part in production on a large, social scale, and domestic work no longer claims anything but an insignificant amount of her time.[42]

Lenin writes in a similar vein that "women are still in an actual position of inferiority because all housework is thrust upon them.[43] Needless to say, what the founders of Marxism had to say about the "woman question" has come to have relevance in the United States.

Social problems abound in the United States that are the direct consequence of subordinating social concerns to profit making. These problems are all too familiar, according to critic Felix Greene.[44] Capitalism has ravished the continent. The United States has killed off 85 percent of its wildlife and destroyed 80 percent of its forests; millions of acres of farmland have been misused and lost. Pollution is rampant. New York City dumps 200 million gallons of raw sewage into the Hudson River each day. Medical care for poor citizens has been neglected. Three million children have untreated speech disorders. Crime and violence have come to be an almost accepted part of urban life. Armed robbery in Washington, D.C., runs 1,760 percent higher than in London; the number of homicides per year in Detroit is several times higher than for all of England. Drugs, inadequate housing, racial prejudice— the list goes on and on.

The charge that these problems are consequences of the free enterprise system is perhaps too facile an explanation. But America is plagued by serious social problems that make the charge difficult to dismiss. The United States prides itself on enjoying a very high standard of living. Average Americans enjoy far more material benefits than any people in history. But the Marxist critic questions even this achievement. How much of what we

[41] "The German Ideology," in Tucker, *Marx-Engels Reader*, p. 123.

[42] *The Woman Question: Selections from Marx, Engels, Lenin, Stalin* (New York: International Publishers, 1970), pp. 10–11.

[43] Ibid., p. 52.

[44] Greene, *The Enemy*, pp. 3–43.

consume corresponds to *real* needs? Herbert Marcuse charges our consumer-propelled economy with the creation of mostly false "needs."[45] Advertisements keep us in a state of perpetual dissatisfaction with what we do have. So new "styles" become the selling point. Advertising seeks to convince us of our "need" for ever-drier deodorants, electric toothbrushes and combs, and automatic garbage compactors. We can no longer even be sure of what kind of vacation we would naturally like, because advertisements have programmed us to "like" what they are selling.

The charges made by Marxists against our economic and political system are many. The wealth produced by industry profits owners and executives far more than workers. Financial investment multiplies the disproportionate distribution of wealth. Factory work stunts the capacities of workers engaged in it. Initiative, self-determination, and a voice in decision making are possible in sales and management but not in the labor force. Competitive self-interest characterizes work at every level. Poverty and unemployment become stigmatized and are considered to be one's own fault. A wealthy, powerful elite controls the highest public offices. Laws favor the wealthy and protect their incomes by tax loopholes. Women are made subservient. Pollution, crime, drugs, racial discrimination, and false needs are by-products of an economy directed only toward more and more goods and profits. The system stands condemned.

But has any system done a better job? Would communism provide a better way of life? The instinctive response of most Americans is "no." The Communist nations of the world have hardly achieved utopia. Their economies still lag far behind our own. Their political regimes appear intolerably regimented and coercive. Anyone watching the persecution of Jews in the USSR or Soviet treatment of dissidents will hardly desire to live under such a political system. The inefficiency and bureaucracy of the Soviet economy and the still undeveloped state of the Chinese economy make them inadequate models for change in the economic system of the United States. Even severe problems resulting from trade and federal deficits will not prompt most Americans to overthrow their present political and economic system for socialism. But not being willing to trade places with Russians or Chinese would not be equated with not being willing to learn from them. For they have constructed economic systems that give priority to eliminating some of the social problems which beset our own.

Watching the achievements and failures of Marxist socioeconomic systems can tell us much about the aspirations and efforts of the peoples of the world. Observing people in Marxist societies tells us about both the perceptions of those people as to what system is most appropriate for them and the

---

[45] Herbert Marcuse, *One Dimensional Man: Studies in the Ideology of Advanced Industrial Society* (Boston: Beacon Press, 1964), pp. 225–46.

reality of how a collective socioeconomic system is able to work. Giving priority to eliminating poverty and increasing employment is a quite different goal for an economic system. Although it has its tradeoff costs, such goals certainly appeal to most people.

Cooperative Versus Competitive Market System

Designing economic programs to deal with the problems of an unjust distribution of wealth and income is generally considered to result in a loss of efficiency and productivity. Government programs require planning and administrators. They are expensive and do not always achieve their intended goals. Moreover, such programs can have a negative effect on the incentive to work for both low- and high-income people.

On the other hand, critics accuse capitalism not only of objective exploitation and alienation of the worker but also of encouraging competitiveness and selfishness. While even the USSR and China now acknowledge the value of competition among production units, self-seeking and excessive competition among individuals can severely hinder the long-term efficiency of a firm and a society.

Two ideals of a democratic society, justice (or equality) and efficiency, are thus often placed in opposition to one another. That is, in the minds of most people, increasing one requires sacrificing some of the other.[46] The ideals of *justice* are basic to any society, especially to a free, democratic one: All men and women have a right to the basics of food and education; all men and women should have an equal opportunity to work and should be treated fairly at work; all people should be treated equally before the law; and there should be no great disparity among families in income and wealth.

The ideal of *efficiency* is a pragmatic goal of the United States. It includes the following convictions: A more efficient and productive society yields more jobs and income for all; all individuals should work hard according to their abilities; rewards should be proportionate to an individual's work and merits; and people, material, and capital should be able to move freely.

These two goals are basic for Americans. As a society we pride ourselves on being both a just and an efficient society. Although it is true that we have failed in one or the other from time to time, it is also true that both remain explicit and real goals for Americans. Total achievement of one may occur only at the expense of the other, yet we also know that it is unwise to undermine seriously either justice or efficiency. Both are essential to American society.

During the 1960s and 1970s, up to 1981, American society moved toward more justice and equality. The civil rights movement, the women's

---

[46] See Arthur Okun, *Equality and Efficiency: The Big Tradeoff* (Washington, D.C.: Brookings Institution, 1975).

movement, and affirmative action plans and their successes attest to that. It is often said that this occurred at the cost of efficiency. Often corporate managers complain of a growing sense of "entitlement" among workers ("a job and a promotion is owed to me"). Perhaps this is true to some extent, yet the evidence shows that lessened American productivity has much deeper roots than worker laziness and excessive government regulation. Although managers with a narrow viewpoint sometimes exclusively blame these two causes, they less often recognize that more basic causes of the lack of productivity gains are their own attitudes, policies, and practices. The current relative decline of American productivity is the unhappy outcome of the drive for immediate, short-term, bottom-line results; this, in turn, often stems from executives who are more concerned about their own successful careers than about the long-term success of their firms.[47]

Currently, productivity is not rising rapidly in the United States. We define productivity as output per person-hour. That is, productivity increases as the amount of labor expended to produce a good or service decreases. Interestingly, we do not define productivity as a function of capital or even energy used. Yet capital and energy are scarce and becoming more valuable. Perhaps we need new terminology (maybe *capital productivity, energy productivity*) to describe moving toward fuller employment and using less energy to produce the same goods.

The notion that any modern economy can be "unregulated" is mistaken. Every economy operates according to a predetermined set of priorities and resulting rules.[48] The only relevant question is, on what priorities are the rules devised? For example, every society assesses taxes and provides subsidies in order to be of the greatest benefit to the people as a whole. That is, legislation, taxes, and other government activities are directed to the common good.

Most government actions directed to the common good require that some individuals or groups must sacrifice some immediate benefits. For example, taxing people to pay for fire protection and parks is a cost to some who may never use the fire department or the park. Thus, this demands a political decision that fire protection and parks are an important good for which all people should pay whether or not they directly benefit from these services.

Such political decisions in a democracy require an objective, even-handed approach to assessing the common good. Legislative decisions are made that will infringe upon, and hence will not be popular with, certain segments of the population. These groups may be quite powerful, either because of their money, their influence, or both. Such legislative decisions are becoming harder to make because of political action committees that contrib-

---

[47] See, for example, Robert Hayes and William Abernathy, "Managing Our Way to Economic Decline," *Harvard Business Review*, July-August 1980, pp. 67–77.

[48] Lester C. Thurow, *The Zero-Sum Society* (New York: Basic books, 1980), p. 128.

ute to a candidate's campaign, special interest groups, and other lobbyists. It is now more difficult for a representative or senator to support legislation that would result in a long-term benefit for most people if it results in a short-term cost for a powerful segment. For example, Congress has been unable to enact an energy plan that would effectively lower the amount of petroleum we use and hence must import. The $50 billion or so that we spend annually for imported petroleum is a principal cause of pollution *and* our balance of payments deficit, but Congress does not have the courage to tax petroleum or otherwise provide incentives so that we would use less.

Enlightened self-interest can lead the enterprising entrepreneur to provide the products and services that people want—and to do so efficiently. But enlightened self-interest also encourages individuals to become more selfish. An infant is born self-oriented, but as it grows it comes to recognize the importance of other people. This realization comes gradually with maturity. Excessive stress on self-interest can stunt a person so that he or she remains at the stage of adolescence, with its focus on "me and mine." Hence enlightened self-interest must often be guided in order to achieve the common good, especially in contemporary society, where so many of our actions affect others (e.g., pollution, noise, and the use of scarce resources). These issues will be discussed more fully in the following chapters.

The case for private ownership of large firms is justified primarily in the name of efficiency. The large disparities in income and wealth that we witness in the United States are also defended on the basis of efficiency: Money motivates people to work and to work harder. The private sector *is* generally more efficient than the public sector. That large disparities in income and wealth also bring about greater efficiency is more difficult to establish. Moreover, here we find one of the most clear-cut conflicts in basic American values: justice versus efficiency.

FREE ENTERPRISE QUESTIONED FROM WITHIN

People typically—often without much reflection—consider rising gross national product and rising median family income as earmarks of a successful society. Since it is true that we have been successful in the production and consumption of material goods, it is probably not so surprising that we would like to make that the measure of success for all cultures. Frederick Winslow Taylor, the founder of scientific management, put it succinctly when he said, "In my judgment the best possible measure of the height in the scale of civilization to which any people has arisen is its productivity.[49]

[49] Frederick W. Taylor, *Hearings Before the Special Committee of the House of Representatives to Investigate the Taylor and Other Systems of Shop Management,* vol. 3 (Washington, D.C.: Government Printing Office, 1912), p. 1471.

Another point of view was presented a generation before Taylor, when England was at its height as an industrial and trading power. Matthew Arnold raised the same issue, alluding to those who said that England's greatness was based on its railroads and its coal:

> If England were swallowed up by the sea tomorrow, which…, a hundred years hence, would most excite the love, interest, and admiration of mankind—and which would most, therefore, show the evidences of having possessed greatness?

Would it be the England of the preceding two decades, a period of industrial triumph, or would it be an earlier period when culture was more valued? Arnold answered for his contemporaries:

> Never did people believe anything more firmly than nine Englishmen out of ten at the present day believe that our greatness and welfare are proved by our being so very rich.

And then he goes on to give his own response:

> The use of culture is that it helps us, by means of its spiritual standard of perfection, to regard wealth as but machinery, and not only to say as a matter of words that we regard wealth as but machinery, but really to perceive and feel that it is so.[50]

This same issue faces Americans in the 1990s. How are we to judge the success of our civilization? What is our goal and what are our criteria for judging whether or not we are successful? Frederick Taylor says it is productivity; Matthew Arnold says productivity and wealth are merely tools to achieve something more. In this perennial debate, on which side do we stand? Or must we fashion some middle ground? If so, what elements will go into it? The point of this book is to provide some basis for resolving the issue.

Schumpeter's Prediction of the Decay of Capitalism

Fears of the decay of free enterprise and the capitalist system were voiced as long ago as the Sixteenth Century by religious reformers John Calvin and John Wesley. Those who fashioned the ideals underlying the Protestant ethic were able to foresee the ultimate collapse of that system (see Chapter 3). However, for most people up to the last decade or so, in the midst of single-minded efforts and vast economic growth in the United States, it

---

[50]Matthew Arnold, *Victorian Prose*, ed. Frederick William Roe (New York: Ronald Press, 1947), p. 399.

was difficult to imagine free enterprise collapsing. However, some feared the collapse of the system once the goals of more material goods, greater financial rewards, and better efficiency in production would be attained. One of the earliest economists to predict such a collapse was Joseph Schumpeter, who publicized his view in the early 1940s.

In his *Capitalism, Socialism and Democracy*, Schumpeter provides a brilliant and detailed description of the undermining and decay of capitalism. He points out that the very success of the capitalist economic mechanism in providing goods and income paradoxically lessens dependence on and concern for the system. As free enterprise is successful, human needs are satisfied and investment opportunities tend to vanish. That same success undermines the need for, and so the position and prestige of, the entrepreneur, who is no longer dominant or even highly respected in society.[51]

Contributing to the growing hostility to capitalism are the intellectuals. Academics and intellectuals are quick to see inequities and evils in any system. The problems are there for any perceptive eye to see, and it is the vocation of the intellectual to be a cultural critic. Moreover, Schumpeter would say that most intellectuals have had no experience in trying to manage an organization; at best they serve as staff or as consultants. The ultimate responsibility for making an organization work has never been theirs, so they do not possess the practical wisdom of those who have gotten their hands dirty. In addition, they have a captive audience in the universities and thus have a ready-made forum for their critical views. Schumpeter was convinced that the intellectuals were undermining capitalism.[52]

He was also convinced that these criticisms generated increasing government regulation to constrain the free movement of people and capital. Schumpeter is at pains to point out that he is not opposed to this change, but it is no longer capitalism. Moreover, the professional manager does not have the same long-term will and vision as the owner he or she replaces.[53] A manager need not stay and fight for the integrity of a firm or system; he or she can move on to another job that offers greater financial return. Schumpeter's indictment is a broad-gauged one; he even goes into some detail as to how capitalism and its attendant attitudes tend to undermine family life and child rearing. In his view, capitalism faces imminent death.

Schumpeter picks out another weakness of capitalism: It has no compelling, motivating, all-embracing ideology and set of values. It is a pragmatic system, designed and pursued for a narrowly conceived end—eco-

---

[51] Joseph A. Schumpeter, *Capitalism, Socialism and Democracy* (London: Allen & Unwin, 1943), pp. 131–39.
[52] Ibid., pp. 143f.
[53] Ibid., p. 156.

nomic growth. He then contrasts capitalism with Marxism. Marxism has a vision of the world and a systematic ideology; it calls on its followers to sacrifice for the sake of the poor and the oppressed and for a more equal distribution of goods. Its vision is sufficient to inspire people and to initiate revolutions. According to Schumpeter, Marxism has all the marks of a religion: vision, doctrine, rules, and a call for self-sacrifice. In contrast, capitalism promises only a higher standard of living and in itself cares nothing for the poor and disadvantaged. It is effective in production but crass and parochial in its view of people and their world.

Decades later, the economist Paul Samuelson updated and paraphrased Schumpeter's penetrating assessment: "I told you so. The successes and rationalism of bourgeois capitalism will breed a swarm of discontented intellectuals—to fan the flames of hostility toward an efficient but unlovable system with no mystique to protect it."[54] Schumpeter's critique was widely quoted in his own day, but it is even more relevant now.

Argument for Free Markets: A Rebuttal

A counterargument to critics is a defense of capitalism and free markets. The most respected and articulate contemporary spokesperson for this free market ideology is the economist Milton Friedman. He considers freedom the most important value in any economic or political system, and he sees economic freedom as absolutely essential to political freedom.

Friedman's position in defense of the free market and in opposition to government intervention goes all the way back to Adam Smith. His is the now familiar conviction that allowing every person the opportunity to buy and sell openly and without restriction will ensure that people will obtain the goods and services they need at the lowest possible price. Free competition in the marketplace will bring about the greatest efficiency in producing the goods society is willing to pay for. The corporation, as the currently predominant economic institution, is a focus of Friedman's concern. He sees that institution as solely an economic one, responsible primarily to its stockholders. The corporation, or more properly corporate management, has no right to dispose of stockholders' profits in any manner that does not directly benefit the corporation. Management has no right to contribute to universities, to install pollution-control equipment, or to spend to make the workplace safer unless in some way these actions benefit the corporation itself, at least in the long-term.

Friedman is convinced that government has no role in central economic planning. He speaks disparagingly of the government exercising control over

---

[54] Paul A. Samuelson, *Newsweek*, April 13, 1970, p. 75.

the market in the "public interest."[55] Moreover, on the whole he finds that public interest groups have a negative influence:

> Whatever the announced objectives, all of the movements in the past two decades—the consumer movement, the ecology movement...the protect-the-wilderness movement, the zero-population-growth movement, the "small is beautiful" movement, the antinuclear movement—have had one thing in common. All have been antigrowth. They have been opposed to new developments, to industrial innovation, to the increased use of natural resources.[56]

Although the details of Friedman's indictment are not entirely accurate, it is clear that he believes these public interest movements have hurt rather than helped the operation of the market.

There are only a limited number of strategies available to address such problems as product reliability, worker safety, and industrial pollution. If government legislation and regulation are to be kept to a minimum, and if public interest groups do more harm than good, then the only alternative for solving such problems is management initiative. Yet Friedman is also convinced that management has no right to take the initiative on *these* issues out of a recognition of the common good. Friedman vehemently denies that corporations do have, or even *can* have, social responsibilities: "The only entities who can have responsibilities are individuals; a business cannot have responsibilities."[57] To presume that a corporation can have social responsibilities

> shows a fundamental misconception of the character and nature of a free economy. In such an economy, there is one and only one social responsibility of business—to use its resources and engage in activities designed to increase its profits so long as it stays within the rules of the game, which is to say, engages in open and free competition, without deception or fraud.[58]

He is convinced that the growing sense of corporate social responsibility undermines basic freedoms:

> Few trends could so thoroughly undermine the very foundations of our free society as the acceptance by corporate officials of a social responsibility other than to make as much money for their stockholders as possible. This is a fundamentally subversive doctrine. If businessmen do have a social responsibil-

---

[55] Friedman and Friedman, *Free to Choose*, pp. 54–56, 95.

[56] Ibid., p. 191.

[57] Milton Friedman, "Milton Friedman Responds," *Business and Society Review* 1 (Spring 1972): 6.

[58] Friedman, *Capitalism and Freedom*, p. 133.

ity other than making maximum profits for stockholders, how are they to know what it is?[59]

He then points out the difficulty in making such a determination, citing the fact that some German businesspeople contributed to the Nazi party in the early 1930s. Managers thus wrongly presumed an authority and a wisdom they did not possess.

Friedman argues for the abolition of all corporate taxes and for ensuring that corporate profits are returned to the stockholders, who can then as individuals decide how they will spend their money. It is *their* money, so it should be their decision whether or not to use it for community purposes. His position is simple, straightforward, and consistent: The interests of stockholders, consumers, and citizens as a whole are best served if the corporation sticks to its traditional role of producing goods and services and does that as efficiently and inexpensively as possible. This is the best long-run service that the business firm can provide for society. He does, however, recognize the problem of unemployment and disability, and he was one of the first to propose a guaranteed minimum income (or "negative income tax," as he calls it) for all those of wage-earning age in the economy. He would substitute a minimum income for the variety of welfare, disability, and unemployment programs that have proliferated, all of which now require separate, expensive, and inefficient administrative apparatuses.

The same principles apply to such diverse areas as schooling and medical care. Friedman does not think the government should be in the business of education, for public education then becomes a monopoly insulated from the challenges to excellence and efficiency that come from free competition. Rather, the government should provide redeemable tuition certificates for parents and children to use at the school of their choice. As with the production of goods and services, he is convinced that better and more effective education will result when there is free competition.[60] His position on the medical profession and the monopoly that certification gives to the American Medical Association is the same. Better, more efficient, and cheaper medical service would result if there was no monopoly. If anyone with some medical knowledge could hang out a shingle, the public would eventually find out who was giving better service and who should not be patronized. Friedman criticizes the guru status we have bestowed on the medical profession and claims that this does not produce the most effective and efficient treatment.

Milton Friedman acknowledges that his views on the corporation and the socioeconomic system do not possess the depth, insight, or balance of his Nobel Prize–winning work in economics. Especially in his later work, he fails

[59] Ibid.
[60] Friedman, *Freedom to Choose*, pp. 150–188.

to grapple with the basic criticisms of free enterprise: It encourages selfishness and results in costs to third parties and in serious inequities. Furthermore, Friedman has little patience for any of the major alternative solutions: government regulation, public interest group pressures, or voluntary actions by management. He is even less interested in cooperative methods of organizing an economy, which were very popular in the last century and continue to be popular, although to a lesser extent.

ALTERNATIVES TO CAPITALISM: EARLY AMERICAN COOPERATIVES

Rejecting the dominant individualist, free enterprise values, many people in the United States organized their economic life cooperatively rather than competitively. In fact, many immigrants, after having experienced life-threatening work, exploitative bosses, and child labor, came to the New World precisely to pioneer cooperative living. Hundreds of cooperative communities were formed in the United States during the last 150 years.[61] These communities counted their members in the hundreds and sometimes thousands. The members shared work and income equally. They were opposed to the competition encouraged by capitalism and felt that only through cooperation could a truly human and Christian community develop.

The Shakers were a religious group that at one time had nineteen separate communities scattered throughout New England and the Midwest; their land holdings totaled nearly 100,000 acres.[62] The suburb of Cleveland called Shaker Heights takes its name from the Shaker community that was there. Its beautiful Shaker Lakes were built as millponds by the Shakers. The men and women lived in separate communities; there was little contact between them at work or socially. There was no marriage; new members had to be converted. In the early days there were converts, and the number of Shakers eventually reached 6,000. They called themselves the *Millennial Church*. It was outsiders who, observing the long, loud, and active shaking movements in their prayer services, dubbed them *Shakers*.

Most of the members of these communities farmed, but some began manufacturing. Notable among communities where manufacturing occurred is the Oneida Community in New York State, which was founded by the

---

[61] Rosabeth Moss Kanter, *Commitment and Community* (Cambridge, Mass.: Harvard University Press, 1972); see also David French and Elena French, *Working Communally* (New York: Russell Sage Foundation, 1975) and an earlier account by William A. Hinds, *American Communities* (Chicago: Charles Kerr, 1902).

[62] Hinds, *American Communities*, p. 27; see also Marguerite F. Melcher, *The Shaker Adventure* (Princeton, N.J.: Princeton University Press, 1941), p. 302.

minister John Humphrey Noyes in 1848. Although it is no longer a commune, it has paradoxically developed into a multimillion-dollar international company and is now the largest maker of stainless steel tableware in the United States.[63]

Probably the best known communal experiment was New Harmony, a community started by Robert Owen in Indiana. Owen, a wealthy British factory owner, was the first in England to limit the workday to ten hours. He both advocated and initiated (among his employees) other work and social reforms. Owen's dream was a community in which all work, life, and leisure would be shared. Unlike most other early commune organizers, Owen's vision was not religious in origin. In 1825, Owen purchased a set of buildings built by a religious community called the Rappites and renamed it New Harmony. He advertised for members and accepted almost all comers; more than 900 came, among them some well-known professional people. But because of his other obligations, Owen himself found little time to be at New Harmony in the early days. Farming and other basic skills were scarce among the community members, and lack of a common vision and subsequent discord brought the community to an end in 1827, after only two years of existence. It was a highly publicized, expensive, and noble experiment, but it was shorter lived than most cooperative communities.

All these early cooperative communities began with strong leadership, and most were religious in origin. For a commune to survive, it must continue to attract vigorous and talented people, not merely the weak and those who are looking for a refuge from the problems of the outside world. Self-discipline and order are necessary to solve the multitude of differences that arise in a community, yet these are impossible to sustain without a shared vision. Most of the communes failed after the original leader was gone and the early goals and inspiration for the community began to fade.

From the above, it should be clear that the communes we find in the United States today are not a new social phenomenon.[64] They are a reflection of a deep-rooted need in people for humane relationships, cooperation, and communication based on shared values.

There are many current attempts to encourage greater cooperation and commitment among members of business firms in order to attain better product quality, create a more humane workplace, and achieve greater prof-

---

[63] Hinds, *American Communities*, pp. 173–214. Concerning its more recent economic success, see "It Started Out as a Commune in 1848, and Today Oneida Is a Thriving Business," *Wall Street Journal*, April 4, 1973, p. 8.

[64] For a sociological analysis of American communes, see Benjamin Zablocki, *Alienation and Charism: A Study of American Communes* (New York: The Free Press, 1979). A well-written, carefully researched first-hand account of scores of modern communes of the 1960s in the United States is Robert Houriet's *Getting Back Together* (New York: Coward, McCann & Geoghegan, 1971).

itability. A producer cooperative[65] is an entire work setting built on cooperative ideals. Participative management, employee stock ownership plans, flexible work schedules, and profit sharing are all used to build greater commitment and cooperation among workers in organizations that are based on the free market model.[66]

SUMMARY AND CONCLUSIONS

Karl Marx perceptively pinpointed the weaknesses of the capitalist economic system. He and his followers have shown that capitalism possesses a series of undesirable characteristics. According to Marx, capitalism results in

1. exploitation of the worker
2. alienation of the worker
3. imperialism (exploitation of other countries)
4. capitalist domination of the state

Although Marxists are at their best in criticising capitalism, they also propose another method for organizing a society. That system is used in the Soviet Union, the People's Republic of China, Cuba, and many other countries, whose citizens add up to more than half of the world's population.

For many Americans, evaluating communism begins and ends with the claim that "we have more and better consumer goods available, and more money with which to buy them. Moreover, we are free; they are not." True, but communist nations also possess much that we lack: more cooperativeness, less unemployment, less disparity of wealth, fewer broken families, less everyday violence, less drug abuse, and less crime.

Each system has its strengths and weaknesses. A totalitarian and bureaucratic system is hardly desirable to most Marxists. Poverty, unemployment, and crime are certainly not advocated by the defenders of free enterprise. But the comparison of communism and capitalism does raise the question of priorities and how they are formulated. Who decides what goals of a society are to be given priority? In a Communist nation, the party and the government set priorities, both economic and political. The system is designed to encourage cooperation, to provide greater participation, and to eliminate unemployment. While meeting these goals, the system also encourages production and economic growth. With free enterprise, conscious prior-

---

[65] Douglas E. Booth, "The Problems of Corporate Bureaucracy and the Producer Cooperative as an Alternative," *Review of Social Economy* 43 (December 1985): 298–315.

[66] For additional information about each of these cooperative strategies, see Gerald F. Cavanagh and Arthur F. McGovern, *Ethical Dilemmas in the Modern Corporation* (Englewood Cliffs, N.J.: Prentice-Hall, 1988), chap. 3.

ities are set only in the political sphere. Government can regulate and subsidize, but it generally does not set specific economic goals. Free enterprise advocates defend this nonintervention as more efficient. In theory, free enterprise recognizes only one priority: "Will it return a profit?" The system does not ask how important the need is that the product fulfills; it has no method of rating products or services on any scale of values other than dollars.

Perhaps profits should be the sole concern of business. If that is true, who sets national economic priorities in the United States and implements them? Do individual consumers have the vision to look after the long-term economic and social good of society? How did we decide that automobile travel was better than using urban rapid transit systems? How did we decide that we should spend more on dog food and cosmetics than on helping hungry peoples feed themselves? As we will see in Chapter 8, it is not clear where the responsibility for such decisions lies. Those advocating greater business responsibility have pointed to the moral and social consequences of some business policies, including those regarding energy and resource use, toxic waste, product safety, and plant closings. But the issue of national priorities goes beyond just these policies.

Efficiency and justice are both important goals for Americans. Competition encourages flexibility and efficiency. A concern for others and cooperation undergird justice. However, paradoxically much of the current declining efficiency in the United States is attributed to self-centered competition, both by individuals and by firms.

In short, a value that we cultivated in the name of efficiency and success now results in making us less efficient and less successful. Moreover, in the process we can become blind to the values of cooperation and justice. Perhaps at least this much can be gained from considering the Marxist critique of free enterprise and the goals Communist nations set for themselves: the motivation to examine our own personal and national priorities. It also helps us to see the limits and the inadequacies of our own ideology so that we may improve.

DISCUSSION QUESTIONS

1. How do you respond to each of the seven questions posed at the beginning of the chapter?
2. What evidence does Karl Marx provide that capitalism exploits the worker? Is the argument valid? Does income tax rectify the inequality?
3. What evidence does Marx use to sustain his claim that capitalism alienates the worker? Evaluate this claim with respect to the United States in the 1990s.
4. Does capitalism bring about exploitation of other countries? Why or why not?

5. What does Marx mean by "capitalist domination of the state"? Does such domination occur?
6. Do the four major problems of capitalism cited by Marx stem primarily from capitalism or industrialization? Why?
7. Americans think of Marxism as materialistic. Is it more materialistic than capitalism or free enterprise? Do the goals that Marxism holds out for the average worker transcend materialism?
8. How does one measure the success or failure of a society? By its gross national product? By the average per capita income of its members? By its literature or art? By its care for the poor and disadvantaged? What other criteria should be used?
9. Why did Joseph Schumpeter say that capitalism would decay? Compare his views on this subject with those of John Calvin.
10. Describe the origins and characteristics of early American communal societies.
11. What elements in a communal society tend to support its continued existence?
12. Outline the comparative advantages of cooperative and competitive socioeconomic systems. Does the current American concern for worker participation run contrary to competitive free enterprise?

CASE: SUPERIOR'S REPORT

Sara McIntyre, a young management accountant at Tuloc, Inc., receives an expense report for reimbursement from Elmer Cole, vice president of the division. The report requests $2,400 for a two-day trip to the East Coast, and several of the items have no receipts and seem inflated to McIntyre. What should McIntyre do? What are her obligations and to whom?

EXERCISE: INTERNATIONAL MANAGEMENT CONSULTANT

In the future it is essential that businesspeople understand other peoples and other cultures. National leaders and corporate chief executive officers tell us this. The purpose of this project is to acquaint you with the climate for living and doing business in another country. Fellow students from other countries are a great resource for learning about their countries. You will consult one for help.

Procedure

I. Find a student consultant from another country who will help you. In order not to overburden the student, he or she may be used as a consultant only once.
II. Examine one of the issues of this course, for example:
   A. Equal employment opportunity (minorities or women)

    B. Air or water pollution
    C. Marketing or advertising practices
    D. Safety of products or workplace
    E. Bribery, kickbacks, tax evasion, or other practices
    F. Operation of foreign firms within the country
    G. Host government regulations
    H. Other (check with instructor)
III. Prepare a summary report on a single sheet of paper indicating the following:
    A. Country chosen
    B. Name of international student consultant
    C. The issue or problem examined, with some background
    D. Any special industry or firm involved
    E. Proposal to address the difficulty

CHAPTER FIVE
THE INFLUENCE
OF BUSINESS
ON PERSONAL VALUES

Man is by instinct a lover, a hunter, a fighter, and none of those instincts are given much play at the warehouse!

Tennessee Williams
*The Glass Menagerie**

Freedom is not the power of doing what we like, but the right of being able to do what we ought.

Lord Acton

The groups and organizations we are members of—from family to corporation—have a profound influence on our personal values, goals, and ethics, although we are seldom explicitly aware of this influence. Personal values, which are among the basic components of personality, develop from exposure to others. Values are often received uncritically from parents, peers, teachers, and the media. A listening and interested parent encourages values that are quite different from those engendered by a parent who is annoyed, distracted, or absent.

Later, during working years, we often so identify·with an organization that success within it becomes a primary measure of personal worth. Performing well at IBM or Citibank tells me what sort of a person I am. When I am with a firm that encourages pride in good work, autonomy, new ideas, and risk taking, that can give me self-confidence and joy in doing my work. On the other hand, personal values are often compromised by a business

---

*Tennessee Williams, *The Glass Menagerie*, ed. Gilbert L. Rathbun (New York: Random House, 1965). Quoted with permission.

climate that condones unethical acts.[1] Moreover, sometimes an individual identifies too closely with work and makes that the total measure of self-worth. Realization of the inadequacy of that measure often does not come until midlife, and then it brings with it profound anxieties, frustrations, and even serious physical ailments.[2]

Ford Motor Parts and Service Division calls itself "the loving and caring division." Domino's Pizza encourages their employees to use the Golden Rule in the workplace. This reinforces human values learned in the family and neighborhood and encourages concern for people—whether they be neighbors, co-workers, suppliers, customers, or subordinates. It also helps the individual within the organization to maintain an integrated personality, not separating the values of family life from those of the workplace.

Some organizations, including business firms and even universities, show little social concern. As we will see later in this chapter, managers of such institutions tend to be more self-centered and show less concern about social conditions and less willingness to make personal gain secondary to helping those in need. The values of these managers contrast with the self-image most Americans have of themselves as generous. When such values are not explicit and are held uncritically, they contain the seeds of potential conflict and anxiety. Leaders of organizations who make decisions based on self-centered and often uncritically held values are in danger of causing severe social disruption. (Note the greedy insider trading activities of some financial bankers or the "kiss and tell" books by friends and ex-members of the Reagan administration.) This is paradoxical, since managers conceive of themselves as objective, rational, and not led by personal whim. A good manager insists on a careful analysis of all the facts before coming to a judgment. The use of market surveys, outside consultants, product planning groups, and computer analyses indicates the high priority rational decision making has within firms. Yet these same managers are often unaware of how much their unexamined personal values bias their decisions.

Managers are thus unaware that the decision-making process itself rests on unexamined assumptions. For beneath this structure lie certain presuppositions about the purpose of the firm—to maximize profits, to expand market share, and so on. These very ideological assumptions which rational decision making is based on are often accepted unquestioningly, much as we accept traditional cultural norms.

---

[1]William C. Frederick and James Weber, "The Values of Corporate Managers and Their Critics: An Empirical Description and Normative Implications," in *Research in Corporate Social Performance and Policy*, ed. William C. Frederick, vol. 9 (Greenwich, Conn.: JAI Press, 1987) pp. 131–51; see also the summary "Nature or Nurture? Study Blames Ethical Lapses on Corporate Goals," *Wall Street Journal*, October 9, 1987, p. 21.

[2]For a more complete description of work and job satisfaction issues, see Cavanagh and McGovern, *Ethical Dilemmas in the Modern Corporation*, pp. 34–63.

Each organization develops a life and norms of its own. An organization's own struggle for survival and growth can give superficial legitimacy to many activities that would not be undertaken if subjected to more careful and conscientious scrutiny. These activities often conflict with the personal values of honesty, integrity, and concern for others that are possessed by members of the organization. This conflict may then cause members to reflect on the inconsistency of these personal and organizational values. The inadequacy of an exclusive reliance on market values often does not appear until the goals of the firm come into conflict with the goals of the larger society. Many of these issues will be discussed in greater detail in Chapter 8.

This chapter will examine personal values in the workplace, including the following topics:

1. the influence of organizational values, climate, and expectations on the values of individuals
2. goals and motives of individuals and how motives are affected by personal values and ethics
3. accomplishment and satisfaction within the organization, as well as stress, anxiety, and frustration, and how these contribute to personal health or illness

THE ORGANIZATION'S FORMATIVE INFLUENCE: SOCIALIZATION

Any group of people working together must share goals and values, otherwise they experience confusion and conflict. Hence socialization is essential in any human endeavor. However, socialization can also limit and constrain flexibility and new ideas. Formal socialization (see Table 5–1) is the planned and deliberate attempt by the organization to affect the attitudes of members. Informal socialization takes place among members through ordinary interaction.[3] Many values are introduced in orientation and training programs, but they are amplified and solidified by exposure to the expectations of superiors and peers forty hours a week. When coupled with the perceived importance of success in the firm, such socialization brings changes in and reinforcement of values. For example, Disney Productions, both through formal and informal socialization, insures that new members know how to make "guests" feel welcome and comfortable.

[3]For current research on socialization, see Gareth R. Jones, "Socialization Tactics, Self-efficacy, and Newcomers' Adjustments to Organizations," *Academy of Management Journal*, 29 (June 1988): 262–79; Douglas T. Hall, "Careers and Socialization," *Journal of Management* 13 (April 1987): 301–21. For a comprehensive treatment, see Lee S. Sproull, "Belief in Organizations," in *Handbook of Organizational Design*, ed. Paul C. Nystrom and William Starbuck, vol. 2 (New York: Oxford University Press, 1981), pp. 203–224.

TABLE 5-1 Socialization Within the Organization

TYPES OF SOCIALIZATION	METHODS OF SOCIALIZATION
Formal	1. Orientation programs 2. Job descriptions and work procedures 3. Management development and training programs 4. Codes of behavior 5. Performance appraisals and feedback
Informal	1. Expectations of superiors 2. Actions of and conversations with peers 3. Unwritten norms 4. Organizational climate

The organization has its own demands, which arise from the activities directed toward maintaining the health of the organization. These activities are often determined by the market values of profitability, market share, and return on investment. Organizational maturity and stability, without profitability and growth, are not acceptable goals for the long term; chief executive officers have been fired for aiming at such unaggressive goals. Moreover, organizations affect almost every segment of our lives. As some put it, "Because modern organizations have created and have largely defined the American value system, they must be considered the most important socializing agencies in America."[4]

From 1950 to 1980, which were years of American business success, many American firms became large and bureaucratic. They are now trying to be more innovative and flexible in order to meet international competition. But organizations generally change their goals and values only in the face of new demands from the outside. Without such challenges, they tend to continue to operate in ways that were successful in the past, and they thus become more rigid as the years go by.

Organizations are generally effective in selecting individuals and then socializing them into persons who "fit well" into the system. Each organization has a subtle but potent influence on its members' attitudes, values, and ethics. As sociologist Robert Merton puts it,

> The bureaucrat's official life is planned for him in terms of a graded career through the organizational devices of promotions by seniority, pensions, incremental salaries, etc., all of which are designed to provide incentives for disciplined action and conformity to artificial regulations. The official is tacitly expected to and largely does adapt his thoughts, feelings, and actions to the

---

[4]William G. Scott and David K. Hart, *Organizational America* (Boston: Houghton Mifflin, 1979), p. 36.

prospect of his career. But *these very devices* which increase the probability of conformance also lead to an overconcern with strict adherence to regulations which induce timidity, conservatism, and technicism. Displacement of sentiments from goals onto means is fostered by the tremendous symbolic significance of the means [rules].[5]

Most large organizations offer many examples of such inflexible behavior. For example, banks tend to be conservative and bureaucratic. Risk taking and flexibility are not as important for banks. A large, rigid organization develops a life of its own, protecting its own special interests and being jealous of its own position, power, and perogatives. The corporation's way of doing things, especially when it has been successful in the past, can become rigid and ossified. Each individual is expected to "learn Exxon's way of doing things." Managers select for promotion subordinates who have values like their own. Although these managers pride themselves on making objective and rational decisions, there is evidence that personal likes and values play an important role.

In large organizations, coordination between people and business units is essential. As various responsibilities are spelled out in writing, there is less room for individual judgment. Even in decentralized companies that are trying to be more flexible, standard practices and procedures limit new ideas and initiatives. Deviant values are eliminated, either in the selection process or through socialization. It thus becomes clear which values are accepted and which are not, for example, whether it is OK to wear a tie or not, to come to work early, or to file for overtime.

In any organization, the competitive, achievement-oriented manager wants to be noticed quickly as a success. Such a manager tends to focus on short-run efficiency and performance, as these are more easily measured and will provide early favorable data for top management. Market values tend to crowd out personal and social values.

Accomplishment at Work

Most people hope that their work will provide satisfaction and fulfillment. Satisfaction generally comes from doing a job well and contributing to the happiness of others. This conviction that one's life is worthwhile gives one not only satisfaction but also energy to focus on one's work. Large organizations and efficiency demand specialization of tasks and interchangeability of personnel. As work is divided up and depersonalized, much of the joy of successfully accomplishing tasks is taken away. Whether manufacturing products or providing services, workers rarely produce finished goods by themselves. They perform one small portion of the entire job, because

---

[5]Robert K. Merton, "Bureaucratic Structure and Personality," in *Organizations: Structure and Behavior*, ed. Joseph A. Litterer, 3d ed. (New York: Wiley, 1980), pp. 232–33.

specialization of labor lowers costs. The large firm often furthers this segmenting of labor, creating a greater distance between the individual worker and the finished product.

As a result, in contemporary industrial society something that "is vital and essential for human life is left out, neglected, suppressed and repressed."[6] Satisfaction, pride in work, and a sense of ownership are lacking. Sociologists call this vacuum "alienation"; theologians call it "estrangement." The goals of industrial society—production and growth—take precedence over the goals of individuals. When nonhuman objectives are valued over persons, the result is isolation, loneliness, and alienation. Even though there are more technological conveniences and more wealth, life seems even less fulfilling.

Our expectations have been raised by advertising and politicians only to be dashed by reality. In the act of accumulating wealth and developing sophisticated technology, we often lose any sense of achieving and contributing to something worthwhile. We have emphasized material wealth more than the person. This tension is one of the causes of the "career crises" we hear about so often. It is important for all who are employed, whether with their hands or their minds, to have meaningful work.

One reason for this lack of satisfaction is that our work ethic no longer has a foundation. When the Protestant ethic was the basic value system of Americans, personal values supported work values. As Daniel Bell sees it, this is not the case today:

> What this abandonment of Puritanism and the Protestant Ethic does...is to leave capitalism with no moral or transcendental ethic. It also emphasizes...an extraordinary contradiction within the social structure itself. On the one hand, the business corporation wants an individual to work hard, pursue a career, accept delayed gratification—to be, in the crude sense, an organization man. And yet, in its products and its advertisements, the corporation promotes pleasure, instant joy, relaxing and letting go. One is to be "straight" by day and a "swinger" by night.[7]

This paradox is demonstrated in self-seeking individualism, which tears apart families, neighborhoods, and business firms.

Money and Markets as American Goals

Corporate and material values influence many Americans. To foreign observers, it sometimes appears as if everything Americans do is directed toward providing and acquiring material goods. A few manifestations of this

---

[6]Walter A. Weisskopf, *Alienation and Economics* (New York: Dutton, 1971), p. 16.

[7]Daniel Bell, *The Cultural Contradictions of Capitalism* (New York: Basic Books, 1976), pp. 71–72.

orientation are advertising, the centrality of corporate life, and individual-ized suburban homes. Americans act as if they believed that "happiness is a new car or a new home." We conceive of ourselves in terms of the goods we purchase and use. For example, consider the attitudes of today's college students, who reflect the values of their parents and the larger culture. More than 75 percent of college freshmen surveyed around the country believe that being financially well off is a very important goal. This number has increased every year from a low of 40 percent in 1970. Compare this with another goal. In 1970, 83 percent of college freshmen thought that developing a meaningful philosophy of life was very important; by 1987, the percentage had dropped to 39 percent.[8]

Economic goals and corporations can have a profound influence on our political values as well. Business lobbying often has a decisive influence on legislation that affects domestic and foreign policy. Economics is clearly dominant when we threaten war to prevent our oil supply from being cut off.

Karl Marx was the first to charge that an industrial society separates people from their work and alienates them. We examined Marx's critique in the last chapter. Here we will focus on the fact that working is not an attractive and rewarding activity for many Americans. And it is not only assembly line workers who do not like their jobs. There are countless other positions in service, banking, and other organizations that provide little job satisfaction. Lack of satisfaction often occurs because the work is cut into small segments, supervisors are autocratic and distant, and there is little pride in the final product. In many of these jobs, workers are used like single-purpose tools. Such jobs thus demand little intelligence or imagina-tion, and the workers have little control over the work or the work setting. Productivity and efficiency are valued over pride, responsibility, and the joy that can be gotten from work.

Job satisfaction can also be hindered by job specialization. A firm spends thousands of dollars training an employee for a specific position. As years go by, the employee desires a job that is more challenging. However, the firm has a large investment in this employee. It is to the firm's advantage not to make a change, since it will cost money to train another employee and take time for the new employee to gain competence. Therefore, the firm does not make a change and the old employee remains in the position. The result is boredom, dissatisfaction with the job, and frustration with self and the company.

Only now, when faced with poor quality and low productivity, have American firms begun to encourage more input from workers through job redesigning, job enrichment, and quality circles. Such programs were pro-posed many years ago by "fuzzy-minded human relations people," but only

----

[8] "Freshman Found Stressing Wealth," *New York Times*, January 14, 1988, p. 9.

now—with our backs up against the wall—are they being instituted by most American firms. Workers on the production line often have the best ideas on how to produce the product efficiently.

Executives often suffer from a lack of concern for people. Managers think that their attention must be restricted to the short-term, bottom-line goals of better productivity, higher return on investment, and a larger share of the market. The individuals who are attracted and make it to the corporate executive suite have a great need for success. To attain their goals, they must be able to make decisions unencumbered by emotional ties to persons or groups. They must always be ready to move to a new location and leave old friends and associations behind. They must have sufficient detachment from their friends and neighborhoods. In fact, for many there is little point in making deep friendships or getting involved in local activities; it would only make parting more difficult. In his study of the executive personality, William Henry concludes,

> The corporate executive is a special type, spawned on impersonality and hurried into the task of defending his individuality in the diffuse and open competition of nonfamily life. His energy to prove his competence again and again is extreme, and his need to re-create a safe and personalized nest is minimal.... Undeterred by other than the purely conventional in personal life, he is able without sense of loss to devote his entire life to the executive task.[9]

Those attracted to corporate executive work are generally people who do not depend on close personal relationships. They obtain their major satisfaction from completing a task. Their personal values set the tone for the organization; these values are communicated to others in the firm. It is clear that the successful people are more task- than person-oriented.

Winners and Self-Developers Among Managers

After interviewing managers in large, high-technology companies, Michael Maccoby concluded that such people were not primarily interested in skills, power, or loyalty but rather in "organizing winning teams."[10] Hence he characterized current successful managers as "gamesmen." Gamesmen develop many positive intellectual characteristics to aid in "winning the game" (e.g., analysis, problem solving, and policy development), but at the same time they allow their emotional life to atrophy. They are more detached and emotionally inaccessible than previous types in the corporate hierarchy.

---

[9] William E. Henry, "Executive Personality and Large-scale Organizations," in *The Emergent American Society*, ed. W. Lloyd Warner et al., vol. 1 (New Haven: Yale University Press, 1967), p. 275.

[10] Michael Maccoby, *The Gamesman: The New Corporate Leaders* (New York: Simon & Schuster, 1976), p. 34.

Gamesmen do not have a "developed heart." They lack compassion and appreciation for suffering—they cannot even bear to look at suffering. Maccoby calls them "weak hearted." Most younger managers are weak-hearted gamesmen. For Maccoby, a strong-hearted manager is able to understand and to empathize with the suffering that may come from a particular business decision. The strong hearted make the best executives in Maccoby's judgment.

Gamesmen also have little sense of social responsibility. Unaware of and hence unconcerned about the social and human effects of their actions on others, they operate on the primitive notion that the growth of their organization will automatically benefit poor people. They refuse to consider undesirable secondary effects.

Although most of the gamesmen that Maccoby interviewed indicated that they wanted friendship and help from their friends, fewer than 10 percent said that helping others was a personal goal. This contrasts with more than half of a group of factory workers who mentioned helping others as a personal goal. Maccoby found managers in Mexico to be "more aware than Americans that their careers protect them from the poor, but even the Mexican executives are not aware that within their enclaves they are becoming more alienated from themselves." Around their houses they have built walls, and on top of those walls they put broken glass or spikes to prevent the intrusion of "outsiders." In a similar way, many affluent U.S. neighborhoods now have walls and guardhouses to separate the inhabitants from common people.

Gamesmen set out to be "winners." Their alert, aggressive behavior does make them successful in focused tasks at work. However, they trade off much of their affective life. The fatal danger of gamesmen is to be trapped in perpetual adolescence, striving to be a winner at the game throughout adulthood.[11]

In a more recent study, Maccoby has identified a growing group among young managers: self-developers.[12] Self-developers value opportunities to learn, grow, and gain a sense of competence and independence in an egalitarian workplace. Wary of being swallowed up by work, they are less likely to become corporate chiefs than are gamesmen. More concerned with learning and cooperation, they are motivated to succeed in family life as well as in their careers and to balance work with play. In the future, with fewer layers of middle management, it will be important that people be able to manage themselves. The self-developers seem to have the necessary qualities. Managers of this new type seem better adapted to business in the 1990s than do gamesmen.

---

[11] Ibid., pp. 109, 203.
[12] Michael Maccoby, *Why Work?* (New York: Simon & Schuster, 1988).

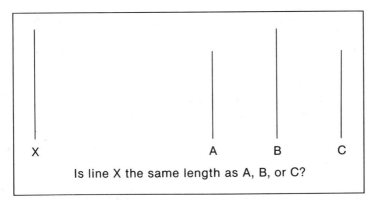

Is line X the same length as A, B, or C?

FIGURE 5-1   Line Perception Experiment

Dissent in the Organization

The importance of the individual and of independent judgment have always been explicitly recognized by Americans. But although we mouth our support of independent judgment, experience and research indicate that it does not hold the high priority we claim for it. In fact, the attitudes of the group have a profound influence on the individual through informal socialization. Individuals are often willing to deny their own perceptions and judgments because of the attitudes of their group.

One of the classic experiments in studying the influence of groups on the judgment of members was done by Solomon E. Asch.[13] Asch gathered groups of seven to nine engineering students at MIT for "psychological experiments in visual judgment." Members of each group were shown two cards simultaneously; one card bore a standard line, the other bore three lines, one of which was the same length as the one shown on the first card (See Figure 5–1). They were asked, which line is the same length as line X—A, B, or C? In each group, all but one member were "confederates" (i.e., instructed ahead of time to pick the same incorrect line). The remaining member was "naive" and was the only real subject of the experiment. The question at issue was, How often would a group member pick the right line even in the face of unanimous agreement by the rest of the group that another was the right one? It was visually quite clear which line was the same length as X, and ordinarily only 1 percent of the subjects would pick the wrong line. The subject was seated near the end of the group so that most of the others had responded by the time it was the subject's turn to do so.

For our reputedly individualistic society, the findings are significant: Faced with incorrect answers by the majority, 75 percent of real subjects erred

[13]Solomon E. Asch, "Opinions and Social Pressure," in *Science, Conflict and Society* (San Francisco: Freeman, 1969), pp. 52–57.

as well. Only 25 percent braved conflict with the group and held to their own perceptions. As Asch points out, when a majority of reasonably intelligent and educated young students will call black "white" when faced with the opinions of the group, it is obvious that we are losing much of the benefit of individuals' independent assessments of reality. The opinions, norms, and values of the majority can become a tyranny. We can see this readily in Soviet Russia or Nazi Germany but are less able to see it in our own society.

In spite of their positive contributions, persons who exercise independent judgment are not always popular in an organization. This was shown in experiments with problem-solving groups. A "deviant," a person whose values and attitudes did not coincide with those of the group, was placed in half the groups. In every case, the groups with a deviant had a better solution to the problem they were given than did the homogeneous groups. Each group was then asked to eliminate one member of the group before receiving the next problem. In every case, the deviant was thrown out, and this in spite of the fact that it was fairly clear the deviant had contributed significantly to the work they had done.[14]

Groups seem to value harmony and unity more than new information and challenge. The suppression of dissent among those in working groups results in failure, often disastrous failure, as important information and options are not brought forward. Hence it is important to provide a vehicle for the expression of dissent.[15] For example, the lack of a means by which the Morton Thiokol engineers could have warned the managers of the Challenger space launch about the dangers of a launch at below freezing temperatures resulted in disaster and loss of life. In response to other problems and in order to lessen the danger of such blockage of vital information, General Dynamics has established an ombudsman and an ethics hotline at each company facility. Both can be called anonymously to ask questions or to report information.

Other experiments have shown that in a group, individual competitive behavior (individuals looking exclusively to their own success and satisfaction) often leads to disruption and inefficiency in the group's effort. Competitive behavior leads to greater efficiency when the job can be done entirely by an individual and does not require the help of others. So, in spite of the American myth, in most settings, including business, cooperative behavior leads to greater efficiency than does competitive behavior.[16]

[14] Elise Boulding, *Conflict: Management in Organizations* (Ann Arbor, Mich.: Foundation for Research on Human Behavior, 1964), p. 54.

[15] John D. Stanley, "Dissent in Organizations," *Academy of Management Review* 6, no. 1 (1981); 13–19.

[16] Alfie Kohn, "How to Succeed Without Even Vying," *Psychology Today*, September 1986, pp. 22–28.

In sum, corporations tend to inculcate and thus perpetuate their own values. Like other organizations, corporations have the goals of survival and growth. These goals, plus the characteristic goals of long-term profit and high return on investment, have a profound influence on the attitudes and values of a corporation's members. Members learn to accept the rules of the game that exist implicitly in their organization. Although creativity is of long-term benefit to the firm, it is not easily tolerated. The material goals of the firm often force individuals into judging the success of their work in numerical terms: numbers of products and dollars of profit. The bias toward the concrete and measurable is widespread because of the objectivity that is allowed. But this bias can easily undermine long-range and human values, such as creativity, trust, and openness.

WHY PEOPLE WORK: MOTIVATION AND IDEOLOGY

Why people work is no mere academic question. Thousands of studies of motivation are done each year, and there are few academic quests that have such practical implications. Executives regularly ask how to better motivate their associates and workers.

One of the challenges for the concerned executive and the researcher is to determine if and how a firm can pursue its objectives effectively and at the same time encourage the development of its members as persons. Social scientists have demonstrated that an individual can grow toward full maturity and achieve self-actualization only in an interpersonal atmosphere of complete trust and open communication.[17] Open, trusting interpersonal relationships are essential to maturation. Working relationships can seldom attain the necessary openness and trust. Moreover, if the working climate inhibits personal growth, it will result in frustration and, eventually, a poor working environment. Managers are therefore especially concerned about the quality of working relationships within the organization.

Many business executives recently have become interested in supporting the personal growth of their employees. At 3M and Digital, for example, executives know that the abilities of their employees can best be tapped by means of such support. It has even been shown that such support can indirectly improve flexibility, innovation, and product quality. The case for shared decisions and for encouraging individual initiative and creativity has been building for decades. One indication of the concern firms have for these

---

[17] Herbert A. Shepard, "Changing Interpersonal and Intergroup Relationships in Organizations," in *Handbook of Organizations*, ed. James G. March (New York: Garland, 1987), pp. 1122–37.

issues is the size of their training staffs and the amount of time and effort they spend on encouraging shared decision making and cooperation on the job. The new young managers identified by Michael Maccoby specified self-development as their chief aim. When a firm recognizes and builds on that motivator, both the firm and the individual can benefit. A variety of theories of motivation have been proposed over the years. Here we will examine a few that take account of the role of values and ideologies.

In his seminal *Human Side of Enterprise*, Douglas McGregor contrasts two sets of *assumptions* about individuals and their desire to work.[18] The first is a view that has heavily influenced past management styles; he calls it *Theory X:*

1.   People do not like to work and will avoid it if they can do so.
2.   Therefore, in order to get them to do their work, they must be coerced, controlled, directed, and threatened with punishment.
3.   People have little ambition, wish to avoid responsibility, prefer to be directed, and want security.

In contrast to this traditional view, McGregor presents and argues for his own view, which he calls *Theory Y:*

1.   Work is as natural to people as play or rest.
2.   Individuals will exercise self-direction and self-control in the service of objectives to which they are committed.
3.   Commitment to objectives is a function of the rewards associated with their achievement (especially satisfaction of ego and self-actualization).
4.   People learn, under proper conditions, to accept and even ask for responsibility.

Each of these divergent views of the values and goals of people obviously would have a profound influence on the organizational climate and management style of any organization in which it predominated. Theory X provides the foundation for a formal, highly structured, control-oriented organization. One disadvantage that characterizes such organizations is goal displacement. This takes place in bureaucratic organizations when members turn procedures into goals. Petty officials tend to make adherence to the rules and preservation of their office the purpose of their work, and this is most often at the expense of the persons or processes they are serving. For example, a government official is asked to process ten people per hour, and the official dutifully does so—even on a day when the line is five times longer than normal. Most recent strategies to increase motivation are based more on Theory Y.

[18] Douglas McGregor, *Human Side of Enterprise* (New York: McGraw-Hill, 1960), p. 33.

Personal Growth Within the Organization

Individuals in firms now ask for more communication, more participation, and more opportunity for individual initiative. Yet executives are not always able to perceive the importance of providing challenging and satisfying work, encouraging a sense of ownership, allowing flexibility, and motivating employees to make their best effort.[19] It is important to note that everyone benefits from the working environment that results. These policies not only serve the individual need for self-development but also provide the foundation for improved product or service quality, new ideas, and greater efficiencies.

When psychologists ask why people work, they now generally look at values. What sort of values move the employee to work?[20] Most older theories of motivation popular with businesspeople described moving forces within the individual but rarely discussed values, goals, or ideologies. These older theories generally presupposed traditional goals. By ignoring values and goals, motivational theorists implied that they were unimportant; they thus did business a disservice. But businesspeople now know that there is an intimate, complex relationship between ideology and motivation. *In Search of Excellence* demonstrates that product quality and production efficiencies depend on the values and goals of the firm as articulated by the chief executive.[21]

Among the questions we might ask about popular theories and practices of motivation are these: To what extent do they imply values and goals? Do they presuppose goals or predispose one toward certain goals? Do these theories aid in a search for values and goals or mask their absence? The current increased interest in motivation has coincided with, and perhaps partially caused, an increased interest in values, ethics, and ideologies.

Ideologies are, as we have seen, products of deliberate reflection and articulation. However, social scientists warn us to be suspicious of stated reasons for actions. It is easy, they remind us, to neglect unconscious or subconscious motives that have a powerful influence on our activities. We may think we know why we do something and respond with an answer when asked. But according to psychologists, we may not have given the real reason at all. In short, the inquiry into values tends not to be aided by psychologists who imply that straightforward verbal statements are generally self-deceiving and untrue. We now turn to some psychologists who have

---

[19] "Managers Underrate Employee Values," *Administrative Management*, July 1987, p. 8.

[20] For an overview of the literature on motivation, see Richard M. Steers, *Introduction to Organizational Behavior* (Glenview, Ill.: Scott, Foresman, 1988), esp. pp. 153–76, 181–209.

[21] Thomas J. Peters and Robert H. Waterman, Jr., *In Search of Excellence* (New York: Harper & Row, 1982); see also Thomas J. Peters, *Thriving on Chaos: Handbook for a Management Revolution* (New York: Alfred A. Knopf, 1987) and Robert W. Waterman, Jr., *The Renewal Factor: How to Best Get the Competitive Edge* (New York: Bantam, 1987).

theories of motivation that are highly influential and who also explicitly inquire into the effect of the values of businesspeople.

Need for Achievement and Power

David C. McClelland is a pioneer in examining the need for achievement and the need for power. He has pointed out that the success of an individual or a society is generally positively correlated with a high need for achievement. A person's need for achievement can be measured; it can even be increased, according to McClelland. However, it is not our purpose to go into the details of McClelland's work. In this instance, as with others that follow, we will be content with a brief examination of how the relationship between motivation and values is treated.

McClelland examines the long-range impact of a person's ideology on motivation. He cites Max Weber on the contribution of the Protestant ethic to attitudes that support modern capitalism.[22] Protestantism encouraged independence and self-reliance. Since the church was no longer the central agency for communicating values, individuals became independent.

Attitudes of independence, self-reliance, and the need for achievement are very much influenced by the manner in which parents bring up their children. From the content of children's stories, fantasies, daydreams, and dreams, McClelland is able to determine whether there is a high or a low need for achievement. Since parents' own values and ideology influence which stories they tell their children and which books they give them, parents thus have a profound effect on their children's motivation. In experimental work, researchers found that boys who showed a high need for achievement had mothers who expected their sons to master a number of activities early in life—to know their way around the city, be active and energetic, try hard to get things for themselves, do well in competition, and make their own friends.[23] On the other hand, the mothers of boys with a low need for achievement reported that they had restricted their sons more. These mothers did not want their sons to make important decisions by themselves or to make friends with children not approved by their parents.

McClelland theorizes that the Protestant Reformation encouraged a new character type possessing a more vigorous and independent spirit. This spirit of self-reliance was then passed on in families, especially through child rearing patterns. Furthermore, McClelland holds that it is precisely self-reliance that forms the foundation for modern capitalism. He cites evidence that the need for achievement is increased as an effect of an ideological or

---

[22] Max Weber, *The Protestant Ethic and the Spirit of Capitalism*, trans. Talcott Parsons (New York: Scribner, 1958).
[23] David C. McClelland, *The Achieving Society* (Princeton, N.J.: Van Nostrand, 1961), pp. 46–50.

religious conversion, whether it be to Fundamentalism, Marxism, or Catholism.[24] In the wake of the reflection and forced reassessment a conversion entails, a felt challenge and a resulting need for achievement emerge. According to McClelland, religion, ideology, and values are inextricably intertwined with motivation, especially the need for achievement. Their relationship is especially close when a person reassesses and changes his or her values.

In modern society, the need for achievement is generally exercised in the marketplace. McClelland cites Florence in the late Middle Ages as an example of a society where the need for achievement was expressed in art, that is, in something other than economic development. In modern societies, however, for good or ill, business is the major outlet for this need. So it is not surprising that McClelland's practical criterion for the success (and hence implicit goal) of the achiever today is economic growth. In using this criterion, McClelland seems to accept unquestioningly the traditional business ideology and the prevailing social norm—that economic growth is the best final goal of a people.

McClelland denies that the businessperson with a high need for achievement is motivated by money. Nevertheless, he does agree that achievement is measured in terms of money.[25] As he notes, money is a *symbol* of success. An increase in salary, which is often demonstrated to friends and neighbors by a more expensive car, clothes, and a larger home, is the reward that comes to those who have achieved; it is a sign of success. (Some observations by Erich Fromm on money as a measure of personal success will be examined later in this chapter.)

People with a high need for achievement are more likely to achieve when they can be their own boss. Someone who begins a business—an entrepreneur—is motivated by a high need for achievement. Executives with a high need for achievement tend to centralize power and want credit for their achievements.[26] Given that 80 percent of new jobs are created in firms with less than 100 employees, American business (and hence the United States as a whole) depends heavily on individuals with a high need for achievement.[27]

Most of McClelland's work was done with males. More recent experimental work shows that males have a high need for achievement and a high need for power, whereas females have a high need for affiliation (relations with others). Females tend to show achievement through nuturing and sup-

---

[24] Ibid., pp. 406–17.

[25] Ibid., pp. 232–37.

[26] Danny Miller and Cornelia Droge, "Psychological and Traditional Determinants of Structure," *Administrative Science Quarterly* 31 (December 1986): 554.

[27] David L. Birch, *Job Creation in America: How Our Smallest Companies Put the Most People to Work* (New York: The Free Press, 1987).

port.[28] Women in the firm who have done graduate preparation for their business careers face a greater dilemma than do men. Although a woman's career is quite important to her, marriage and having children increase in importance as a woman progresses in her career.[29] This calls for major decisions and sometimes creates stress.

McClelland later turned his attention to the need for power and influence. The need for power is the desire to have an impact, to be strong or influential. McClelland found that top managers in companies possess a need for power even higher than their need for achievement. This need for power must be "disciplined and controlled so that it is directed toward the benefit of the institution as a whole and not toward the manager's personal aggrandizement."[30]

Managers with a high need for power who do not exercise it with self-control can be very disruptive: "They are rude to other people, they drink too much, they try to exploit others sexually, and they collect symbols of personal prestige such as fancy cars or big offices."[31] A recent study found that people with a high need for affiliation are better liked by their subordinates and have a higher level of job performance.[32] Where McClelland identified predominant need patterns that differ from individual to individual, the psychologist we will examine next developed a hierarchical model of all human needs that, according to him, is applicable to all persons.

Self-Actualization

Abraham H. Maslow proposed that motivation arises from a hierarchy of needs. Maslow based his theory of motivation on observations of healthy, mature persons. For individuals to develop their own internalized philosophical and religious values, "lower needs" (food, water, safety, and security) must be somewhat satisfied. Maslow found that as lower needs were satisfied, they ceased to be motivators. The person then moved on to "higher needs" (belongingness, love, self-esteem, and self-actualization), so that

---

[28]See Janet T. Spence, "Achievement American Style," *American Psychologist,* December 1985, pp. 1285–95. For limitations of McClelland's thesis, see R. Scott Frey, "Need for Achievement, Entrepreneurship, and Economic Growth: A Critique of the McClelland Thesis," *Social Science Journal* 21 (April 1984): 125–34.

[29]Brooke Banbury-Masland and Daniel J. Brass, "Careers, Marriage, and Children: Are Women Changing Their Minds?" *Business Horizons,* May-June 1985, pp. 82–86.

[30]David C. McClelland and David H. Burnham, "Power Is the Great Motivator," *Harvard Business Review* 54, no. 2 (1976): 101.

[31]Ibid., p. 103.

[32]Edwin Cornelius and Frank Lane, "The Power Motive and Managerial Success in a Professionally Oriented Service Industry Organization," *Journal of Organizational Psychology,* February 1984, pp. 32–39.

healthy persons are primarily motivated by their needs to develop their capacities and actualize their potentialities to the fullest.[33]

The higher needs are not always strong, according to Maslow. In spite of the fact that in the long run they are important for the person, they often do not emerge in people who do not have enough to eat or a roof over their heads. In Maslow's words, "The human needs for love, for knowledge or for philosophy, are weak and feeble rather than unequivocal and unmistakable; they whisper rather than shout. And the whisper is easily drowned out."[34]

Maslow maintains that as individuals become more mature and accepting, they will establish their own values. He concludes that a firm foundation for a value system is furnished by open acceptance of one's own self, "of human nature, of much of social life, and of nature and physical reality." A society made up largely of self-actualizers is characterized by more free choice and nonintrusiveness. Under these conditions, "the deepest layers of human nature would show themselves with greater ease."[35]

Maslow goes on to describe the personal characteristics of the people he has examined—those whom he calls *self-actualizers.* They tend to be "strongly focused on problems outside themselves"; they are problem-centered rather than ego-centered. Most often these mature, self-actualized individuals have "some mission in life, some task to fulfill," a task outside themselves that enlists most of their energies. Significantly, especially for our purposes, such tasks are generally nonpersonal or unselfish; they are directed primarily toward the good of others. Furthermore, self-actualizers "are ordinarily concerned with basic issues and eternal questions of the type that we have learned to call philosophical or ethical."[36] They have wide horizons; their major concerns are not ego-centered, tribal, or petty. They seem to have a stability that enables and encourages them to address large ethical and social issues.

Maslow describes in detail their basic values. Self-actualizers "are strongly ethical, they have definite moral standards, they do right and do not do wrong." They are less confused about their basic values. It is easier for them to distinguish right from wrong, although their judgments do not always coincide with those of the accepted, conventional, surrounding culture.

Maslow holds that as persons grow and mature, they will become less selfish and more concerned with other people and larger problems. Their values will become clearer, more explicit, and highly ethical. Indeed, although Maslow finds that these people are not always theists and that many

---

[33] Abraham H. Maslow, *Motivation and Personality,* (New York: Harper & Row, 1954), pp. 35–58.

[34] Ibid., p. 276.

[35] Ibid., pp. 276–78.

[36] Ibid., pp. 159–60.

have little loyalty to an institutional church, they are nevertheless the sort who could be described as godly or devout people.[37]

Maslow is convinced that ethical values emerge as an individual matures. In fact, he implies that the development of unselfish goals and internalized ethical principles can *only* occur as a person matures. He therefore has little sympathy for a study of values, ethics, asceticism, or a spirituality that seeks to develop unselfish ethical principles and goals. In Maslow's view, people must become self-actualizers before unselfish goals and policies can be developed. However, it is doubtful whether the problems that face our country and our world can wait for this maturity to come about. Indeed, it is doubtful whether such maturity ever *will* characterize most leaders and policymakers.

The above motivation models involving need for achievement, need for power, and need for self-actualization continue to influence organizations and generate research. Meanwhile, newer theories of motivation have been developed that take into account a wider variety of personality traits, attitudes, and needs. They are called expectancy/valence or path-goal theories.[38] We are unable to go into the details of these theories. However, it is noteworthy that an individual's personal attitudes and values are traced and given weight in these theories. The close relationship between motives and personal values is again acknowledged and underlined.

The above theories of motivation build upon the attitudes and values of the individual. The values and goals of the organization in which the individual is working are not as clearly considered. Psychologists may respond that the goals of the firm are beyond their concern and competence. This may be true, yet an organizations's goals and values have considerable influence on each participant's motivations. If values are in conflict, it will lead to frustration for the person and inefficiencies for the organization. Moreover, neglect of values and goals leaves the impression that they are unimportant. In the past, we took organizational goals for granted; now we find ourselves in the awkward position of wanting to probe these goals, yet have few tools and little expertise for doing so.

Moving Blindly with Unexamined Assumptions

After working with Maslow, Douglas McGregor dug into the accepted ideology and the conventional assumptions that lay beneath thinking and literature on management and motivation. He was incisive in penetrating the

---

[37] Ibid., pp. 168–69. Some empirical verification of Maslow's model is provided by Jean Davis-Sharts, "An Empirical Test of Maslow's Theory of Need Hierarchy Using Hologeistic Comparison by Statistical Sampling," *Advances in Nursing Science,* October 1986, pp. 58–72.

[38] For a summary of these views, see Henry L. Tosi, John R. Rizzo, and Stephen J. Carroll, *Managing Organizational Behavior* (Boston: Ballinger, 1986), pp. 240–45, 564–69.

"let's be practical, theorizing has no place in management" mentality, and he shows that "it is not possible to reach a managerial decision or take a managerial action uninfluenced by assumptions, whether adequate or not."[39] Any decision maker makes assumptions and has implicit goals and values. The relevant question is whether these assumptions and implicit goals and values are adequate. McGregor pinpoints one of the most glaring deficiencies of this self-imposed managerial blindness: "The common practice of proceeding without explicit examination of theoretical assumptions, leads, at times, to remarkable inconsistencies in managerial behavior."[40]

It is not easy to cast a cool, clear eye on our own assumptions and values. All of us engage in various shortcuts in considering our own and others' values. Rationalization, stereotyping, and other mechanisms block our ability to perceive what exactly these values are.[41] Sometimes these barriers also block our ability to reflect on the goals and the values of the organization. We may convince ourselves, for example, that the growth of the organization benefits some people and thus automatically compensates for damage done to others. We may think that businesspeople waste their time speculating on abstract values and goals. They are irrelevant to successful performance, and it is better to concentrate on the work before us.

On the other hand, it is now clear that there is no such thing as value-free management. Proceeding to carry out the goals of an organization without explicitly knowing what values undergird those goals is itself to have chosen to make decisions on the basis of a value. This value can be characterized as unquestioning acceptance of the values of the organization, unquestioning faith that the present goals of the organization are justifiable, and unquestioning faith that in a conflict with the larger society or with another organization, one should pursue the goals of one's own organization. McDonnell Douglas's overcharges to the government, Firestone's resistance to recalling its fatally dangerous series 500 tire, Gulf + Western's ostentatious introduction of a battery for electric automobiles (when under criticism for unethical activities) that fizzled—all bear testimony to the shortsightedness and ultimate inefficiency of this sort of "value-free" and blind management.

SOURCES OF SATISFACTION
AND PRESSURE TO PERFORM

We have examined how the structure and climate of the organization affect the values of the manager. In this section, we will focus on the business manager as a person and on her or his values.

[39] McGregor, *Human Side of Enterprise*, p. 7.

[40] Ibid; see also Bruce H. Drake and Eileen Drake, "Ethical and Legal Aspects of Managing Corporate Cultures," *California Management Review* 30 (Winter 1988): 107–23.

[41] Steers, *Introduction to Organizational Behavior*, pp. 115–23.

In one classic empirical study of the backgrounds, education, and attitudes of business executives, the executive is characterized as a mobile person, able to leave and take up a new job in a new community rather easily:

> The mobile [manager] must be able to depart: that is, to maintain a substantial emotional distance from people, and not become deeply involved with them or committed to them; and [the manager] must be an energetic person and one who can focus energy on a single goal.[42]

These top mangers are not always sensitive to the needs of other people. Even though their own success in often built on decisions that result in considerable loss to others, this does not seem to bother them. They are not "distracted into personal duels, for they do not allow themselves to become so involved with others." When United Airlines or U.S. Steel (now USX) layed off 1,000 people, top management did not allow that to affect them, even though 1,000 families were severely hurt.

Mobility and lack of consideration for others enable these executives to approach managerial decisions dispassionately. This objectivity contributes to making them successful. But their success does not allow them the satisfaction one might expect. There is rarely time to relax or to look back on their successes, "for an essential part of the system is the need for constant demonstration of one's adequacy, for reiterated proof of one's independence."[43]

What sort of an upbringing would give a person the qualities of mobility and emotional distance from others and the need to constantly demonstrate personal adequacy? Researchers found that these executives tended to have strong, demanding mothers and weak or even absent fathers. Although the mothers of these successful executives are even-tempered and hard working, they are also stern, rigid, moralistic, and controlling. They hold out high standards of achievement and parcel out their love as a reward for success. At the same time, the fathers are distant from their children; they do not provide support or reinforcement. These executives see their fathers as rather unreliable figures and could not identify with them. If they were to win their mothers' love and respect, they must prove themselves; they must be successful at what they are doing. They can never be fully sure that they have achieved enough. The overwhelming majority of the families of these executives are upper or middle class: 76 percent of the fathers were owners, executives, professionals, or white-collar workers. The executives are conservative in their politics. Moreover, when they have any involvement with community activities, it tends to be with conservative movements, such as the Chamber of Commerce and conservative charities.

[42] W. Lloyd Warner and James Abegglen, *Big Business Leaders in America* (New York: Atheneum, 1963), pp. 81–82.
[43] Ibid., p. 83.

A 1987 study verified that the chief executive is still typically white, male, married, never divorced, and politically conservative. Noteworthy is that most of the chief executives in the study had a master's degree in business administration, and 60 percent did not have a specific career goal in mind when they began with the firm.[44]

When the chief executives were asked what they would look for in their successors, they did not give high priority to such attributes as the ability to get along well with people of different races and classes. They would generally look for people who were much like themselves in background and attitudes. Organizations and their attitudes tend to be self-perpetuating. The ordinary struggle for growth and survival urges people and organizations to seek "their own kind." Although there are now some large black-owned and managed firms and a few women in executive positions, both blacks and women are still severely underrepresented in chief executive positions.

The surveys discussed above remain the best available sources of information on the characteristics of chief executive officers of American firms. The next survey will undoubtedly show additional changes. What changes would you expect?

Selling of Self: Careerism

Although the goals and values of a businessperson are influenced by background, education, and age, they are also heavily influenced by the person's estimate of what sort of personal values will "sell" in the marketplace. The market concept of value, how much a person can obtain through entering the employment market, has a considerable influence on notions of self-worth.[45] Today we call selling oneself *careerism*.

For example, imagine the case of a businesswoman looking for a new position. She will be concerned about how she appears to prospective employers. Dressing for success and using proper grammar and terminology will be important. She might be less concerned about personal goals of achievement, satisfaction, and happiness. In short, her attention will tend to be focused on pleasing someone else rather than on her own values and goals. The more she sees self-esteem as dependent on how much she is worth in the market, the less control she will have over her own life. Suppose she thinks that she is not valued for the person she is and that her adequacy is determined by unpredictable and insensitive market forces—the price others put on her in the marketplace. If that is the case, when she receives an increase in salary, it will be less the money itself that delights her than the fact

---

[44] "Profile of Leadership Emerges in Study of Top Corporate Executives," *Journal of Accountancy*, March 1987, pp. 36–38.

[45] Erich Fromm, "Personality and the Market Place," in *Man, Work, and Society: A Reader in the Sociology of Occupations*, ed. Sigmund Nosow and William Form (New York: Basic Books, 1962), pp. 446–52.

that someone has recognized the she has done a good job. Without the salary increase, she might sink into depths of low self-esteem and even self-pity.

Furthermore, since the market is often the principal determiner of self-worth and since value in the market is subject to many changing, unpredictable forces and fads, she must remain flexible. Her present value may collapse, simply because there are too many with the same talents on the market. She must then be able to shift to a new career. (The phenomenon of glutted labor markets encourages businesspeople to maintain flexibility and maximum exposure.) No matter how much she may like her present work or locale, it is not to her advantage to sink deep roots. If she becomes known as a one-talent person, her value, and hence her self-esteem, will be severely limited. This situation does not encourage developing expertise, loyalty, or settling into and becoming involved in a community.

This notion of self-worth makes a businessperson dependent on others for his or her own self-esteem. Self-worth stems not from accomplishments or the affection of others but rather from the impersonal forces of the employment market, in this case, from company superiors. Someone who accepts this view can be called "other-directed." The heavy influence of a changing external environment on personal values contributes to making Americans practical and pragmatic. They will rarely dispute principles for their own sake and consider martyrdom to be folly. Thomas More's beheading under Henry VIII makes superb drama in *Man for All Seasons.* Americans find the episode quaint but difficult to fully understand and smacking of fanaticism. Indeed, businesspeople find disputes over principles time-consuming and unproductive and will rarely allow themselves to be caught up in what seems to them to be philosophical battles.

Loving, Caring, and Decisiveness

Another aspect of the tension that businesspeople experience is the conflict between the characteristics that are rewarded on the job and those that make for a good spouse and parent. Here we will discuss but one example. Imagine a typical manager—aggressive, decisive, and fact-oriented. He makes decisions, not on the basis of intuition or feelings, but on the basis of facts and defensible reasoning. However, this talent of examining only the facts and then reasoning from them does not work so well when the manager is at home with his wife and children. For example, when his spouse asks to go to a movie, it is not necessarily because she wants to see a particular film; she may simply desire to be alone with her husband for a few hours away from the house and children.

The fact-oriented manager may also have difficulty determining what his son or daughter is saying beneath the flurry of words and argument. He has trained himself to look for the facts and so he takes the words at face value. Furthermore, he might often be impatient with his wife and children for not saying what they really mean. He finds it impossible to sift through the words to determine what his wife, son, or daughter is really saying—often nonverbally. Moreover, in his impatience he is often unable to be open enough to encourage them to communicate what they really are thinking and feeling. He is sometimes aware of this inability and the resulting conflict, and this causes additional tension and anxiety.

A person like the manager above has what is called a *Type A personality*, which is characterized by impatience, restlessness, aggressiveness, and competitiveness. Type A persons also tend to have many irons in the fire and to be under considerable time pressure. Sixty percent of managers in the average organization are Type A. The Type A manager is two to five times more likely to have heart disease or a fatal heart attack as other mangers. Interestingly enough, it has been shown that although Type A managers have the talents and attitudes that enable them to rise in the organization, chief executive officers are generally not Type A; they are more patient and willing to examine the long-term ramifications of decision.[46]

Authority

Following orders within an organization is essential to any organization's success. To what lengths will a person go in following orders when those orders seriously conflict with his or her own moral values? Evidence of a person's willingness actually to do harm to another individual when instructed by authority to do so was provided by a series of controversial laboratory experiments.[47] Subjects were told by an academic authority figure dressed in a white coat that they were to engage in experiments in memory and learning. Each subject was placed at a shock generator with thirty intervals marked, starting with 15 volts (slight shock) and going up to 450 volts (danger—severe shock). Another person (the learner), who was strapped in a chair with electrodes on his or her wrists, could be seen in an adjoining room through a glass partition. (The learners were in on the experiment and were not really subjected to shocks.) The subject was then instructed to shock the learner, increasing the intensity for every wrong answer the learner gave. As the shock level rose, the learner cried out in increasing pain, yet almost two-thirds of the subjects administered the highest level of shock.

Each subject would become nervous, agonize, and rationalize, but most nevertheless administered the highest level of shock under the auspices of authority. The experiment has been criticized as being unethical. Indeed, it did play with people's consciences. However, it also gave us frightening evidence of what one human being is willing to inflict on another when it seems to be legitimized by some authority.

[46] Steers, *Introduction to Organizational Behavior*, pp. 507–8.
[47] Stanley Milgram, *Obedience to Authority* (New York: Harper & Row, 1974).

Obedience in this experiment drops if the subject is in the same room as the learner or if the subject must actually touch the learner to administer the shock. The more impersonal the situation, the more willing the subject is to do harm to another. Ancient warfare involved face-to-face contact; modern warfare is closer to the above experimental situation and easier to wage. A person can push a button thousands of miles away and never have to witness the death and destruction caused by the resulting nuclear explosion.

Sometimes lower-level managers are instructed to do something that violates their ethics. The above experiment shows that about 60 percent of us will perform actions at serious variance with what we know is right if someone in authority instructs us. Yet this sort of obedience has its cost in tension, anxiety, stress, and the attendant physical ailments.

Modern organizations are designed to produce results in an impersonal fashion. Pollution, exploitative advertising, and firings are the direct result of decisions and policies made by executives. Such problems and questionable activities occur more often when executives do not view the victims of their actions and can thus feel that they themselves did not directly bring about the undesirable results. In the minds of some executives, the system demands that they act impersonally if they are to see to it that their firms survive and grow.

SUMMARY AND CONCLUSIONS

People's values are heavily influenced by business and corporations. During the working day, the expectations and behavior of supervisors influence the behavior of employees. In the evening, corporations, their products, and their values are sold to everyone through television programming and advertising.

Successful businesspeople generally are ambitious, achievement- and power-oriented, disciplined, and adaptable. Younger managers are intent on being "winners" and "self-developers," often at the expense of empathy for others. The business manager ingests many of these values when he or she joins the firm. The prevailing values of competition, free market, and opposition to government intervention are learned early, along with the specific values of the particular firm. Hence the goals of managers are largely determined for them—whatever goals must be accomplished for success *within* the firm. Moreover, when managers contribute to policymaking, their goals come to include those that must be accomplished to insure success *for* the firm. Just as early in life the rules of the game were set by someone else, so now the economic rules of the game come from outside.

Evidence is accumulating that people's personal goals are changing. Individuals now desire more than salary and status. They desire challenging work, participation in decision making, the respect and approval of friends, the ability to identify with their community, and a stimulating and fulfilling life. A business firm can help in the achievement of many of these goals if its senior executives use wisdom in directing it.

DISCUSSION QUESTIONS

1. Does rational decision making rest on values and ideological assumptions? What are they?
2. Since Americans often claim their actions are "value-free," what is the benefit in inquiring about values?
3. Is it acceptable for a firm to attempt to socialize its members? How does it do so? What are the unexpected costs of socialization?
4. Outline the pros and cons to the individual of having salary and status as goals. Do Americans "sell" themselves? Are *you* concerned with making yourself more "marketable"?
5. Do business managers tend to be more interested in people, power, or tasks? Are executives more conformist or more innovative?
6. What do Solomon Asch's experiments on the influence of groups tell us?
7. What sort of upbringing do people with a high need for achievement tend to have? What in a culture encourages a high need for achievement? Are those elements present in contemporary U.S. culture?
8. What special problems in achieving do many women have?
9. Is a high need for power a help or a hinderance to effective leadership? Explain.
10. What values develop as a person matures and becomes self-actualized? What role does concern for other people play in the set of values of a self-actualized person?
11. Describe the family life and values of the mobile manager.
12. What are the benefits and costs of "selling" oneself? What sort of values does this engender in a person?
13. Describe the values that are most valuable to someone in organizational life and the values that are developed in family life. Is there a conflict here? How can it be resolved?
14. What is the effect of authority on a person's willingness to inflict pain, or even the danger of death, on another? Describe an experiment regarding this subject. Do parallel situations occur in an organization? In a country? Explain.

CASE: THE PURCHASING MANAGER'S CAR

Jim Angot is the purchasing manager for Nihco, Inc. He is responsible for buying two $1 million computers. Nihco has a written policy prohibiting any company buyer from receiving a gift in excess of $50 and requiring that all gratuities be reported. The company has no policy on whistle-blowing. A salesperson for a computer manufacturer offers to arrange it so that Angot can purchase a $20,000 auto for $6,000. The auto would be bought through a third party. Should Jim decline the offer? Should he tell his superior? Should he tell the salesperson's superior?

CHAPTER SIX
MATURITY AND MORAL DEVELOPMENT

Greed in business is healthy. You can be greedy and still feel good about yourself.

Ivan Boesky

Let us be concerned for each other, to stir a response in love and good works. Do not stay away from the meetings of the community, as some do, but encourage each other to go...

Hebrews 10:24–25

Every business firm exists in a particular society and culture. The values of that culture influence the ethics of the firm—the judgments within the firm of what is right and wrong. This chapter provides a bridge from the values of society as affected by history and environment (Chapters 1–5) to the ethics of the firm (Chapter 7). In the last chapter we examined the influence of the organization on the values of the individual. In this chapter we will examine (1) the moral development of the individual person and (2) the stress and illness that stem from a lack of internalized values and goals. We will then look at methods of making personal values explicit and conclude by reviewing the arguments for the proposition that ethics should be an integral part of business decisions.

First let us examine some examples of executives under stress. James E. Olson, chairman and chief executive officer (CEO) of AT&T, died suddenly on April 18, 1988 at age sixty-three. He had just cut one billion dollars from AT&T's operating costs the year before and had overseen the largest corporate restructuring in American history—the breakup of the AT&T system into numerous operating systems.[1]

Jerome Kohlberg, founding partner of Kohlberg, Kravis & Roberts, one

---

[1] *Business Week,* May 2, 1988, p. 34.

of the largest and most aggressive investment firms involved in unfriendly takeovers, withdrew from an active role in his firm, citing "the overpowering greed that pervades our business life" while acknowledging that his own firm participated in that greed.[2]

Eli Black, CEO of United Brands, broke the window of his forty-fourth-floor office in Manhattan with his attaché case and jumped to his death on February 3, 1975. Two months later the Securities and Exchange Commission revealed that United Brands paid a $1,250,000 bribe to a government official in Honduras for a reduction in the export tax on bananas. Black knew about the bribe.

Each of these executives faced stress, anxiety, and a conflict in values. They are particularly visible examples of the strains and anxieties that face businesspeople every day. This chapter will examine the sources of and some solutions to the conflicts that arise. Some of the data in this chapter are taken from psychology and sociology. The application to people in the business world is often obvious.

LACK OF MATURITY BRINGS STRESS

People who are mature and morally developed are more relaxed, can enjoy life more, are able to more fully utilize their talents, and are generally more liked and respected by their families and peers. Moreover, they are also considered wise and are more often consulted by others. Crises, stress, and illness often plague the person who has failed to achieve maturity and moral development.

Midlife Identity Crisis

A person who has not internalized his or her own values is often pressed into making important life and career decisions in ignorance and before clarifying goals or examining alternatives. This then often leads to a midlife identity crisis.

John Z. DeLorean was vice president in charge of all General Motors car and truck divisions in North America. DeLorean quit because he felt that the GM committee system was too unwieldy. It dispersed authority and responsibility, and he felt that as a result no one could show initiative. Whether one agrees with DeLorean or not, his case is not unique. The *Wall Street Journal* ran a series of articles on scores of people who left well-paid corporate jobs to do something quite different at a fraction of their former pay. These people

---

[2]"For What Shall It Profit a Man," *Business Week*, July 6, 1987, p. 104; Jim Hightower, "Where Greed, Unofficially Sanctioned by Reagan, Has Led," *New York Times*, June 21, 1987, p. E25.

found their work in the corporation to be confining, and most turned to a simpler and less-structured life. Typical is Ross Drever, age fifty-two, who quit as director of Amsted Industries' research division at a $100,000 salary. He now works a cranberry bog in Three Lakes, Wisconsin. He says, "I have a lot of suits and shoes I'll never use again."

These managers felt they were giving too much time to a job that gave them little satisfaction. They made a radical change; they left comfortable jobs, homes, and friends to carve out a new life. These men and women show us how some at midlife examine their own values and goals and act on what they find.

This reassessment often occurs in men and women around the age of forty. One looks around and asks if this is the way one would choose to lead the rest of one's life. Time is running out; there may be only two or three decades of healthy work life left.

A midlife identity crisis can be traumatic—to family, to fellow workers, and to the person experiencing it. On some occasions the person experiencing the midlife transition panics and seeks a dramatic change. The individual sometimes breaks all connections with the past, leaves spouse and children behind, and goes off with different friends. This sort of radical break can cause much hurt and disruption to families, neighbors, co-workers, and other relatives. Such a reaction to the midlife reassessment is desperate and immature. The frequency of these sharp midlife breaks shows that too few of us have sufficiently probed our own goals in order to chart our own course. Too often we allow higher starting salaries to determine our career and our life goals for us.

The midlife journey generally involves a gradual, life-giving reassessment, especially if the person has internalized his or her own goals and values. The journey becomes a crisis if the person's goals and values have not been examined and if the person's life has been determined by "opportunities" (salaries and the lead of others) instead of by his or her own choices and initiatives. The moral: Make your values and goals your own. The more you clearly recognize what your heartfelt goals are, the greater the chance that the midlife reassessment will be a tranquil one.

Stress and Illness

Self-esteem depends on the positive and negative feedback a person receives from others. In the American culture, those who gain the esteem of their peers are considered successful. Such people are typically competent, goal-oriented, conscientious, ambitious, and hard working, qualities which we identified with the Protestant ethic in Chapter 3.[3]

---

[3] See H. J. Wahler, "Winning and Losing in Life: A Survey of Opinions About Causes," *Mental Hygiene* 55, no. 1 (1971): 94.

The culture, through family life, schools, churches, government, and business, is able to communicate its values to the individual. A culture does this in order to give itself direction and integrity. Otherwise it cannot develop. Without this socialization process, it is not possible to know what one person may expect of another in everyday dealings. We examined the socialization process within the firm in the last chapter.

Although some cultural expectations are not now as strong in the United States as they were a generation ago, there is more consensus as to the route to success in business. People who are not successful according to the norms are often judged inferior by others. Such lack of success is thus often a source of stress. Additional job-related stress is caused by conflict and confusion over a person's responsibilities[4] or when the job calls for actions that are at variance with an individual's values and ethics. In these cases, either a compromise is reached or something is sacrificed. The result is anxiety and frustration.

Those who are judged successful according to the prevailing norms (i.e., viewed as competent, ambitious, and hardworking) may by that very fact suffer anxieties. In the last chapter, we saw how successful corporate managers are mobile; they are able to leave their present jobs and homes in order to move on to "better" positions. Psychologists tell us that anxiety is caused by moving from the known to the unknown. Having mastered one environment, it is unsettling to be asked to move to a new one. It is true that in order to mature, one must take risks and change. Yet being uprooted every few years—leaving behind not just the confidence built in mastering a job but also friends, relatives, and knowledge of the community—can undermine the willingness to commit oneself to a new job or neighborhood. People in such situations may be forced in upon themselves and may come to depend more on their aggressiveness and individuality than on the help and cooperation of co-workers, friends, and neighbors. When they choose to grow in this fashion, they force their spouses and children to undergo the same cyclic trauma of arriving and departing, along with the pain and anxiety it involves.

The unknown, even more the uncontrollable, produces anxieties. Ulcers and stress are often manifestations of anxiety; they usually result when there are two conflicting demands on the individual. Neuroses have been experimentally induced in animals exposed to ambiguous stimuli. After the same

---

[4]See "Stress: The Test Americans Are Failing—It's Taking a Greater Toll on CEOs, Managers, Factory Workers," *Business Week*, April 18, 1988, pp. 74–76. Among the top items CEOs worry about are (in descending order) their own health and fitness, their company's future, the lack of time for family or leisure pursuits, their children's problems, job-related stress, keeping up with technology, product quality, and personal investments; from John H. Sheridan, "What Worries Today's Executives," *Industry Week*, November 30, 1987, pp. 27–32. See also Thomas V. Bonoma and Gerald Zaltman, *Psychology for Management* (Boston: Kent, 1981), pp. 128–41.

or very similar stimuli, the animals were sometimes rewarded and sometimes not (or sometimes rewarded and sometimes punished). Gastric ulcers developed in caged laboratory rats who spent one month subjected to ambiguous stimuli. During forty-seven hours of every forty-eight-hour period, they had to endure an electric shock every time they went to the food box or the water cup. They needed the food, but also feared the shock. Furthermore, since they were not shocked during the remaining hour, they were never sure they would get a shock along with their food. The conflict of wanting the food and yet being afraid of the pain, plus a lack of control over the situation, produced the ulcers. Control rats, which were simply deprived of food and water for forty-seven of the forty-eight hours, did not develop ulcers.[5]

Cats that were first fed and then shocked following the same buzzer exhibited a wide variety of aberrant physical activities, such as restless roving, clawing at wire cages, butting the roof with their heads, and ceaseless vocalizing—all indicating a high degree of anxiety. These cats were then given the opportunity to drink milk that had been laced with alcohol. Half the animals quickly learned that the alcohol relieved the symptoms of their anxiety, and they invariably chose the 5 percent alcohol mixture served in a distinctive cocktail glass. The cats preferred the alcohol as long as their tensions persisted and they remained neurotic. When the animals experienced uncontrollable psychic pain, they sought relief in periodic withdrawal, and their neurotic symptoms disappeared under the influence of the alcohol.

People, too, attempt to escape from the pain that arises from uncertainty and the inability to control their immediate environment. That escape can be healthy or can result in suppression and in a refusal to face the issues that are causing the problem. The stress that ensues can bring on ulcers, high blood pressure, a heart attack, or even cancer.

Large amounts of stress cause poor job performance. Therefore, job-related stress has taken on new importance for businesspeople.[6] Stress and the illness, absenteeism, and health care costs that are related to it have become immense expenses for firms.[7] In addition, in a few notable court cases, firms have been held responsible for work-related stress. However, not all stress is bad for the individual or for job performance. In fact a moderate amount of stress correlates with better job performance; the "fight or flight"

[5] Bernard Berelson and Gary A. Steiner, *Human Behavior: An Inventory of Scientific Findings* (New York: Harcourt, Brace & World, 1964), pp. 276–79; see also "The Crippling Ills That Stress Can Trigger," *Business Week*, April 18, 1988, pp. 77–78.

[6] John M. Ivancevich and Michael T. Matteson, "Optimizing Human Resources: A Case for Preventive Health and Stress Management," *Organizational Dynamics*, Autumn 1980, pp. 5–55; Saroj Parasuraman, "An Examination of the Organizational Antecedents of Stressors at Work," *Academy of Management Journal* 24 (March 1981): 48–67.

[7] Wayne F. Cascio, *Costing Human Resources: The Financial Impact of Behavior in Organizations* (Boston: Kent, 1982).

response releases a moderate amount of stimulants and thus enables a person to better achieve the objective. Stressful situations can also lead people to seek quiet places in order to reflect on themselves and on their values and goals, enabling them to emerge from the stressful situations healthier and in better control of their lives. Exercise and relaxation are advocated to reduce stress.[8] Quiet time, reflection, meditation, and prayer are being rediscovered. They are effective in dealing with normal stress and in helping people to become mature. Stress and anxiety are lessened when people internalize their own values (i.e., make the values their own). In the process, people become more mature and morally developed.

MORAL DEVELOPMENT

We all know or have read about people who are willing to work unselfishly for the benefit of others, even when it demands personal sacrifice. Some people in every community spend their lives providing for the sick and homeless with food and shelter. Some executives habitually take into account the effect of their decisions "on the little guy." Some leaders will take the blame for the blunders of subordinates. We consider such people to be morally good; they have a high level of moral development.

On the other hand, we also know others who consider only their own welfare. Often well educated and articulate, they are manipulative and generally skillful in hiding their self-centeredness (some, of course, are straightforward in their greediness).

Moral development is somewhat like physical development. Individuals grow physically, psychologically, and morally. As an infant's body develops, it must physically progress through the stages of creeping, crawling, toddling, walking, and finally running. Likewise, a person morally progresses through certain identifiable phases. As a result of moral development, the person has a growing ability to recognize moral issues and to distinguish right from wrong. This ability to make moral judgments and to engage in moral behavior increases with maturity. People are not born with moral abilities; they must be cultivated and developed, much like abilities of other kinds.

Scholars have observed moral development for centuries and have classified the stages of development in various ways. Philosophers have been aware of moral development and have proposed theories to explain it.[9] Child

---

[8]For an excellent overview of how firms such as GM, J&J, Bank of America, IBM, and Xerox have introduced wellness programs and how they deal with these issues, see William M. Kizer, *The Healthy Workplace: A Blueprint for Corporate Action* (New York: Wiley, 1987).

[9]John Dewey, "What Psychology Can Do for the Teacher," in *John Dewey on Education: Selected Writings*, ed. Reginald Archambault (New York: Random House, 1964).

psychologist Jean Piaget was the first to collect data from the observation and interviewing of children.[10] Psychologist Lawrence Kohlberg was concerned with moral development over the life span.[11]

Stages of Moral Growth

Kohlberg considered moral development to proceed through three levels, with each level consisting of two stages. Let us now examine these levels and stages.

LEVEL I: PRECONVENTIONAL

At this level a child is able to respond to rules and social expectations and can apply the labels *good, bad, right,* and *wrong.* The child sees rules (1) as something imposed from the outside and (2) largely in terms of the pleasant or painful consequences of actions or in terms of the power of those who set the rules. The child views situations from his or her own point of view. The child does not yet have the ability to identify with others, so the child's point of view is largely one of self-interest.

Stage 1: Punishment and Obedience Orientation.   The child does the right thing to avoid punishment or to obtain approval. There is little awareness of the needs of others. The physical consequences of an act determine its goodness and badness regardless of the wider consequences.

Stage 2: Naively Egoistic and Instrumental Orientation.   The child is now aware that others also have needs and begins to defer to them in order to obtain what he or she wants. Right actions are those which satisfy the child's own interests. Right is what is fair, an equal exchange, a deal. Human relations are viewed as being like the relations of the marketplace.

LEVEL II: CONVENTIONAL

Maintaining the expectations of one's family, peer group, or nation is viewed as valuable in its own right regardless of the consequences. The person at this level does not merely conform to expectations but is loyal to those groups and tries hard to maintain and justify that order. The person is now able to identify with another's point of view and assumes that everyone

[10] Jean Piaget, *The Moral Judgment of the Child* (Glencoe, Ill.: The Free Press, 1948).

[11] Lawrence Kohlberg, "The Cognitive-Developmental Approach to Moral Education," in *Readings in Moral Education,* ed. Peter Scharf (Minneapolis: Winston Press, 1978), pp. 36–51.

has a similar point of view. The person conforms to the group's norms and subordinates the needs of the individual to those of the group.

Stage 3: Interpersonal Concordance: "Good Boy—Nice Girl" Orientation. Good behavior is behavior which pleases or helps close family and friends and is approved by them. Right action is conformity to what is expected; the person conforms to stereotypes of what is majority or "natural" behavior. Behavior is frequently judged by intention: "He means well." One earns approval by being a "good boy" or a "nice girl."

Stage 4: Law and Order Orientation.   Right behavior consists in doing one's duty, showing respect for authority, and maintaining the social order for its own sake. Loyalty to the nation and its laws is paramount. The person now sees other people as individuals yet also as part of the larger social system which gives them their roles and obligations. The person enters this stage as a result of experiencing the inadequacies of Stage 3.

LEVEL III: POSTCONVENTIONAL, AUTONOMOUS, OR PRINCIPLED

The person no longer simply accepts the values and norms of the groups to which he or she belongs. There is a clear effort to find moral values and principles that impartially take everyone's interests into account. The person questions the norms and laws that society has adopted and redefines them so that they make sense to any rational individual. Proper laws and values are those to which any reasonable person would be committed whatever the society or the status held within that society.

Stage 5: Social Contract Orientation.   The individual is aware that people hold a variety of conflicting views, but even relative rules must be upheld in the interest of the social contract. Laws are agreed on and must be followed impartially, although they can be changed if need be. Some absolute values, such as life and liberty, are held regardless of differing individual values or even majority opinion. Utilitarianism ("the greatest good for the greatest number") is the characteristic ethical standard. The morality of this stage is the "official" morality of the U.S. government and the Constitution.

Stage 6: Conscience and Principle Orientation.   Right action is defined by decisions of conscience in accord with universal ethical principles which are chosen by the person because of their comprehensiveness, universality, and consistency. These ethical principles are not specific, concrete moral codes like the Ten Commandments but are instead universal moral principles dealing with justice, public welfare, the equality of human rights, respect for the dignity of individual human beings, and the belief that persons are ends in themselves and should not be used merely as means. The person's motivation for doing right is constituted by a belief in the validity of universal moral principles and a personal commitment to these principles.

Reasoning and Moral Development

Observations of mature people show that *all* such persons move through these stages. Individuals do not move to a higher stage until they have passed through each of the lower stages. However, not all people reach the higher stages; some remain stuck at a lower stage for their entire lives. Kohlberg finds that most Americans never do reach the higher stages but remain at stage 3 or 4.[12] For example, Kohlberg believes that former president Richard Nixon never got beyond moral stage 3 or 4. Nixon never really understood the U.S. Constitution, which is a document built on stage 5 thinking. Psychiatrist Karl Menninger, founder of the Menninger Institute, agrees with Kohlberg's assessment of Nixon and adds him to the list of what he calls evil men, which includes Adolph Hitler, Lyndon Johnson, and James Watt (the anti-environmental Secretary of the Interior in Ronald Reagan's first term).[13] Does the fact that Nixon is again emerging as a public figure mean that we have forgotten about his misdeeds and lack of moral development?

Some claim that schools should be value-free and not concerned with moral development. Kohlberg responds that this is nonsense. All teaching communicates values. Choosing to be value-free is itself taking a value position. The important question is: What are the values that should be communicated?

Kohlberg thinks that moral judgment is the single most important factor in moral behavior. It is impossible to be morally mature without the ability to confront various options and to make intelligent judgments on the rightness and wrongness of each. Moral judgment in turn depends on moral reasoning. Thus, a person's ability to reason sets a limit to the moral stage that can be achieved. If people are unable to reason, they will be restricted to one of the lower stages of moral development. On the other hand, people's ability to reason is generally more advanced than their moral development, so reasoning does not pose a limit for most people.

Kohlberg's research was done only with males. To complete the model,

---

[12] Ibid., p. 38.

[13] "Famed Psychiatrist Karl Menninger Analyzes the World, Finds It Needs Help," *Wall Street Journal*, December 23, 1985, pp. 1, 8; see also Karl Menninger, *Whatever Became of Sin?* (New York: Hawthorn Books, 1972).

TABLE 6-1 Moral Development and Ethical Theory: An Overview

THEORIES OF MORAL DEVELOPMENT AND CORRESPONDING STAGES[a]				ETHICAL THEORIES CORRESPONDING TO STAGES OF MORAL DEVELOPMENT[b]
JEAN PIAGET'S THEORY	JOHN DEWEY'S THEORY	LAWRENCE KOHLBERG'S THEORY		EDWARD STEVENS' THEORY
0. Premoral		0. Premoral		Group A
1. Heteronomous (age 4–8)	I. Preconventional	I. Preconventional		1. Social Darwinism
		1. Punishment and obedience orientation		2. Machiavellianism
2. Autonomous (age 8–12)		2. Naively egoistic and instrumentalist orientation		3. Objectivism (Ayn Rand)
	II. Conventional	II. Conventional		Group B
		3. Interpersonal concordance: "good boy–nice girl" orientation		4. Conventional morality
		4. Law and order orientation		5. Legalistic ethics
	III. Autonomous	III. Postconventional, autonomous, principled		6. Accountability model of ethics
		5. Social contrast orientation		Group C
				7. Pragmatism
		6. Conscience and principle orientation		8. Marxism
				9. "Economic humanism"

[a]Adapted from Lawrence Kohlberg, "The Cognitive-Development Approach to Moral Education," in *Readings in Moral Education*, ed. Peter Scharf (New York: Winston Press, 1978), pp. 36–37.
[b]Adapted from rough congruence presented by Edward Stevens, *Business Ethics* (New York: Paulist Press, 1979).

Carol Gilligan examined the moral development of women. She found that, especially in the later stages, their moral development differs from that of men. Whereas men tend to judge good and bad on the basis of reasoning and principles, women more often consider relationships, caring, and solidarity. Women (and in many cases men) at the higher stages of moral development often decide right from wrong on the basis of what effect the proposed action would have on relationships, love, and caring.[14]

The above theories of moral development have been both supported and challenged,[15] but most challengers agree that moral development takes place in generally the way described. Moreover, Kohlberg has studied moral development in great detail and provided a useful model.[16]

The stages of moral development described by Kohlberg are similar to those described by Dewey and Piaget. One business ethics book uses Kohlberg's levels of moral development as a outline, and the author, Edward Stevens, proposes that some popular ethical theories can be explained by the fact that their originators were stuck at one of Kohlberg's lower levels.[17] For example, Stevens finds that both social Darwinism (see Chapter 2) and Ayn Rand's objectivism flow from a primitive, preconventional view of moral development (see Table 6–1).

Individualism and the Common Good

Ethical acts and moral development presuppose that moral good exists and that there is some agreement on what it is. Robert Bellah and his coauthors investigated the American view of a good society in their critically acclaimed *Habits of the Heart: Individualism and Commitment in American Life*.[18] They interviewed a wide variety of Americans from coast to coast and found that our society places obstacles in the path of determining the moral good and of achieving a national consensus on important issues. The principal

[14] Carol Gilligan, *In a Different Voice: Psychological Theory and Women's Development* (Cambridge, Mass.: Harvard University Press, 1982). Robbin Derry found justice and caring moral orientations in both men and women and so did not verify the sex split; see Robbin Derry, "Moral Reasoning in Work Related Conflicts," in *Research in Corporate Social Performance and Policy*, ed. William C. Frederick, vol. 9 (Greenwich, Conn: JAI, 1987), pp. 25–49.

[15] See, for example, Gerald Baxter and Charles Rarick, "Education for the Moral Development of Managers: Kohlberg's Stages of Moral Development and Integrative Education," *Journal of Business Ethics* 6 (April 1987): 243–48; see also Thomas Lickona, "What Does Moral Psychology Have to Say to the Teacher of Ethics?" in *Ethics Teaching in Higher Education*, ed. Daniel Callahan and Sissela Bok (New York: Plenum Press, 1980), pp. 103–32.

[16] For a more detailed description of maturity, including Kohlberg's moral development model, see Robert Kegan, *The Evolving Self: Problem and Process in Human Development* (Cambridge, Mass.: Harvard University Press, 1982), esp. pp. 50–71.

[17] Edward Stevens, *Business Ethics* (New York: Paulist Press, 1979).

[18] Robert N. Bellah et al., *Habits of the Heart: Individualism and Commitment in American Life* (New York: Harper & Row, 1985).

virtue for most Americans is freedom. Freedom has long been a primary American value, as we have seen in Chapters 2 and 3. As the authors put it,

> Freedom is perhaps the most resonant, deeply held American value. In some ways, it defines the good in both personal and political life. Yet freedom turns out to mean being left alone by others, not having other people's values, ideas, or styles of life forced upon one, being free of arbitrary authority in work, family, and political life. What it is that one might do with that freedom is much more difficult for Americans to define. And if the entire social world is made up of individuals, each endowed with the right to be free of others' demands, it becomes hard to forge bonds of attachment to, or cooperation with, other people, since such bonds would imply obligations that necessarily impinge on one's freedom.[19]

Making freedom such an important value has given Americans a respect for other individuals and has encouraged creativity and innovation. However, it also has its costs:

> It is an ideal freedom that leaves Americans with a stubborn fear of acknowledging structures of power and interdependence in a technologically complex society dominated by giant corporations and an increasingly powerful state. The ideal of freedom makes Americans nostalgic for their past, but provides few resources for talking about their collective future.[20]

Such a definition of freedom leaves both the person and the society little inclination or vocabulary to address common concerns. The traditional term *common good* refers to the good of society as a whole. It has almost fallen out of usage, because its meaning is difficult for most contemporary Americans to understand or appreciate.

Alexis de Tocqueville (see Chapter 2) showed how the value of freedom becomes individualism. Moreover, such an understanding of life is generally hostile to older ideas of the moral order. The center of our current moral order is the individual, who is given full freedom to choose careers, commitments, and a life, not on the basis of obligations to others or of truths outside the individual, but on the basis of self-satisfaction as the individual judges it. Commitments—from marriage and work to political and religious involvement—are made as a way to enhance individual well-being rather than out of obedience to moral imperatives. If it is satisfying to me, I will do it; if it is not satisfying, I will withdraw. In a word, what is good is what someone finds rewarding. If preferences change, so does what is considered good. Even the most fundamental ethical virtues are treated as matters of personal preference. Hence, the basic ethical rule is that individuals be able to pursue

---

[19] Ibid., p. 23.
[20] Ibid., P. 25.

whatever they find rewarding as long as they not interfere with the actions and values of others.[21]

Such a value system places obstacles in the path of discussing issues that face groups of people. It provides no "public philosophy," no means of addressing large value questions. If every person is "defined by their preferences, but those preferences are arbitrary, then each self constitutes its own moral universe, and there is finally no way to reconcile conflicting claims about what is good in itself." We thus turn away from the moral norms of the Puritans, Jefferson, and even Benjamin Franklin. "Utility replaces duty; self-expression unseats authority. 'Being good' becomes 'feeling good.'"[22]

Each person will thus decide what is the moral good for him- or herself, and there will be no common ground for judging moral growth. A person becomes his or her own exclusive judge on the most important questions in life. Our individualistic notion of the moral good is thus isolated from the influence of religious values, family values, and the values of the Founding Fathers and the U.S. Constitution. If these sources are no longer given a role to play, it will be more difficult to hold personal or common goals for moral development. However, because of a felt need, there have been some valuable recent efforts to probe our shared values, common goals, and even the common good in U.S. business life.[23]

Good Habits Create Virtue

A morally mature person is able to and will develop good habits, commonly called virtues (for definitions, see Figure 6–1). A conscientious person develops good habits by deliberately and repeatedly doing good acts. Developing virtue takes time and effort, but once good habits are in place, through the active effort of the person, virtuous acts come easily and naturally. That is, a person, by intentionally developing good habits through good acts, makes additional good acts easier to do.

A good manager has developed many good habits, many virtues, in the process of becoming a good manager. For example, a manager who habitually listens to and encourages subordinates develops the virtue of being receptive and eventually listens and encourages almost automatically. A manager who makes little effort to develop the habit of listening and encouraging will find each new case difficult and challenging. Such a manager will

---

[21] Ibid., pp. 6, 47. For a discussion of the meaning of freedom in business, see Michael Keeley, "Freedom in Organizations," *Journal of Business Ethics* 6 (May 1987): 249–63.

[22] Bellah et al., *Habits of the Heart*, pp. 76–77.

[23] Oliver F. Williams and John W. Houck, eds. *The Common Good and U.S. Capitalism* (Lanham, Md.: University Press of America, 1987); Robert B. Dickie and Leroy S. Rouner, *Corporations and the Common Good* (Notre Dame: University of Notre Dame Press, 1986).

Habit: An acquired behavior pattern that is almost automatic.
Maturity: The state of being fully developed as a person.
Moral Development: An increased ability to distinguish right and wrong.
Virtue: A good habit; spontaneous attraction to the good.

FIGURE 6–1　Moral Development Terms

find that it takes far more time and energy to become a *good* manager—if that will ever be possible.

EXAMINING PERSONAL VALUES

One approach to the problem of unclear, ambiguous, or conflicting personal values and goals is to make an explicit attempt to clarify them. A scale that has been used for two generations for the purpose of measuring personal values is the Allport-Vernon-Lindzey value scale. This scale attempts to discriminate personal values according to six potentially dominant personality characteristics: theoretical, economic, aesthetic, social, political, and religious.[24]

The authors of the scale administered the value test to college business students, who came out significantly higher on economic and political values and significantly lower on aesthetic, religious, and social values as compared with college students as a whole. The business students were participants in the Advanced Management Program at the Harvard Business School. Their predominant values were economic, theoretical, and political (see Table 6–2). For the population as a whole, these same values tended to average around 40 on the scale.

A person whose values are predominantly economic is primarily oriented toward what is useful and practical. A theoretical person is primarily concerned with the discovery of truth. A political person is characterized by an orientation to power—influence over people. The religious person is one "whose mental structure is permanently directed to the creation of the highest and absolutely satisfying value experience." The aesthetic person is primarily interested in the artistic aspects of life—form and harmony. The highest value for the social person is love of people.

When we compare the relative strengths of the six values for businesspeople and business students, the dominance of economic, theoreti-

---

[24]Gordon Allport, Philip Vernon, and Gardner Lindzey, *Study of Values* (Boston: Houghton Mifflin, 1931).

TABLE 6-2   Personal Values in Business

| VALUE | SCORE | |
	BUSINESS STUDENTS	BUSINESSPERSONS
Economic	46	45
Theoretical	43	44
Political	46	44
Religious	34	39
Aesthetic	39	35
Social	33	33

Sources: For students, Gordon Allport, Philip Vernon, and Gardner Lindzey, *Study of Values* (Boston: Houghton Mifflin, 1931), p. 14; for businesspersons, William D. Guth and Renato Tagiuri, "Personal Values and Corporate Strategy," *Harvard Business Review*, 43 (September-October 1965): 126.

cal, and political orientations is characteristic of both groups, and there is a significant gap between these values and the remaining three value orientations. Social values are the lowest by a wide margin for both businesspeople and business students. Religious values are stronger for older businesspeople, whereas aesthetic values are stronger for students.

The values of managers from five countries—Japan, Korea, India, Australia, and the United States—were measured and compared by George W. England.[25] The value systems of these managers in widely varying cultures were more similar than different. Among the minor differences, the Japanese were more pragmatic and more homogeneous in their values and Indian managers were more moralistic.

More interesting were the significant differences between the values of younger and older managers. Compared with their senior peers, younger managers across all cultures tended to

1. place less importance on organizational goals
2. place less importance on co-workers and more on themselves
3. place less importance on trust and honor
4. place more importance on money, ambition, and risk
5. be slightly more pragmatic

The picture that emerges is of the competitive gamesman, someone primarily concerned with his or her own life and career and less concerned with the organization, trust, honor, or other people. Since this survey, the values of

[25] George W. England, "Managers and Their Value Systems: A Five-Country Comparative Study," *Columbia Journal of World Business*, Summer 1978, p. 35.

businesspeople as a whole have shifted more in the same direction, probably because the values of the younger managers have become predominant.

The Allport and other value scales were originally designed as research tools to learn more about personalities and their values. The questions in these scales are now widely used by interviewers and guidance counselors to determine the attitudes and potential vocational interests of students and employees. However, there are two important limitations in using the scales as indicators of a person's ability to perform well in a particular future career. The first is that the tests measure only *relative* values. One person could possess exactly the same value profile as another, yet possess each value much more strongly. The second is that counselors, based on the value profiles of successful businesspeople, often advise individuals with relatively high scores on social values to stay out of business. It is true that those businesspeople who have previously taken the test show low scores on social values. But to give career advice merely on the basis of how people in business have scored in the past prevents new values and creativity from entering the profession and hence makes old patterns even more rigid.

The value profile of the businessperson has for generations been more pragmatic, materialistic, and self-centered than that of the average American. Concern for people was the value of least importance to managers a generation ago, and this same low concern for others is still prevalent among today's managers. Recent value probes of younger managers show them to be even more concerned about themselves and less about the organization or other people. Since most firms now emphasize cooperation and concern for customers, fellow employees, and quality, the attitude of younger managers presents a significant problem for American business. If young people coming into business are so self-centered, it will take much effort to socialize them to have greater concern for other people.

Measuring Personal Values

Another examination of the values of working people found six distinct sets of values: conformist, manipulative, sociocentric, existential, tribalistic, and egocentric.[26] The first four of these value sets were most common among managers. The conformist set was common among older, lower-level, and less-educated managers. The manipulative set was found most often among the well-educated, high-income workers in large retail organizations in the northeastern United States. Those with sociocentric values tended to be well-paid, well-educated company presidents over sixty years old.

One paradox of this study is worthy of special attention. Company presidents tend to have sociocentric values: They allow the development of

---

[26] Vincent S. Flowers et al., *Managerial Values for Working* (New York: AMACOM, 1975).

friendly relationships between people. For them, "working with people toward a common goal is more important than getting caught up in a materialistic rat race."[27] Ironically, sociocentric managers are significantly underrepresented in jobs just two levels below the presidency. Therefore, the values that get a person to within sight of the top job are not the same values that will push her or him along further. Those searching the organization for potential successors to the CEO will find *few* candidates among those in the best preparatory slots in the organization: plant managers, directors, and similar positions.

In every examination of values, American managers are shown to be pragmatic—very concerned with efficiency and productivity. Interestingly, female managers seem to be even more pragmatic than male managers. Furthermore, female managers are more career-oriented than their male counterparts: 60 percent of female managers say that they get more satisfaction out of their career than their home life, whereas only 37 percent of male managers feel this way.[28] Also important, 61 percent of all managers respond that an improvement in the quality of life in the United States will come by means of a return to basic values, especially commitment and integrity. Over all, 80 percent of managers believe that their company is guided by "highly ethical standards." However, this belief is stronger among top management, and more cynical views tend to be held by those of lower rank.[29] Clear, strong, engaging values are essential to good leadership. "A leader needs a philosophy, a set of high standards by which the organization is measured, a set of values about how employees, colleagues, and customers ought to be treated, a set of principles that make the organization unique and distinctive."[30] Indeed, where members of a firm share values, the members tend to be more ethical. Or, putting it the other way, where values are not shared, managers are more likely to take bribes, falsely report earnings, steal company secrets, and the like.[31]

The above variations underscore the need not to stereotype the values of businesspeople. Problems develop when we make decisions based on stereotypes: (1) the biases often present an erroneous image of businesspeople; (2) they tend to steer people of differing values away from business as a

[27] Ibid., p. 2.

[28] Warren H. Schmidt and Barry Z. Posner, *Managerial Values and Expectations: The Silent Power in Personal and Organizational Life* (New York: American Management Association, 1982), pp. 28–29, 52–53.

[29] Warren H. Schmidt and Barry Z. Posner, *Managerial Values in Perspective* (New York: American Management Association, 1983), pp. 29–41.

[30] James M. Kouzes and Barry Z. Posner, *The Leadership Challenge* (San Francisco: Jossey-Bass, 1987), p. 187.

[31] Barry Z. Posner, James M. Kouzes, and Warren H. Schmidt, "Shared Values Make a Difference: An Empirical Test of Corporate Culture," *Human Resources Management* 24 (Fall 1985): 299.

career; and (3) the biases tend to perpetuate themselves (i.e., they are self-fulfilling). Hence, it is important not to fall into the stereotype trap. It is even more important for each individual, whether business-oriented or not, to examine his or her own personal values. Note that the exercise at the end of Chapter 1 is intended to aid in doing just that.

Personal Experience Gives Direction

In earlier generations, children growing up in a family would witness their father and mother working in or near home, whether as a shoemaker, baker, or farmer. They saw not only the skill and effort required in work but also the joy of accomplishment. Since commercial work is now generally done away from home, children rarely have direct contact with it and only hear about it through comments, often complaints.

The attitudes of all Americans, especially young people, are influenced by the media. Consider business as it is presented in literature, on television, and in films. Most TV and film writers have no direct experience with business. As a result, their portrayal is often caricature. There is rarely a TV program or film that presents business and work objectively, let alone favorably. The businessperson is generally pictured as shallow, grasping, narrow, and petty, concerned only with status and wealth. One hopes that the success of the Bill Cosby show will encourage a more positive TV view of the father and the family.

Thus the biased perceptions of the TV writer are exaggerated on film and passed on. While the values tests described above support some of the media stereotype, these same tests show that older managers have strong religious and social values and that top executives have a much more balanced set of values. Yet these latter facts are almost never reflected in the media. Thus biased perceptions have a powerful influence on all of us, especially the young and most impressionable.

Helping Behavior

It is not merely businesspeople and business students who hold social values in relatively low esteem; their attitudes reflect the values of much of American culture. As laboratory experiments have shown, individuals in American culture are heavily influenced by the values and activities of others. Norms of right and wrong are inculcated by the family, television, the neighborhood, and the environment in any culture, but the attitudes of bystanders in the immediate vicinity also have an unduly large influence on Americans. Several laboratory experiments were prompted by the murder of a young woman in New York City. She was stabbed to death in full view of many apartment dwellers. Later investigation showed that at least 38 people saw or heard the attack but not one tried to help; no one even phoned the police. This story shocked the country, and some researchers decided to try to determine what elements influence helping behavior.

In one experiment, each subject was led to believe that there were several other subjects placed in adjoining rooms connected by an intercom.[32] Sometimes the subject was told there was one other subject, sometimes that there were two other subjects, and sometimes that there were five. In reality, the subject was the only person involved. During a discussion over the intercom on a topic of current interest, one "participant" suffered what seemed to be an epileptic seizure; that person choked, stuttered, and called out for help. The greater the number of persons the subject thought were present, the less likely the subject would be to help and slower to help. Apparently, the subject felt the problem could be left to others. If the subject thought there was no other person to help, the subject was more likely to feel the responsibility to respond to the participant calling for help.

Similar results were obtained when individuals were placed in a room and asked to fill out a questionnaire. Subjects were either alone in the room, with two other subjects, or with two confederates who were instructed to remain impassive. After a few minutes, smoke began to pour into the room through a small wall vent. Results of this experiment again showed that when other individuals are present, someone is less likely to respond in a socially responsible way. When subjects were with passive confederates, they reported the apparent fire only 10 percent of the time.

It seems clear that individuals will act responsibly when they feel the responsibility directly. When another unknown person is present, they are not as apt to stick their necks out. Nevertheless, these and other studies show that people *will* help others, even if they don't expect anything in return. Furthermore, people will tend to respond more quickly and in a more responsible way if they have been the recipients of help themselves or if they have previously been successful in helping others.

Periodic surveys of values of Americans over the last few decades show new values emerging.[33] As people achieve a degree of economic security, their attention turns toward nonmaterial needs, namely, the need for challenging and significant work, the need for the respect and approval of friends, the need for identification with the community, and the need for a stimulating and fulfilling life. That this shift is especially true of the young, the well educated, and the affluent has special importance for business values. These personal needs are being carried into the working place. Moreover, as some of these people become managers, they will undoubtedly seek

[32] Leonard Berkowitz, *A Survey of Social Psychology* (New York: Holt, Rinehart & Winston, 1980), pp. 374–75.

[33] Angus Campbell, *Sense of Well-Being in America: Recent Patterns and Trends* (New York: McGraw-Hill, 1981).

to reshape the work environment so that it can better satisfy these needs. At the same time, the organizations need to be more cooperative in order to attract the young, educated, and talented people they require if they are to be competitive in world markets. The values that managers and organizations might well possess in the future will be discussed in greater detail in Chapter 9. Let us now examine the need for businesspeople to develop a greater ability to identify ethical issues and to do ethical reasoning.

NEED FOR ETHICS IN BUSINESS

No human institution can long exist without some agreement on what is right and what is wrong. Managers recognize the need for ethical norms to guide their everyday actions. Decisions made at every level of the firm are influenced by ethics, such as those regarding dealings with subordinates and peers, use of company property, quality of work, worker and product safety, truth in advertising, and use and disposal of toxic materials. Executives increasingly recognize the importance of ethics:

1. Almost two-thirds (63 percent) of executives are convinced that high ethical standards strengthen a firm's competitive position.[34]
2. Almost three-quarters of U.S. firms now have a code of ethics.[35]
3. More than 100 boards of directors of large firms have established an ethics, social responsibility, or public policy committee.[36]
4. Speeches of chief executive officers and annual reports often allude to the importance of ethics in business decisions.

Managers understand that without ethics the only restraint is the law. Without ethics, any business transaction that was not witnessed and recorded could not be trusted. Government regulation may be felt to be constraining and unnecessary, but less regulation requires managers to possess and exercise ethical skills in their decision making. The alternative is *more* legislation. Putting it succinctly: Shall we be honest and free or dishonest and policed?

---

[34] *Ethics in American Business: An Opinion Survey of Key Business Leaders on Ethical Standards and Behavior* (New York: Touche Ross, 1988), p. 1; see also R. Edward Freeman and Daniel R. Gilbert, Jr., *Corporate Strategy and the Search for Ethics* (Englewood Cliffs, N.J.: Prentice-Hall, 1988); Bruce H. Drake and Eileen Drake, "Ethical and Legal Aspects of Managing Corporate Cultures," *California Management Review* 30 (Winter 1988): 107–23.

[35] According to a survey by Opinion Research Corporation, 73 percent of the larger corporations in the United States now have a written code of ethics. See *Chronicle of Higher Education*, August 6, 1979, p. 2.

[36] "Business Strategies for the 1980's," in *Business and Society: Strategies for the 1980's* (Washington, D.C.: U.S. Department of Commerce, 1980), pp. 33–34.

Business managers do act ethically under the following conditions: (1) when they believe that a moral principle has a bearing on a situation, and (2) when they perceive themselves as having the power to affect the situation.[37] And not only top managers but also middle managers act ethically, especially when they understand the ethical issues and see that they have some influence on the outcome. However, as a group, middle managers are almost twice as likely to be unethical as either top managers or lower-level managers.[38]

A significant minority of American firms have been involved in both unethical and illegal activities. During the last decade, 11 percent of the largest U.S. firms were convicted of bribery, criminal fraud, illegal campaign contributions, tax evasion, or some sort of price fixing. Firms with two or more convictions include Allied, American Airlines, Bethlehem Steel, Diamond International, Firestone, Goodyear, International Paper, J. Ray McDermott, National Distillers, Northrop, Occidental Petroleum, Pepsico, Phillips Petroleum, Rapid-American, R. J. Reynolds, Schlitz, Seagram, Tenneco, and United Brands. Leading the list with at least four convictions each are Braniff International, Gulf Oil, and Ashland Oil.[39] But crime and immorality are punished as the market price of a firm's stock declines when the news of the criminal act is made known.[40] The ultimate punishment is to be taken over (as Gulf was by Chevron) or to go bankrupt (as Braniff did).

Most of the major petroleum firms illegally contributed to Richard Nixon's reelection campaign for president of the United States: Standard of California, Exxon, Sun, Ashland, Gulf, and Getty. The chairman of Phillips personally handed Nixon $50,000 in Nixon's own apartment. Many firms were also involved in multimillion-dollar foreign "irregular" payments: Exxon, Lockheed, McDonnell Douglas, United Brands, Mobil, Gulf, and Phillips. The presidents of Gulf, American Airlines, and Lockheed lost their jobs because of the unethical payments. Other chief executives just as guilty—those heading Northrop, Phillips, and Exxon—were excused by their boards. Firms based in the United States are, of course, not alone in engaging in unethical behavior. The Japanese electronics firm Hitachi and its executives

---

[37] See the field research reported in the series of three articles by James A. Waters and Frederick Bird: "Everyday Moral Issues Experienced by Managers," *Journal of Business Ethics* 5 (October 1986): 373–84; "The Nature of Managerial Moral Standards," ibid., 6 (January 1987): 1–13; "The Moral Dimension of Organizational Culture," ibid., 6 (January 1987): 15–22.

[38] "Middle Managers Most Likely to Be Unethical," *Management Accounting*, December 1987, p. 3.

[39] Irwin Ross, "How Lawless Are Big Companies?" *Fortune*, December 1, 1980, pp. 56–64; see also Robert K. Elliott and John J. Willingham, *Management Fraud: Detection and Deterrence* (New York: Petrocelli Books, 1980).

[40] Wallace Davidson and Dan Worrell, "The Impact of Announcements of Corporate Illegalities on Shareholder Returns," *Academy of Management Journal* 31 (March 1988): 195–200.

stole trade secrets from IBM. After being caught, the firm and executives pleaded guilty and agreed to pay damages to IBM.[41]

Corporate Pressure or Personal Greed

Embezzlement, fraud, and political back scratching benefit the individual and are most often done out of personal greed. Bribery, price fixing, and compromising product and worker safety are often responses to pressure for bottom-line results. They are often done "for the sake of the firm." A study of the ethics of managers showed that 59 to 70 percent "feel pressured to compromise personal ethics to achieve corporate goals."[42] This perception increases among lower-level managers. A majority felt that most managers would not refuse to market below-standard and possibly dangerous products. However, on the more encouraging side, 90 percent supported a code of ethics for business and the teaching of ethics in business schools.

Pressure and organizational climate can influence the ethical judgments of managers. Behavior that the manager finds unethical at home or before taking a job is sometimes readily considered acceptable once the job is taken. Two studies that are considered below question whether some American executives have a sufficient sensitivity to ethical issues and whether their work environment hinders moral development.

Public affairs officers in firms have the direct responsibility for dealing with many stakeholders: customers, suppliers, the local community, and shareholders. These officers constitute a principal conduit through which the firm is informed of new social concerns. Even though these public affairs officers spend more time with these various stakeholders than do other company officers, they tend to be poor listeners. Evidence shows that the more contact company officers have with various segments of the public, the less sensitive they become to their concerns.[43]

Another ethically sensitive area for a business is lobbying and corporate political activities. The more involved company officers were in these activities, the more dulled their conscience became. There are numerous ethically dubious actions that are taken by political officers. For example, they sometimes invite members of Congress and their families on company-paid vacations in return for votes on legislation. Evidence shows that company officers who are closest to such activities are less sensitive to the moral and ethical

---

[41] "IBM Data Plot Tied to Hitachi and Mitsubishi," *Wall Street Journal*, June 23, 1982, p. 4; David B. Tinnin, "How IBM Stung Hitachi: Espionage," *Fortune*, March 7, 1983, pp. 50–56.

[42] Archie Carroll, "Managerial Ethics," *Business Horizons*, April 1975, pp. 75–80.

[43] Jeffery Sonnenfeld, "The Executive Differences in Public Affairs Information Gathering," in *Academy of Management Proceedings, 1981*, ed. Kae H. Chung (San Diego: Academy of Management, 1981), p. 353.

issues involved. The manager who is more involved is more likely to declare as acceptable an activity that fellow managers would say is unethical.[44]

Laboratory research has shown that unethical behavior increases as the climate becomes more competitive and that it increases even more if such behavior is rewarded. Conversely, a threat of punishment tends to deter unethical behavior. Whether a person acts ethically or unethically is also very strongly influenced by the individual's personal ethical values and by informal organizational policy.[45]

Instances of unethical behavior by managers point to the need for:

1. a sensitive and informed conscience
2. the ability to make ethical judgments
3. a corporate climate that rewards ethical behavior and punishes unethical behavior

Technical education does not create better ethics. For example, in Nazi Germany, officials with PhDs from the best German universities ordered mass murders. As a society becomes more technical, complex, and interdependent, the need for ethics increases exponentially.[46] In simpler societies, people have daily contact with others they might be inclined to cheat, and this provides a built-in sanction. In large, complex organizations or when people are dealt with over the telephone or through a computer, ethical sensitivities and ethical reasoning play a far more important role in preventing wrongful actions.

Enlightened Self-Interest and Ethics

Some advocates of free enterprise argue that if managers pursued enlightened self-interest (for definition, see Figure 2–1), the result is greater honesty and better ethics. The argument is that high ethical standards are in the long-term interest of the firm. There is a good deal of plausibility in such a simple and straightforward position.

There are also serious problems with this view. *Enlightened* is an elastic term and does not have the same meaning for everyone. Also, even if there was perfect agreement on the meaning of *enlightened*, self-interest still could easily slip into selfishness. Our normal human selfish desires (original sin, if you will) distort our perceptions of what is in our long-term interest and the

[44] Steven N. Brenner, "Corporate Political Actions and Attitudes," in Chung, *Academy of Management Proceedings, 1981*, pp. 361–62.

[45] W. Harvey Hegarty and Henry P. Sims, Jr., "Unethical Decision Behavior: An Overview of Three Experiments," in *Academy of Management Proceedings, 1979*, p. 9.

[46] See W. Michael Hoffman, "What Is Necessary for Corporate Moral Excellence?" *Journal of Business Ethics* 3 (June 1986): 233–42.

resulting misperceptions are often encouraged by a free enterprise philosophy and by most conservative ideologies.

Some altruism is necessary. That is, one must consider the benefits and harms that others might experience, and one must also be willing on occasion to sacrifice one's own benefits for the sake of others. Altruism can engender good habits and virtue within individuals, and it can be a protection for society as a whole. In many instances, enlightened self-interest provides a shortcut method of solving problems, but, as with all shortcuts, it cannot handle all cases. In addition, in espousing the ideology of enlightened self-interest, managers feel compelled to justify every move they make by pointing out how it will increase the profitability of the firm. Perhaps the justification is important for many shareholders, but such a doctrinaire position makes ethics subordinate to economics and causes managers to acquire a rigid, simplistic mind-set.

Instances will arise when ethical treatment of others, perhaps people outside the firm, will be at a net cost to an employee or to the firm. Since many popular forms of free enterprise ideology do not permit consideration of others for their own sake, businesspeople who adhere to these forms are close to falling over the cliff into immorality. Moreover, many do fall, as we have already seen, and they are more likely to fall if they hold that enlightened self-interest should always determine one's actions. Examples of both ethically good and poor behavior will be presented in Chapter 8. In sum, enlightened self-interest will take one a long distance toward being more ethical—but not the whole way.

When considering the ethics of a situation, each person takes a basic stance toward other people. There are five possible ways one can consider oneself in relation to others:[47]

1. self alone
2. self first
3. self equally with others
4. others first
5. others alone

People who only consider themselves alone are egoists. People who consider themselves first but also consider others are more enlightened. Equitable consideration of oneself and others is suggested by the Golden Rule ("Do unto others as you would have them do unto you"). Considering others first or others alone are generous forms of altruism. Good parents at the very least consider their children first. Consideration only of others is the

---

[47] Adapted from Garth Hallett, *Reason and Right* (Notre Dame, Ind.: Notre Dame Press, 1984).

attitude of a selfless, generous, saintly person (for example, Mother Theresa). It goes without saying that such people are not common.

Taste, Bias, and Culture

Even though managers recognize the importance of ethics, in the popular mind ethics is hard to distinguish from taste, bias, or culturally determined attitudes. Difficult ethical dilemmas are resolved arbitrarily, for there seems to be no objective values or criteria that can be used to help judge the issues. We noted the effect of the predominant American value of freedom on this earlier in the chapter (see "Individualism and the Common Good"). If each person provides his or her own unique ethical norm, it is impossible to decide that one action is ethical and another is not. Moreover, even experts in ethics differ among themselves, thus encouraging the popular notion that ethics is not an objective discipline and no common norms exist.[48]

Almost everyone recognizes the need for some ethical criteria to be used by managers, yet it is also clear that developing these criteria is no easy task. We are faced with different value systems, various perceptions of facts, and different judgments on tradeoffs. Moreover, even if we could develop adequate ethical decision-making criteria, this would not automatically make decision making easy. Ethical issues are not easily framed in terms of measurable data, unlike financial (return on investment) or marketing (share of market) issues. Nevertheless, a developed sensitivity and an understanding of ethical principles provides a foundation for making correct ethical judgments and is good insurance against serious ethical blunders (e.g., ITT's attempt to overthrow the democratic government of Chile in 1973 and Lockheed's bribery of foreign officials). Increasing the ethical abilities of managers will also generally enable a firm to be a better producer, employer, and citizen and thus a more trusted and valued contributor to society.

From the above we can conclude the following:

1. A sense of what is right and wrong, plus ethical criteria for making judgments, is essential to any human social organization, including business enterprises.
2. However, ethical norms and criteria are not easily derived. Moreover, there is often disagreement on the facts of any given case, the relevant criteria, and the various tradeoffs.

Both the importance of the task is recognized and the difficulty of accomplishing it.

---

[48] See William C. Frederick, "Embedded Values: Prelude to Ethical Analysis" (University of Pittsburgh Working Paper WP-446, 1982).

Young People and Morals

Those who believe that human beings are by nature good would hold that young people are good until tarnished by modern civilization. The data indicate otherwise. An earlier section of this chapter on moral development presents evidence that infants are born self-centered and that persons mature in their ethical sensitivities.

Moreover, studies show that many young people are easily led into unethical acts. A large-scale study of more than 3,000 Illinois teenagers done over a six-year period revealed some startling facts. One-third of all fourteen-to eighteen-year-olds had been involved in a serious crime. Thirteen percent admitted taking part in a robbery, 40 percent acknowledged keeping stolen goods, and 50 percent admitted shoplifting. Moreover, many of the conventional "predictors" for criminal behavior did not hold true. Except with respect to the most violent behavior, the delinquent was just as likely to be a girl as a boy, to be white as black, to come from a small town as from an inner city. Peer groups were found to have the most influence on young people, more so than parents. In fact, in 80 percent of the cases, parents did not know about the offenses their children had committed. One research team member spent two years with youths in a wealthy Chicago suburb and reported a "near vacuum of morality enclosed by the perimeter of the edict to achieve.... Anything that jeopardizes their occupational future is bad. The rest really doesn't matter." Peer pressure has a strong influence on all sorts of adolescent attitudes and conduct.[49]

There is also considerable unethical behavior in colleges and universities. A study that examined ethics on campuses found a significant and apparently increasing amount of cheating by students in academic assignments; a substantial misuse by students of public financial aid; theft and destruction by students of valuable property, especially library books and journals; inflation of grades by faculty members; awarding of academic credits by some departments and institutions for insufficient and inadequate work in order to attract students; and inflated and misleading advertising by some institutions in search of students.[50]

In sum, the need for ethics in business is clear. The daily news stories of unethical activities remind us of the need for accepted ethical norms. Most business executives and managers are ethical. However, many of these men

---

[49] Donna R. Clasen and Sue Eicher, "Perceptions of Peer Pressure, Peer Conformity Dispositions, and Self-reported Behavior Among Adolescents," *Developmental Psychology* 22 (April 1986): 521–30; on earlier data, see "Kid Crime: Host of Juveniles Admit Serious Acts," *Detroit Free Press*, January 24, 1977, pp. 1, 2.

[50] George Stevens and Faith Stevens, "Ethical Implications of Tomorrow's Managers Revisited: How and Why Students Cheat," *Journal of Education for Business* 63 (October 1987): 24–29; "Ethical Conduct Needs Improving," *Higher Education in National Affairs*, April 20, 1979, p. 1.

and women cannot intelligently discuss ethical problems and hence cannot defend their judgments. They do not possess the terminology, the concepts, or the models for effectively discussing ethical issues. The next chapter will provide some language, concepts, and models as an aid to managers.

SUMMARY AND CONCLUSIONS

Emphasis on success and winning can cause stress and serious physical ailments. Particularly prone to heart attacks, ulcers, or other illnesses are the 60 percent of managers who are Type A: impatient, aggressive, restless, and pressured. Their ambition, task orientation, and quick action allow them to move up rapidly in the organization. Yet these same qualities are ultimately a barrier to getting to the top. Chief executives generally are patient and have the ability to listen to and weigh alternatives and to work with other people.

Maturity and moral development go hand in hand. Just as people grow emotionally and psychologically, so do they also grow morally. Without maturity and moral development, people risk traumatic challenges in middle age. On the other hand, people who have reflected on and internalized their own values and goals do not face the same anxiety, stress, and the debilitating diseases that stem from stress; rather they deal with the midlife reassessment with assurance and dignity. By being aware of their own personal values and goals and how these relate to the values and goals of others, they are in a better position to live, love, and enjoy life and work.

The person who is morally developed is better equipped to deal with ethical dilemmas. That person has the equilibrium necessary to gather the facts, search for the most appropriate ethical criteria, and make a reasoned ethical judgment.

Much current evidence suggests there is a need for ethics in business. The prevalence of corporate crime and of unethical and greedy acts by individuals, as well as the lack of ethical models within our American culture, argues for developing our ethical sensitivities and our ability to make ethical judgments. Chapter 7 presents some useful tools—concepts, models, and language—for ethical reasoning.

DISCUSSION QUESTIONS

1. What are the symptoms of a midlife identity crisis? Under what conditions will the effects of the midlife transition be less traumatic?
2. What causes anxieties and stress? What physical ailments do these lead to? What do the above described experiments with rats and cats tell us? What role does alcohol play?

3. What is the relation of moral development and maturity? What does moral development have to do with ethics?

4. What are the advantages and the disadvantages of the American view that freedom is the most important value? How does this view affect the moral good? How does it affect moral development?

5. Why is this view of freedom an obstacle to discovering the "common good" or developing a public philosophy?

6. Business executives tend to have less social concern than others. What processes tend to perpetuate their lack of concern?

7. What is the effect of authority on a person's willingness to inflict pain or even put someone in danger of death? Describe the experiments on this subject. Do parallel situations occur in an organization? How so?

8. Under what circumstances is an individual more likely to come to the aid of another person? Describe the results of the experiments dealing with this issue.

9. What events of the last decade underscore the need for business ethics? List the ways that firms have responded positively to this need.

10. What are the principal limitations of free enterprise or self-interest ideology? How do the limitations differ for self-interest that is "enlightened"? Does enlightened self-interest insure that a person will act ethically? Why? Give an example.

11. Is inflating costs or selling poor-quality goods less bad if the individual does not profit?

12. What do the surveys show about the ethics of young people compared with the ethics of their elders? What seems to account for the difference?

CASE: BANK DEPOSIT INSURANCE

On October 19, 1987, the stock market fell 501 points, a 25 percent decline as measured by Dow Jones. This drop caused major concern among all investors; many bank customers worried about the safety and security of financial institutions. Deposits up to $100,000 are insured by the Federal Deposit Insurance Corporation (FDIC), and those customers whose aggregate balances exceeded $100,000 worried about the insurance protection afforded their funds.

Branch managers are responsible for maintaining deposit totals in their branch offices. You are an assistant branch manager and you have just heard your manager explaining the FDIC coverage to a customer who maintains over $300,000 in your bank. The customer was obviously very concerned about the safety of her funds. The bank manager misinterprets the FDIC guidelines and reassures the customer that her life savings are properly insured when they are not.

The manager's annual performance review and salary increase are partially based on the dollar amount of total deposits in his office. The manager knows that the customer will withdraw the funds that are not insured by the FDIC and that the branch will lose the deposits. You tell the manager that his assurance to the customer was in error.

The manager tells you not to be concerned, since the customer does not understand the financial soundness of the bank and is worried only because of a mistaken fear that banks will close as they did during the Great Depression. Discuss the ethics of the case. Since the customer does not understand the intricate workings of the banking system, is the manager justified in allowing the customer to believe her funds are safe? Is the bank manager's explanation acceptable?

CHAPTER SEVEN
ETHICAL DECISION MAKING IN BUSINESS

Freedom is expendable, stability is indispensable.

Arnold Toynbee

The noble, many-storied mansion of democracy may be dismantled, leveled to the dimensions of a flat majoritarianism, which is no mansion but a barn, perhaps even a tool shed in which the weapons of tyranny may be forged.

John Courtney Murray
We Hold These Truths

The values that are the foundation of business and business ethics were explored in earlier chapters. Business ethics builds on such values as personal and market freedom and responsibility to stakeholders. This chapter goes beyond exploring those values and asks, How does one make ethical judgments about what is right and what is wrong? What norms, language, techniques, and other aids are available for ethical decision making?

Ethics is a system of moral principles and the methods for applying them.[1] Ethics thus provides the tools to make moral judgments. First a few examples of situations that call for ethical judgments:

Beech-Nut, the second largest baby food manufacturer in the United States, sold phony apple juice that was made of beet sugar, corn syrup, and other ingredients but contained little or no apple juice. The company, a division of Nestlé,

---

[1]For an excellent overview of the development of business ethics, see Richard T. De-George, "The Status of Business Ethics: Past and Future," *Journal of Business Ethics* 6 (April 1987): 201–11; see also John E. Flemming, "A Survey and Critique of Business Ethics Research, 1986," *Research in Corporate Social Performance and Policy*, ed. William C. Frederick, vol. 9 (Greenwich, Conn: JAI, 1987), pp. 1–24.

made the phony apple juice for babies for 20 percent less than real apple juice and sold it for four years in twenty states.[2]

Ivan Boesky agreed to pay a $100,000,000 fine for his purchase of securities after receiving inside information on upcoming deals that would increase the price of those securities. He also agreed to provide evidence concerning others involved in his insider trading schemes.[3]

A Pennsylvania man advertised "Blank receipts, 100 restaurant receipts, 50 styles, $5.98. Satisfaction guaranteed." The blank receipts are attractively designed to look like the receipts of restaurants anywhere in America: Captain's Table, Trophy Room, Village Green, P.J.'s, and so on. The purchaser, after filling in the dates, number of diners, and total bill, can use them in reporting expenses. An IRS spokesperson says that selling blank receipts is not illegal.[4]

John Shad, former head of the Securities and Exchange Commission and former vice chairman of E. F. Hutton, contributed $23,000,000 to support the teaching of ethics at the Harvard Business School. Shad was principally responsible for the insider trading prosecutions of Ivan Boesky and many others. Shad is a Harvard Business School alumnus, as are a number of those involved in inside trading.[5]

Each of these cases raises ethical issues similar to those of concern to businesspeople today. They illustrate the central importance of ethics. Most business decisions contain an ethical component. The purpose of this chapter is to better equip the average businessperson to make effective ethical judgments.

FACTS, VALUES, AND DECISIONS

Ethics provides the skills to make ethical decisions.[6] It includes the language, concepts, and models that enable an individual to make moral decisions. The basic method of making ethical judgments involves just three steps: (1) gathering relevant factual information, (2) determining the moral norm that is

---

[2] "Two Former Executives of Beech-Nut Guilty in Phony Juice Case," *New York Times*, February 18, 1988, pp. 1, 27; "What Led Beech-Nut Down the Road to Disgrace," *Business Week*, February 22, 1988, pp. 124–28.

[3] "Ivan Boesky: Crook of the Year," *Fortune*, January 5, 1987, pp. 48–49; "A Man Who Made a Career of Tempting Fate," *Business Week*, December 1, 1986, pp. 34–35. For a fuller account of Boesky and others, see Jeff Madrick, *Taking America* (New York: Bantam, 1987).

[4] "Here's a New Way to Take the IRS Out to All the Finest Restaurants", *Wall Street Journal*, May 4, 1982, p. 27.

[5] "Harvard's $30 Million Windfall for Ethics 101," *Business Week*, April 13, 1987, p. 40.

[6] As LaRue Hosmer puts it, "I do not want to teach moral standards; I want to teach a method of moral reasoning through complex ethical issues so that the students can apply the moral standards they have." LaRue Hosmer, "The Other 338: Why a Majority of Our Schools of Business Administration Do Not Offer a Course in Business Ethics," *Journal of Business Ethics* 4 (February 1985): 17–22.

most applicable, and (3) making the ethical judgment on the rightness or wrongness of the act or policy (see Figure 7–1).

Nevertheless, ethical judgments are not always easy to make. The facts of the case are often not clear-cut, and the ethical criteria or principles to be used are not always agreed on, even by the experts themselves. Hence, ethics seems to most businesspeople, indeed to most Americans, to be subjective, amorphous, ill-defined, and thus not very useful. Just as with politics and religion, there is often more heat than light generated by ethical discussions. This lack of confidence in ethics is unfortunate, since without agreed ethical principles, it is everyone for him- or herself. In such a situation, trust, which is basic to all business and commerce, is undermined.

Dilemmas to Decisions

Let us begin our examination of ethical decision making by assessing a case that was first judged by 1,700 business executive readers of the *Harvard Business Review*. This case was part of a classical large-scale study of business ethics by Raymond C. Baumhart, S.J.[7]

> An executive earning $120,000 a year has been padding his or her expense account by about $6,000 a year.

First some background: An expense account is available for expenses that are incurred in the course of one's work. It is not fair to ask an employee to use personal funds, without reimbursement, for legitimate business expenses.

To return to the case, how ethical is it to pad one's expense account? On numerous occasions over the years hundreds of other managers have been asked to judge the case, and the results have been substantially the same. Replying to an anonymous questionnaire and speaking for themselves, 85 percent of executives think that this sort of behavior is simply unacceptable. Perhaps more important, almost two-thirds of them think their business colleagues would also see such behavior as unacceptable under any circumstances.

Why would padding an expense account be considered wrong by these executives? An expense account is not a simple addition to someone's salary. It is designed to cover the actual expenses that are incurred by employees in the course of doing their work.

Pocketing a company pencil or making a personal long-distance phone call from the office may seem relatively trivial. Perhaps, but fabricating expenses up to 5 percent of one's salary is not trivial; it is a substantial

---

[7]Raymond C. Baumhart, S.J., *Ethics in Business* (New York: Holt, Rinehart & Winston, 1968), p. 21. The dollar figures in the case have been adjusted for inflation. For an updating of Baumhart's findings, see Steven Brenner and Earl Molander, "Is the Ethics of Business Changing?" *Harvard Business Review* 55 (January-February 1977): 57–71.

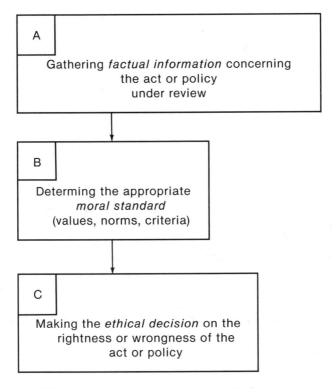

FIGURE 7-1   Steps in Ethical Decision Making

violation of justice. The executive in the case is taking more compensation than he or she is entitled to. Presumably the executive's salary is ample compensation for the work, and the extra $6,000 is not intended as direct compensation, nor is it recognized by law as such.

Circumstances are often cited that might seem to mitigate the injustice. Some might say, "Many others are also doing it" or "My superior knows about it and says nothing." In the cited study, only about a quarter of the executives thought that their peers would justify such actions on these counts. A mere handful (about 10 percent) said that they themselves thought that it would be acceptable in such circumstances. An examination of these circumstances follows.

The Actions of Other People

The fact that many people are doing actions of a certain kind can never in itself justify those actions. For example, the fact that superiors ordered actions and others did them was no legal defense for concentration camp officers at the post–World War II Nuremberg war crime trials. Even though these Nazi officers were under orders, and even though many of their peers felt that killing "undesirables" was alright, it was not accepted as a defense. Even less so is it an ethical defense. Although ethics is influenced by conditions, a moral principle is not established by voting.

Let us assume in the case of the expense account that the executive is a woman. We must acknowledge that it would be to her benefit if she could increase her salary by 5 percent. To have that extra $6,000 would be in her self-interest. Focusing primarily on her self-interest could easily lead her to be less objective in her search for the right action and would make her more prone to look for excuses to do that which would benefit her.

Justice calls for a fair distribution of the benefits and burdens of society. In this case, we are concerned with benefits. When is it ethical to take funds from an expense account? Assuming that the executive's family is not starving because she has an abnormally low salary, justice tells us that the expense account should be used for expenses, not as a salary supplement. Ignorance and coercion can lessen responsibility. However, in this case, the executive could hardly claim that she did not know what an expense account was or that she was coerced into taking the money.

But if she can get away with it, why shouldn't she pad her expense account? Is there any real difference between an executive who is ethical and one who isn't? A basic assumption that almost all businesspeople support is that a businessperson should be ethical. That is, individuals should try to do good and avoid evil, not only on the job but in all aspects of life. The foundation for business transactions is confidence that most businesspeople are trustworthy, truthful, and ethical. If most businesspeople were not ethical, it would be almost impossible to purchase supplies, sell goods or securities, or do most of the buying and selling that we are accustomed to doing in modern society.

Admittedly there can be a short-term financial advantage for an embezzler or a supplier who takes ten million dollars and delivers defective goods. It is because of individuals like this that we have laws, courts, and jails. Yet we also know that not all activities can be regulated, nor can all unethical acts be fully punished (in this life, anyway). If a large percentage of businesspeople did not pay their bills and took advantage of their business partners, the business system would collapse.

ETHICAL NORMS FOR BUSINESS DECISIONS

Ethical criteria and ethical models have been the subject of much reflection over the centuries. Of all ethical theories, utilitarianism is the one businesspeople feel most at home with. This is not surprising, as the theory traces its origins to Adam Smith, the father of modern economics. The main proponents of utilitarianism, however, were Jeremy Bentham[8] and John Stuart Mill,[9] both of whom helped to formulate the theory more precisely. Utilitarianism evaluates actions in terms of their consequences. In any given situation, the one action which would result in the greatest net gain for all concerned parties is considered to be the right, or morally obligatory, action. The theory of rights focuses on the entitlements of individual persons. Immanuel Kant[10] (personal rights) and John Locke[11] (property rights) were the first to fully develop the theory of rights. The theory of justice has a longer tradition, going back to Plato and Aristotle in the fourth century B.C.[12] Theoretical work in each of these traditional theories has continued to the present.[13] For an overview of these three theories—their history, strengths, weaknesses, and areas of application—see Table 7–1.

The Norm of Utilitarianism

Utilitarianism judges that an action is right if it produces the greatest utility, "the greatest good for the greatest number." The decision process is very much like a cost-benefit analysis applied to all parties who would be touched by the decision. That action is right which produces the greatest net benefit when all the costs and benefits to all the affected parties are taken into account. Although it would be convenient if these costs and benefits could be measured in some comparable unit, this is rarely possible. Many important values (e.g., human life and liberty) cannot be quantified. Thus, the best that can be done is to enumerate the effects and the magnitude of their costs and benefits as clearly and accurately as possible.

The utilitarian principle says that the right action is that which produces the greatest net benefit over any other possible action. This does not mean that the right action produces the greatest good for the person performing the action. Rather, it is the action that produces the greatest net good for all those who are affected by the action. Utilitarianism can handle some ethical cases quite well, especially those that are complex and affect many parties. Although the model and the methodology are clear in theory, carrying out the calculations is often difficult. Taking into account so many af-

---

[8] Jeremy Bentham, *An Introduction to the Principles of Morals and Legislation* (New York: Hafner, 1948).

[9] John Stuart Mill, *Utilitarianism* (Indianapolis: Bobbs-Merrill, 1957).

[10] Immanuel Kant, *The Metaphysical Elements of Justice*, trans. J. Ladd (New York: Library of Liberal Arts, 1965).

[11] John Locke, *The Second Treatise of Government* (New York: Liberal Arts Press, 1952).

[12] Aristotle, *Ethics*, trans. J. A. K. Thomson (London: Penguin, 1953).

[13] For example, John Rawls, *A Theory of Justice* (Cambridge, Mass.: Harvard University Press, 1971). See two books of readings: Thomas Donaldson and Patricia Werhane, *Ethical Issues in Business* (Englewood Cliffs, N.J.: Prentice-Hall, 1979); Tom Beauchamp and Norman Bowie, *Ethical Theory and Business*, 2d ed. (Englewood Cliffs, N.J.: Prentice-Hall, 1983).

TABLE 7-1   Ethical Models for Business Decisions

DEFINITION AND ORIGIN	STRENGTHS	WEAKNESSES	EXAMPLE	WHEN USED SUMMARY
UTILITARIANISM				
"The greatest good for the greatest number": Bentham (1748–1832), Adam Smith (1723–1790), David Ricardo (1772–1823).	1. Concepts, terminology, methods are easiest for businesspersons to work with; justifies a profit maximization system. 2. Promotes view of entire system of exchange beyond "this firm." 3. Encourages entrepreneurship, innovation, productivity.	1. Impossible to measure or quantify all important elements. 2. "Greatest good" can degenerate into self-interest. 3. Can result in abridging person's rights. 4. Can result in neglecting less powerful segments of society.	1. Plant closing. 2. Pollution. 3. Condemnation of land or buildings for "development."	1. Use in all business decisions, and will be dominant criteria in 90%. 2. Version of model is implicitly used already, although scope is generally limited to "this firm."

THEORY OF JUSTICE Equitable distribution of society's benefits and burdens: Aristotle (384–322 B.C.), Rawls (1921–).	1. The "democratic" principle. 2. Does not allow a society to become status- or class-dominated. 3. Ensures that minorities, poor, handicapped receive opportunities and a fair share of output.	1. Can result in less risk, incentive, and innovation. 2. Encourages sense of "entitlement."	1. Delivery of shoddy goods. 2. Low wages to Hispanic or black workers. 3. Bribes, kickbacks, fraud.	1. In product decisions usefulness to *all* in society. 2. In setting salaries for unskilled workers, executives. 3. In public policy decisions: to maintain a floor of living standards for all. 4. Use with, for example, performance appraisal, due process, distribution of rewards and punishments.
THEORY OF RIGHTS Individual's freedom is not to be violated: Locke (1635–1701)—property; Kant (1724–1804)—personal rights.	1. Ensures respect for individual's property and personal freedom. 2. Parallels political "Bill of Rights."	1. Can encourage individualistic, selfish behavior.	1. Unsafe workplace. 2. Flammable children's toys. 3. Lying to superior or subordinate.	1. Where individual's property or personal rights are in question. 2. Use with, for example, employee privacy, job tenure, work dangerous to person's health.

fected parties, along with the extent to which the action touches them, can be a tallying nightmare.

Hence several shortcuts have been proposed that can reduce the complexity of utilitarian calculations. Each shortcut involves a sacrifice of accuracy for ease of calculation. Among these shortcuts are (1) adherence to a simplified rule (e.g., the Golden Rule, "Do unto others as you would have them do unto you"); (2) calculation of costs and benefits in dollar terms for ease of comparison; (3) restriction of consideration to those directly affected by the action, putting aside indirect effects. In using these shortcuts, an individual should be aware that they result in simplification and that some interests may not be sufficiently taken into consideration.

In the popular mind, the term *utilitarianism* sometimes suggests selfishness and exploitation. For our purposes, the term should be considered not to have these connotations. However, a noteworthy weakness of utilitarianism as an ethical norm is that it can advocate, for example, abridging an individual's right to a job or even life for the sake of the greater good of a larger number of people. This and other difficulties are discussed elsewhere.[14] One additional caution in using utilitarian rules is in order: It is considered unethical to opt for narrower benefits (e.g., personal goals, career, or money) at the expense of the good of a larger number, such as a nation or a society. Utilitarian norms emphasize the good of the group; it is a large-scale ethical model. As a result, an individual and what is due that individual may be overlooked. The theory of rights has been developed to emphasize the individual and the standing of that individual with peers and within society.

The Norm of Individual Rights

A right is a person's entitlement to something.[15] Rights may flow from the legal system, such as our constitutional rights of freedom of conscience or freedom of speech. The U.S. Bill of Rights and the United Nations Universal Declaration of Human Rights are examples of documents that spell out individual rights in detail. Legal rights, as well as others which may not be written into law, stem from the human dignity of persons. Moral rights have these characteristics: (1) They enable individuals to pursue their own interests, and (2) they impose correlative prohibitions or requirements on others.

Hence, every right has a corresponding duty. My right to freedom of conscience is supported by the prohibition of other individuals from unnec-

---

[14] Gerald F. Cavanagh, Dennis J. Moberg, and Manuel Velasquez, "The Ethics of Organizational Politics," *Academy of Management Review*, 6 (July 1981): 363–74. For a more complete treatment, see Manuel Velasquez, *Business Ethics: Concepts and Cases* (Englewood Cliffs, N.J.: Prentice-Hall, 1982), pp. 46–58.

[15] Velasquez, *Business Ethics*, p. 29; see also Thomas Donaldson, *Corporations and Morality* (Englewood Cliffs, N.J.: Prentice-Hall, 1982).

essarily limiting that freedom of conscience. From another perspective, my right to be paid for my work corresponds to a duty of mine to perform "a fair day's work for a fair day's pay." In the latter case, both the right and duty stem from the right to private property, which is a traditional pillar of American life and law. However, the right to private property is not absolute. A factory owner may be forced by law, as well as by morality, to spend money on pollution control or safety equipment. For a listing of selected rights and other ethical norms, see Figure 7–2.

People also have the right not to be lied to or deceived, especially on matters which they have a right to know about. A supervisor has the duty to be truthful in giving feedback on work performance even if it is difficult for the supervisor to do so. Each of us has the right not to be lied to by salespeople or advertisements. Perjury under oath is a serious crime; lying on matters where another has a right to accurate information is also seriously unethical. Truthfulness and honesty are basic ethical norms.

Judging morality by reference to individual rights is quite different from using utilitarian standards. Rights express the requirements of morality from the standpoint of the individual; rights protect the individual from the encroachment and demands of society or the state. Utilitarian standards promote society's interests and are relatively insensitive regarding a single individual except insofar as the individual's welfare affects the overall good of society.

A business contract establishes rights and duties that did not exist before: The right of the purchaser to receive what was agreed and the right of the seller to be paid what was agreed. Formal written contracts and informal verbal agreements are essential to business transactions.

Immanuel Kant recognized that an emphasis on rights can lead people to focus largely on what is due them. So he formulated what he called "categorical imperatives." The first is that "I ought never to act except in such a way that I can also will that my maxim should become a universal law." Another formulation is this: An action is morally right for a person in a certain situation if and only if the person's reason for carrying out the action is a reason that he or she would be willing to have every person act on, in any similar situation.[16]

Kant's second categorical imperative cautions us against using other people as a means to our own ends: Never treat humanity simply as a means, but always also as an end. One interpretation of the second imperative is this: An action is morally right for a person if and only if in performing the action the person does not use others merely as a means for advancing his or her own interests, but also both respects and develops their capacity to choose for

---

[16]Immanuel Kant, *Groundwork of the Metaphysics of Morals*, trans. H. J. Paton (New York: Harper & Row, 1964), pp. 62–90.

UTILITARIAN

1. *Organizational goals* should aim at *maximizing the satisfactions* of the organization's constituencies.
2. The members of an organization should attempt to attain its goals as *efficiently* as possible by consuming as few inputs as possible and by minimizing the external costs which organizational activities impose on others.
3. The employee should use *every effective means* to achieve the goals of the organization and should neither jeopardize those goals nor enter situations in which personal interests conflict significantly with the goals.

RIGHTS

1. *Life and safety:* The individual has the right not to have her or his life or safety unknowingly and unnecessarily endangered.
2. *Truthfulness:* The individual has a right not to be intentionally deceived by another, especially on matters about which the individual has the right to know.
3. *Privacy:* The individual has the right to do whatever he or she chooses to do outside working hours and to control information about his or her private life.
4. *Freedom of conscience:* The individual has the right to refrain from carrying out any order that violates those commonly accepted moral or religious norms to which the person adheres.
5. *Free speech:* The individual has the right to criticize conscientiously and truthfully the ethics or legality of corporate actions so long as the criticism does not violate the rights of other individuals within the organization.
6. *Private property:* The individual has a right to hold private property, especially insofar as this right enables the individual and his or her family to be sheltered and to have the basic necessities of life.

JUSTICE

1. *Fair treatment:* Persons who are similar to each other in the relevant respects should be treated similarly; persons who differ in some respect relevant to the job they perform should be treated differently in proportion to the difference between them.
2. *Fair administration of rules:* Rules should be administered consistently, fairly, and impartially.
3. *Fair compensation:* Individuals should be compensated for the cost of their injuries by the party that is responsible for those injuries.
4. *Fair blame:* Individuals should not be held responsible for matters over which they have no control.
5. *Due process:* The individual has a right to a fair and impartial hearing when he or she believes that personal rights are being violated.

FIGURE 7-2   Some Selected Ethical Norms

Source: Quoted and adapted from Manuel Velasquez, Gerald Cavanagh, and Dennis Moberg, "Organizational Statesmanship and Dirty Politics: Ethical Guidelines for the Organizational Politician," *Organizational Dynamics*, (Fall, 1983).

themselves.[17] Capital, plants, and machines are all to be used to serve the purposes of individuals. On the other hand, individuals themselves are not to be used merely as instruments for achieving the goals of others. This rules out deception, manipulation, and exploitation in dealing with people.

The Norm of Justice

Justice requires all persons, and thus managers too, to be guided by fairness, equity, and impartiality. Justice calls for evenhanded treatment of groups and individuals (1) in the distribution of the benefits and burdens of society, (2) in the administration of laws and regulations, and (3) in the imposition of sanctions and the rewarding of compensation for wrongs suffered. An action or policy is just if it is comparable to the treatment accorded to others.

Standards of justice are generally considered to be more important than the utilitarian consideration of consequences. If a society is unjust to a minority group (e.g., apartheid treatment of blacks in South Africa), we generally consider that society to be unjust and we condemn it, even if the results of the injustices bring about greater economic productivity. On the other hand, we seem willing to trade off some equity if the results will bring about greater benefits for all. For example, income and wealth differences are justified only if they bring greater benefits for all.

Standards of justice are not as often in conflict with individual rights as are utilitarian norms.[18] This is not surprising, since justice is largely based on the moral rights of individuals. The moral right to be treated as a free and equal person, for example, undergirds the notion that benefits and burdens should be distributed equitably. Personal moral rights (e.g., freedom of conscience, the right to due process, the right to free consent, the right to privacy) are so basic that they generally may not be taken away to bring about a better distribution of benefits within a society. On the other hand, property rights may be abridged for the sake of a fairer distribution of benefits and burdens (e.g., graduated income tax, limits on pollution).

Distributive justice becomes important when a society has sufficient goods but not everyone's basic needs are satisfied. The question then becomes, What is a just distribution? The fundamental principle is that equals should be treated equally and that unequals should be treated in accord with their inequality. For example, few would argue that a new person hired for a job should receive the same pay as a senior worker with twenty years experience. People who perform work of greater responsibility or who work longer hours should be eligible for greater pay. However, it is clear that pay differ-

---

[17] Ibid; see also Velasquez, *Business Ethics*, p. 68.

[18] Jerald Greenberg, "A Taxonomy of Organizational Justice Theories," *Academy of Management Review* 12 (January 1987): 9–22.

entials should be based on the work itself, not on some arbitrary bias of the employer.

Even knowing all of the above, we still wouldn't be able to determine what is a fair distribution of society's benefits and burdens. In fact, quite different notions of equity are generally proposed. For example, the capitalist model (benefits based on contribution) is radically different from the socialist (from each according to abilities, to each according to needs). An important contribution to the theory of justice has been made by John Rawls.[19] Rawls would have us construct a system of rules and laws for society as if we did not know what roles we were to play in that society. We do not know if we would be rich or poor, male or female, African or European, manager or slave, handicapped or physically and mentally fit. Rawls calls this the "veil of ignorance." Constructing a system of rules under the veil of ignorance is intended to allow us to rid ourselves of the biases we have as a result of our status. In such circumstances, each of us would try to construct a system that would be of the greatest benefit to all and that would not undermine the position of any group. Rawls proposes that people under the veil of ignorance would agree to two principles:

1. Each person is to have an equal right to the most extensive liberty compatible with similar liberty for others.
2. Social and economic inequalities are to be arranged so that they are both reasonably expected to be to everyone's advantage and attached to positions and offices open to all.

The first principle is consonant with the American sense of liberty and thus is not controversial in the United States. The second principle is more egalitarian and also more controversial. However, Rawls maintains that if people honestly choose as if they were under the veil of ignorance, they would opt for a system of justice that is most fair to all members of society. Let us now use these ethical norms in making ethical decisions.

SOLVING ETHICAL PROBLEMS

Any human judgment is preceded by two steps: gathering the facts and determining the appropriate criteria (see Figure 7–1). Before any ethically sensitive situation can be assessed, it is essential that all the relevant data be on hand. As an aid to determining the appropriate criteria, we have presented the classical norms of utility, rights, and justice. Figure 7–3 is a schematic diagram of how ethical decision making should proceed. Although it contains greater detail than Figure 7–1, the same three steps (A, B, and C) are underscored. Even Figure 7–3 is simplified, but nevertheless it can aid in handling ethical problems.

[19] Rawls, *Theory of Justice.*

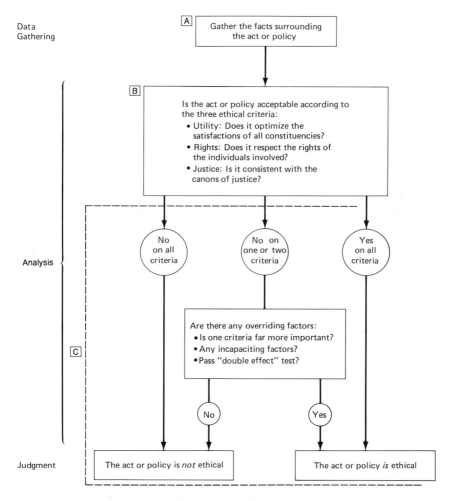

FIGURE 7-3   Flow Diagram of Ethical Decision Making

Source: Adapted from Manuel Velasquez, Gerald F. Cavanagh, and Dennis J. Moberg, "Organizational Statesmanship and Dirty Politics: Ethical Guidelines for the Organizational Politician," *Organizational Dynamics* (Fall, 1983).

Let us apply our scheme to the case of the executive who padded her expense account. We will accept the limited data provided in the case. Using the utility criterion, we judge that although padding her expense account is in the interest of the executive, it does not optimize benefits for others. Her actions hurt shareholders, customers, more honest executives, and people in other firms in similar situations. Padding one's expense account also adds to the expense of doing business and to this extent violates utility. The rights norm is not so useful here: The executive has no right to the extra money, although we might make the case that the shareholders' and customers' right to private property is being violated. With regard to justice, salary and commissions constitute ordinary compensation for individuals. Expense accounts have a quite different purpose. In this instance, most managers responding to the case held that it was unethical for the executive to pad her expense account. John Rawls would maintain that all of us would set the rules in this fashion if we did not know what roles we ourselves would have in society. Hence, we conclude that padding one's expense account is judged unethical on all three ethical norms, and is therefore clearly wrong. Note that 73 percent of the executives who were asked came to the same judgment.

Let us consider the first case given at the beginning of the chapter. When we apply the utility criterion to the action of the executives at Beech-Nut who were responsible for selling pseudo–apple juice, we find there was a short-term gain to the firm and the executives from the added profitability. On the other hand, parents and babies lost, since the babies given the juice did not obtain the vitamins and nutrients that were expected. In the long run, the firm, the executives, and the shareholders also lost, because there was unfavorable publicity and a resulting decrease in business. So the action does not pass on the utility criterion. The rights of parents to the truth were violated, since the product was not what it claimed to be. Perhaps the health of the babies was even endangered, for the mixture might have contained unhealthy chemicals (one former employee testified it did). Beech-Nut did not provide the product they had promised, so the sales contract was breached and justice also was violated. The action was unethical according to all three norms. In fact, the two executives were sentenced to a year in jail and fined $100,000 each, and the company paid a $2,000,000 fine.[20]

What of the second case, in which an entrepreneur advertised official-looking blank receipts of fictitious restaurants? Salespeople and managers could fill out the receipts and submit them for reimbursement. The receipts would "prove" the purchase of meals that never existed. Using our model, what would we say of the ethics of selling such receipts? Or of purchasing them and using them? Respond to this case using the flow chart in Figure 7–3.

Decision Making Using the Model

Let us examine another case:

Brian Curry, financial vice president of Digital Robotics Corporation, is about to retire and has been asked to recommend one of his two assistants for promotion to vice president. Curry knows that his recommendations will be acted on. He also knows that since both assistants are about the same age, the one not chosen

---

[20] "Jail Terms for Two in Beech-Nut Case," *New York Times*, June 17, 1988, pp. 29, 31.

will have difficulty getting future promotions. Debra Butler is the most qualified for the position. She is bright and outgoing and has better leadership ability. Moreover, her father is president of the largest customer of Digital, and Curry correctly reasons that Digital will more likely keep this business if the daughter is made an officer. On the other hand, John McNichols has been with the company longer, has worked seventy-hour weeks, and has pulled the company through some very difficult situations. He has continued putting in extra effort because he was told some time ago that he was in line for the vice presidency. Nevertheless, Curry recommends Butler for the job.

Let us again use our norms and Figure 7–3 to decide this case. Utility tells us that the selection of Debra Butler optimally benefits top management, shareholders, customers, and most of the workers, because she is a better leader. The principal cost is to John McNichols. As for justice, we conclude that because the promotional decision was made on the basis of relevant abilities, it did constitute fair treatment. On the other hand, McNichols worked extra hours because of the promised promotion. Much of his work effort was based on a false promise. McNichols had a right to know the truth and to be treated fairly.[21]

Thus, according to the criterion of utility, the appointment of Butler is morally acceptable, since there will be a net gain for most parties. However, because of the promise made earlier to McNichols, which resulted in extended workweeks, he is being treated unjustly. We can then ask if there are any "overriding factors" that ought to be taken into consideration.

Overriding Factors

Overriding factors are factors which may, in a given case, justify overriding one of the three ethical criteria: utility, rights, or justice (see Figure 7–3). Overriding factors can be examined when there is a conflict in the conclusions drawn from the ethical norms. For example, there might be incapacitating factors. If there are any elements that coerce an individual into doing a certain action, then that individual is not held to be fully responsible. Managers at a H. J. Heinz plant were under great pressure from top management to show a profit. They were not able to do as well as was expected, so they began to juggle the books. This resulted in a cumulative overstatement of profits of $8.5 million. Nevertheless, the managers who falsified the books would probably be judged less unethical than the top managers who exerted the unrelenting pressure. Even though making false entries in the books is objectively unethical, the plant managers did not bear full responsibility because they were pressured by superiors.[22]

---

[21] Marshall Sashkin has developed a set of questions whereby a manager can score him- or herself as being predominantly a user of the utility, justice, or rights norm. See Sashkin, *Managerial Values Profile* (Bryn Mawr, Pa.: Organizational Design and Development, 1986).

[22] "Some Middle Managers Cut Corners to Achieve High Corporate Goals," *Wall Street Journal*, November 8, 1979, pp. 1, 19.

Also, someone might not be able to utilize the criteria owing to lack of information. A manager might think that another employee is embezzling from the firm. However, to report that employee to superiors might ruin his or her reputation. Therefore, even though stealing is a violation of justice, in this instance there is not yet sufficient information to utilize the criteria. In addition, the manager may be sincerely uncertain of the criteria or their applicability in this particular case.

Consider again the case of appointing a financial vice president. Utility calls for recommending Debra Butler for the position. The right to full information and perhaps justice support McNichols' claim. McNichols has worked more hours and harder because of a promised reward. Since the position was promised to him, fair treatment requires giving him special consideration. On the basis of the importance of a verbal promise and of justice, we might conclude that McNichols should get the position.

Because there is now a conflict between these two norms, any overriding factors should be taken into account. Is one criteria more important? The effective operation of the firm is an important ethical goal. How much better a manager is Butler and how would her selection affect the firm's performance and the jobs of others at Digital?

With regard to incapaciting factors, there seems to be little coercion involved, certainly no physical coercion. That Debra Butler's father is president of Digital's largest customer might constitute psychological coercion. However, Curry seems to have made his decision freely.

Another important factor to consider is exactly what sort of promise was made to McNichols? Was it clear and unequivocal? If the "promise" was in fact a mere statement that McNichols had a good chance at the promotion or if Butler's performance is expected to be significantly better than McNichols', then Curry could ethically recommend Butler. However, some sort of compensation should then be made to McNichols.

Another kind of overriding factor occurs when people using different criteria come to varying conclusions on the same case. The so-called principle of double effect can be useful. Let us take an example of firing a worker who is not a very good performer but who is the sole provider of a family. Using the utility norm, we would probably say the firing was ethical. But using the justice norm, we might call it unethical, because an entire family would be deprived of income. There is a conflict between the conclusions reached using the different norms, so the principal of the double effect is appropriate. The principle is applicable when an act has both a good effect (e.g., bringing greater efficiency to the firm and providing honest feedback to the worker) and a bad effect (e.g., elimination of the principal support for the family). One may ethically perform such an act under three conditions: (1) One does not directly intend the bad effect (e.g., depriving the family of income); (2) the bad effect is not a means to the good end but is simply a side effect (e.g., depriving the family of income is not a means of making the firm more efficient); and (3) the good effect sufficiently outweighs the bad (e.g., the benefits of greater firm efficiency are sufficiently greater than the difficulties the family will face). Going back to the preceding case, would the appointment of Butler pass the double effect test?

The above ethical model, which has been used in many books on management,[23] enables the manager to integrate ethical analysis into business decisions. It is intended to stand alongside economic analysis—to complement and correct it.

Loyalty and Whistle-blowing

In addition to ethical analysis, a member of an organization is sometimes faced with a situation where superiors seem to be blind to unethical acts. This presents a difficult dilemma. The following case, where the stakes are high, demands careful analysis and additional criteria:

> An engineer in the design section of an airplane manufacturing firm is convinced that the latch mechanism on a plane's cargo door does not provide sufficient security and that the door has to be redesigned in order to insure against the possibility of a crash. He presents his supervisor with the information and is told that the Federal Aviation Administration (FAA) has given the required approval and that he should not "rock the boat." He goes to the president of the firm and gets the same answer.

Would that engineer be justified in taking this information to the news media? The answer to this question is extremely important. The danger to the lives of hundreds of passengers might argue for going to the news media. On the other hand, the reputation and perhaps the financial viability of the firm are also to be weighed. A mistake in either direction could be disastrous. Thus it is important to do the ethical analysis very carefully.

The right to life and safety is at issue. If indeed the designer is correct that the faulty latch mechanism puts the plane in danger of a crash, then the lives of the passengers would assume paramount importance in the calculations. While the designer owes loyalty to his employer, nevertheless justice requires that future passengers should not unknowingly be in danger of their lives due to the faulty design.

Utilitarians would total up the costs and benefits to all parties affected. Redesigning the aircraft and recalling planes already in service would cost the firm tens of millions of dollars. More immediately, taking the issue to the ill-informed media would result in a serious erosion in reputation for the firm. On the other hand—assuming that 300 people would be aboard the first

---

[23] See, for example, Harold Koontz and Heinz Weihrich, *Management*, 9th ed. (New York: McGraw-Hill, 1988), pp. 611–13; John Schermerhorn, James Hunt, and Richard Osborn, *Managing Organization Behavior*, 2d ed. (New York: Wiley, 1985); Richy Griffin and Gregory Moorhead, *Organization Behavior*, 2d ed. (Boston: Houghton Mifflin, 1989).

plane to crash—how much are 300 lives worth? Utilitarians, too, would undoubtedly conclude that the designer would be justified in taking the issue outside the firm. Even 69 percent of the corporate executives who examined the case thought that the designer was justified in breaching loyalty and taking the issue to the media.[24]

When to Blow the Whistle

Since opportunities for whistle-blowing are becoming more common and the stakes are bigger,[25] it is important to give some attention to the special conditions that would allow whistle-blowing. According to the analysis of Sissela Bok, to be legitimate, whistle-blowing should meet several criteria:[26]

1. The purpose should be moral: to benefit the public interest.
2. What is protested should be of major importance and should be specific.
3. The facts of the case must be certain; they should be checked and rechecked.
4. All other avenues for change within the organization must be already exhausted.
5. The whistle-blower should be above reproach. In particular, the whistle-blower should not gain anything through revealing the information. Ideally the individual should openly accept responsibility for the whistle-blowing.

Let us examine these criteria. The first demands that the purpose of whistle-blowing should not be to attract attention, to seek revenge, or to achieve some personal goal. In many cases, whistle-blowers are trying to wreak vengeance on a supervisor or a company that they believe has been unfair to them. Perceptions regarding one's own grievances can be biased and do not provide a solid basis for whistle-blowing. Instead, the revelation of wrongdoing should be for the common good.

Second, whistle-blowing requires that the wrongdoing is a *serious* breach of ethics. Much is at stake, and the action should not be taken lightly. The unethical act protested should be a specific act, not a vague attitude which is hard to document.

Third, the facts of the case must be ascertained, and the evidence must be double-checked.

The fourth criterion demands that superiors and other higher officials in the organization who might be able to rectify the situation have been informed and that they still refuse to do anything. This requires going to the

---

[24] "Business Executives and Moral Dilemmas," *Business and Society Review*, Spring 1975, p. 52.

[25] Alan F. Westin, ed., *Whistle Blowing* (New York: McGraw-Hill, 1980).

[26] Sissela Bok, "Whistleblowing and Professional Responsibilities," in *Ethics Teaching in Higher Education*, ed. Daniel Callahan and Sissela Bok (New York: Plenum Press, 1980), pp. 277–95: see also Kenneth D. Walters, "Your Employees' Right to Blow the Whistle," *Harvard Business Review* 53 (July-August 1975): 26–34.

president or even the board before going to an outside party. If a federal regulatory agency could be involved, then, assuming all internal avenues have been tried, the agency is to be preferred to the news media.

The fifth criterion is that the whistle-blower should not benefit from the revelation. If one's career is benefited or one makes money from exposing the situation (e.g., money made from writing a best-selling exposé), one's motives are suspect. Considerations of self-interest can unconsciously enter into one's deliberations. To compensate for possible personal bias, a person should seek considerable objective advice so as not to blow the whistle on the basis of misinformation or partial information. The potential whistle-blower should also be aware of all the arguments for and against whistle-blowing before going to an outside party. Ideally, the whistle-blower should be willing to accept responsibility for providing the information. Granted this takes courage, since the person's job may be on the line, yet it can be a test of one's motives. Anonymous informers are justifiably not often trusted.

Let us apply the criteria to the case of the aircraft designer. His purpose in blowing the whistle is to serve the public interest by preventing an airplane crash and saving hundreds of lives. The facts of the situation should be checked. From the description of the case, we do not know that the designer is well informed or even mentally stable. We also do not know whether he has checked his calculations with others who would be in a position to affirm or correct his estimates. The whistle-blower has already gone to his own supervisor and to the president. The FAA does not seem to have found the design problem. However, before going to the media, the designer should check to see if the FAA is aware of the problem. If not, apprising the FAA of the problem could achieve the safety goal without a public splash and thus prevent severe damage to the manufacturer and to the airlines that would eventually be using the plane. Since the whistle-blower has not yet acted, we do not know whether he will identify himself. In the same vein, we know nothing of his character. More than likely, however, no personal advantage will be gained by the whistle-blowing.

In conclusion, the whistle-blower, assuming he has the correct facts, would be justified in going to an external agency. This case is not entirely fictitious. Had someone noted and protested the cargo door latch problem on the DC-10, the Turkish airliner taking off from Paris would not have crashed with the loss of more than 300 lives.[27]

A serious deterrent to whistle-blowing is the well-known fact that most whistle-blowers are penalized by being fired, demoted, or shunted off to an unimportant job. They are labeled as "boat rockers" and "squealers." A series of recent court decisions has begun to provide some protection for whistle-

[27] Paul Eddy, Elaine Potter, and Bruce Page, *Destination Disaster* (New York: New York Times Book Co., 1976), esp. pp. 33–63.

blowers. Employees now cannot be fired for whistle-blowing, at least in certain restricted circumstances.[28]

On the other hand, as any experienced manager or student of organizations knows, only when management fails does whistle-blowing become necessary. The moral problem would not have arisen, for example, with better design of the product, clearer expectations on the job, or better communications. Whistle-blowing becomes an option when supervisors do not listen to subordinates and their legitimate concerns. These concerns are not always well founded, but it is essential that they be heard. Often bureaucratic managers blind themselves to shoddy products and practices in attempting to show higher quarterly profits or to maintain the status quo. In short, legitimate whistle-blowing is a sign that the organization is not performing well, has poor management, or both.

ANOTHER MODEL: MARKET VALUES AND SOCIAL VALUES

The earlier described ethical model for business decision making (see Figure 7–3) is widely used. However, perhaps it does not sufficiently take into account the needs of business. The following second-generation model (see Table 7–2) is an attempt to synthesize the social values of rights, justice, and utilitarianism while taking into account the values and virtues that form the basis of business.[29] The market values of individual responsibility, freedom, and efficiency are desirable goals of individuals and of society. Hence, they are also important ethical values and belong next to the social values of the dignity of the human beings, community, and justice.

The model under discussion is newly devised. It is intended to be used as an alternative to the first model (Figure 7–3). That is, while both models can be used on the same problem, the definitions of the values and the norms used and the methods of application are different and should not be confused. While justice is much the same in both models, the other five values differ significantly.

Market Values and Norms

The free market system requires and supports specific personal values. Many of these values are important in other settings as well. Growth and productivity provide work and income. Freedom, honesty, and individual responsibility are also basic ethical goals. In order for the market to operate, there must be freedom of choice and freedom of movement. The system also

[28] "Armor for Whistle-blowers," *Business Week*, July 6, 1981, p. 97.

[29] For a fuller description with applications, see Cavanagh and McGovern, *Ethical Dilemmas in the Modern Corporation*.

TABLE 7-2 Market Values and Social Values

MARKET VALUES	SOCIAL VALUES
1. *Freedom of the Individual* NORM: Preserve and protect the freedom of all members. Political democracy, free enterprise, and a free market are institutions well suited to achieve this freedom.	1. *Dignity of the Human Person* NORM: Preserve and promote the dignity of all persons; deal honestly with others and treat others as ends, not means; enable people to meet basic human needs (life, health, safety, employment, etc.), so that a dignified human life may be realized.
2. *Individual Responsibility* NORM: Promote personal responsibility; institutions that encourage initiative and individual responsibility are favored. Enlightened self-interest is a useful and realistic motive for achieving this value.	2. *Community* (Common good; solidarity) NORM: Encourage people to care for others, for their neighborhood, work group, and society as a whole; enable all to have a sense of participation and belonging.
3. *Growth* (Productivity) NORM: Promote spirit and institutions that encourage the production of goods and services and economic health. Free enterprise, with its flexibility, competition, and legitimate striving for profits, best achieves innovation and productivity. "Consumer sovereignty" is the best means of distributing goods.	3. *Justice* (Equity) NORM: Strive for fair distribution of benefits, burdens, and power; deal fairly with all persons, including future generations; create structures that promote participation and the common good; change structures that discriminate against any group. Political democracy best achieves justice.

encourages individual responsibility, innovation, and flexibility, since so many decisions are made by individuals, not by government authorities. However, not all market values should be conceived as ends in themselves. Competitiveness, self-interestness, and survival of the fittest are not ethical goods to be sought in every instance. Being primarily guided by the latter values can make someone callous and selfish.

Personal freedom has been discussed throughout this book. Alexis de Tocqueville first pointed to it as a paramount American virtue (see Chapter 2). A wide variety of personal freedoms are vitally important, even taken for granted, by Americans. Political democracy and free markets depend on individual freedom. The ability to freely make, sell, and purchase goods is a foundation of our economy and its efficiencies. The freedom of people to move to another part of the country, indeed to another country, makes it easier for those who are looking for work to find it. There is, of course, a tradeoff—in the breaking up of extended families and the disruption of communities.

Individual responsibility is also an essential ethical value in democratic and market societies. The focus is on individuals and the need for each individual to shoulder responsibility. There must be some growth in society, because men and women must work in order to feed and house their families. However, growth must take place without the waste of resources and without significant pollution in order to be a genuine ethical value. Whether this can be achieved is open to question. The goal is to provide jobs, goods, and a decent source of income without depleting nonrenewable resources and without undue pollution.

Social Values and Norms

Social values and norms are somewhat parallel to rights, utility, and justice in our first ethical model. The dignity of the individual—the central importance of each and every person, regardless of age, sex, race, religion, nationality, income level, or background—is the foundation for all ethical values. Individual rights, justice, and utility stem ultimately from human dignity. Each person must always be treated as an end and never only as a means. One consequence of human dignity is the right of each person to food, housing, and, in sufficiently affluent societies, basic education and medical care. Freedom means little without the means to support a decent life for oneself and one's family.

A sense of community and a concern for the common good are necessary for meeting the needs of the group. Community urges participation at work, and it also encourages people to care for others: family, neighbors, others at work, inhabitants of their city, and members of society as a whole.[30] The concept of community is older than the concept of utility, going back to the Greek philosophers. It makes explicit the needs of society and the norm of examining the effect of an act on the group. There can be a conflict between the values of freedom and community. For example, while I might express my personal freedom by polluting, in doing so I also undermine community. If at work I hoard critical information, I may benefit myself but I hinder the work of others and the success of the firm. I undermine community, retard growth and efficiency, perpetrate an injustice, and fail to respect the dignity of other persons. As we mentioned earlier, justice as a social value is essentially the same as justice in the first ethical model (see Figures 7–2 and 7–3).

One technique for using the six market and social values in decision making is presented in Figure 7–4. For a proposed action, each of the applicable six norms is scored. The basis for each score is the degree to which the

[30]See Robert Bellah et al., *Habits of the Heart*.

Does this act or policy respect:

A. FREEDOM OF THE INDIVIDUAL
Does it encourage freedom?
Score: _____

B. INDIVIDUAL RESPONSIBILITY
Will it encourage personal respon-
sibility?
Score: _____

C. GROWTH AND PRODUCTIVITY
Will it encourage growth and pro-
ductivity?
Score: _____

D. DIGNITY OF HUMAN BEINGS
Does it promote human dignity?
Score: _____

E. COMMUNITY AND THE COMMON
GOOD
Will it have a positive effect on
other individuals, other groups,
and society as a whole?
Score: _____

F. JUSTICE
Does it embody fairness and
equity for all?
Score: _____

Ethical rating of proposed act or policy:
Score each of the six norms on a scale 1–6 (poor to good)
If the norm is not applicable, drop it from the calculations.
Total the scores and divide by number of norms scored.
FINAL SCORE: _____

If the final score is 5 or above, the act or policy *is* ethical.
If the final score is 3 or below, the act or policy is *not* ethical.
If the final score is between 3.1 and 4.9, the act or policy requires addi-
tional analysis.
Is one criteria more important?
Are there incapacitating factors?

FIGURE 7–4   Specification of Market and Social Values

action would achieve or violate the corresponding ethical value. The use of numbers in the scoring should not lead us into thinking that we have exact judgments, however.

Let us take the example of the executive's padding her expense account and apply the method presented in Figure 7–4. By padding the expense account, she did exercise personal freedom (score: 5). On the other hand, she did not encourage personal responsibility and so undermined that value (score: 1). The act of padding somewhat hindered growth by shunting funds into uses that were not optimally productive (score: 3). It failed to respect the dignity of persons, since it involved dishonest reporting and the manipulation of data and other people (score: 2). It also undermined community, since it encouraged a self-centered ethic (score: 2). Moreover, it violated justice, since she took funds that were not due her (score: 2). By averaging the numbers we get a score of 2.2, which indicates that the act was not ethical.

Case of the Flammable Crib

Let us use the second model in a case concerning product quality and safety:

> Assume the president of a firm which manufactures baby cribs has the option of installing either of two pads: a less expensive one which barely meets what she believes are overly lenient federal safety requirements regarding flammability (requirements which she is quite sure were established as a result of pressure from the industry) and a more expensive one which she believes is safe. Assume that the safe pad will not bring a higher price for the crib.

Would the use of the cheaper pad respect freedom? At first glance, one might say yes, since both seller and purchaser are free to buy and sell what they please. On the other hand, the purchaser would probably not be aware of the danger of the cheaper pad. If no one else makes a safer pad and announces that fact to customers, the president of the company would actually be reducing freedom. We might give a score of 3 here. Use of the cheaper pad would demonstrate less personal responsibility on the president's part (score: 2). On the other hand, using cheaper materials would probably stimulate growth. We must acknowledge that even accidents add to the gross national product through the cost of repairs, medical bills, and other expenses (score: 5). Turning to social costs, would the use of the cheaper pad undermine human dignity? Probably so, because the manufacturer is saying that lower costs are more important than child safety (score: 1). The act of using the cheaper pad does not respect community and the common good (score: 2). It could also be considered unjust, since consumers presume that a baby crib is safe (score: 1). Summing the scores and dividing by 6 gives us a total score of 2.3. Hence, we judge that using the cheaper pad is not ethical.

This judgment is also the judgment of corporate executives. In a survey of CEOs, 94 percent would use the safe pad even though it was more expensive.[31] Perhaps these executives used a particular shortcut ethical test for proposed actions, the test of asking oneself the following questions: Would I do it if I knew that the decision was to be featured on this evening's TV news? Could my decision bear the sharp scrutiny of a probing reporter?

Case of Cigarette Smoking

Let us use the second model in assessing the ethics of the following case:

> Philip Morris and R. J. Nabisco (formerly R. J. Reynolds) hold about two-thirds of the market for cigarettes in the United States. The U.S. Surgeon General estimates that approximately 350,000 people a year die prematurely because they smoked cigarettes. Medical scientists estimate that 30 to 40 percent of all

---

[31] "Business Executives and Moral Dilemmas," *Business and Society Review*, Spring 1975, p. 55.

who smoke will die of cancer, cardiovascular disease, or chronic obstructive lung disease caused by their smoking. In the face of these health dangers, the number of people in the United States who smoke has declined every year since 1978. Yet the tobacco industry is still very profitable, even in recent years.[32]

Noting the shrinking market in the United States, the tobacco firms have launched a full-sale campaign to sell cigarettes in poor third world countries. They have employed "image" advertising and widespread distribution. Cigarette advertising invariably shows members of the dominant racial or social group smoking cigarettes, generally in pleasant and enviable surroundings. The cigarettes are often sold, not by the pack, but by the individual cigarette, so the poor can afford to purchase them. Sales have increased dramatically. Philip Morris's sales to poor countries have increased more than 30 percent over the last five years, and they now sell cigarettes in 170 countries.

In this case, there are obvious conflicts between many of the market values and social values. Some market values would seem to support the efforts of the tobacco companies. People want the *freedom* to endanger their own lives if they choose (initial score: 5). As long as tobacco firms continue to market cigarettes, both domestically and in poor countries, that enables individuals to exercise *individual responsibility* (initial score: 4). And tobacco farming, along with the manufacturing and distribution of cigarettes, *produces* wealth and provides an income for many families (score: 5).

On the other hand, turning to social values, selling a product that generally shortens people's lives challenges *human dignity*. Do Philip Morris and R. J. Nabisco value their cigarette profits more than the human lives that they are helping to shorten? (score: 1). Cigarettes endanger the life, health, and safety of smokers, family members, and co-workers and so undermine *community and the common good* (score: 2). Using image advertising is probably deceptive, since data show that better educated and more affluent people smoke less. The suggestion that cigarettes are healthy and consumed by people of high status is probably the key to the ethics of the case. In order to maintain profits, the tobacco firms are selling cigarettes to poor people. This seems to be unfair and an infringement of *justice* (score: 2).

Moreover, since the advertising is deceptive and the people in poor countries do not have full information on the health effects of smoking, we will have to revise our estimate of several of the market value scores. For example, the poor in third world countries are not able to exercise full *freedom*, since they do not have correct information (revised score: 2). Moreover, the lack of information also reduces *individual responsibility* (revised score: 2). One is not held fully responsible for choosing to engage in an activity that one is not fully informed about. The final score is 2.3. Hence, it seems clearly unethical for Phillip Morris and other manufacturers to sell

[32] "Smoking and Cancer: What the Cigarette Companies Really Knew," *New York Times*, June 17, 1988, p. 28.

cigarettes to people who are not aware of the serious health hazards of cigarettes.

ETHICS IN BUSINESS EDUCATION

Our difficulties in arriving at a rational judgment in the above cases stem in part from our lack of familiarity with ethics and the classical ethical traditions. Most managers are not immoral, but probably most are amoral. They simply fail to adequately consider moral consequences.[33] Little formal ethics is now taught in American universities. In fact, the competitive, individualistic environment of American universities and professional schools obstructs the development of an ethical sense, that is, a sense of obligation to other human beings. The president of Johns Hopkins University, Steven Muller, maintains that this is the principal failing of universities today: "We fall short in exposing students to values. We don't really provide a value framework to young people who more and more are searching for it." He goes further:

> The failure to rally around a set of values means that universities are turning out potentially highly skilled barbarians: people who are very expert in the laboratory or at the computer or in surgery or in the law courts, but who have no real understanding of their own society.[34]

A recent survey of key business leaders by a leading public accounting firm found that 94 percent felt that the business community is troubled by ethical problems today. Further, these corporate CEOs, directors, business school deans, and members of Congress said that there was an observable difference in the quality of ethics in various parts of the United States. Areas of the country were ranked from most ethical to least as follows: Midwest, Northwest, New England, South, Southwest, West, and East.[35]

Ethics was not always such an unknown. Ethics, or moral philosophy as it is sometimes called, was the vital center of the curriculum of American universities throughout the nineteenth century. There was always a general ethics course that was required of all seniors and, because of its importance, was usually taught by the college president himself.[36] This course integrated

---

[33] Archie B. Carroll, "In Search of the Moral Manager," *Business Horizons*, March-April 1987, pp. 7–15.

[34] Steven Muller, "Universities Are Turning out Highly Skilled Barbarians," *U.S. News and World Report*, November 10, 1980, p. 57.

[35] *Ethics in American Business: An Opinion Survey of Key Business Leaders on Ethical Standards and Behavior* (New York: Touche Ross, 1988), pp. 1, 10.

[36] Douglas Sloan, "The Teaching of Ethics in American Undergraduate Curriculum, 1876–1976," in *Ethics Teaching in Higher Education*, ed. Daniel Callahan and Sissela Bok (New York: Plenum Press, 1980), p. 2. *Ethics Teaching* contains several other excellent essays on the teaching of ethics.

all that the students had learned and finished preparing them for the working world. More specifically, this course sharpened the ethical sensitivity of students and enabled them to deal better with the ethical problems they were about to face.

Educators during this period judged that no nation could survive and prosper without common social and moral values. For a society such as ours, which was and is so fragmented because of differences in ethnic backgrounds, interests and expertise, and allegiances, it was very important to provide a structure whereby students could unify their learning: "The entire college experience was meant above all to be an experience in character development and the moral life, as epitomized, secured, and brought to focus in the moral philosophy course."[37]

Ethics is no longer a part of the education of most college graduates; now few take an ethics course. However, there is new interest in learning ethics in colleges and business schools. The $23 million contributed to Harvard Business School that was mentioned at the beginning of the chapter is an indication of this new interest. John Shad underscored the need for education in ethics when he noted the decline of ethical values in the United States:

> The erosion of ethical attitudes in America since the end of World War II can be attributed to the dispersion of families, rising divorce rates, the Vietnam War, the "permissive" and "me" generations, the drug culture, the affluent society and, most important, the substitution of television for the family, church, and school as the principal purveyor of social mores.
>
> We should redouble our efforts to induce television sponsors to increase the ethical content in interesting and amusing television cartoons and other programming. The business and financial communities also need to inspire and enforce higher ethical standards.[38]

Shad goes on to present his goals for business schools:

> It is not enough for these schools to certify that their graduates have mastered the fundamentals of their profession. The schools must hone their ability to certify that their graduates have the character and integrity to use the knowledge gained for the benefit—rather than the abuse—of society.[39]

Wharton Business School dean Russell Palmer agrees with Shad on the role of business schools. He speaks for his fellow deans when he says,

> We who run America's business schools are concerned about how people behave in business, and our responsibility to influence positive ethical behavior

[37] Ibid., p. 7.
[38] John S. R. Shad, "Business's Bottom Line: Ethics," *New York Times,* July 27, 1987, p. 19.
[39] Ibid.

is considerable and urgent. We must teach not only the skills of management but also the principles of right and wrong.[40]

Most business education experts want to include ethics in the curriculum of undergraduate and graduate programs. How successfully ethics is being brought into college courses and how effective course work is in helping people distinguish right and wrong is still an open question.

However, there is evidence that examining ethical cases and making ethical judgments before one is exposed to real world pressures to act unethically can actually bring about more ethical behavior. In an experiment, college students were presented with a case involving an ethical dilemma and asked to judge a course of action. The experimenters then presented the actual situation to these same students two weeks later. The students tended to act more ethically than did a control group that had not earlier discussed the case. In an actual situation, the pressures of time and of the job push one to compromise.[41]

When considering a dilemma away from the pressures of the actual situation, a person tends to consider the ethical issues in a more objective and balanced way. Also, people tend to predict ethical behavior more often than is warranted by the facts. Yet when someone predicts they will act ethically, that individual is more likely to follow one's own prediction of one's own good behavior.[42] The surprising conclusion: The informed discussion of ethical issues and the making of ethical judgments very likely have a significant effect in bringing about better ethical behavior.

Nevertheless, the models, concepts, and language presented in this chapter are not designed to affect behavior directly but to aid the individual in the development of ethical decision-making skills. The models and norms are not perfect; they will not solve all ethical problems easily. But they are presented as a foundation for additional reflection, use, and improvement.

SUMMARY AND CONCLUSIONS

Businesspeople want to be ethical; most have good instincts that lead them to the morally right decision. Nevertheless, there is a current rash of bribery, fraud, and trade secret stealing. In many cases, managers say that they could not distinguish the right action from the wrong action. Generations now growing up have even fewer moral skills. The media and advertising teach us

---

[40] Russell E. Palmer, "Let's Be Bullish on Ethics," *New York Times*, June 20, 1986, p. 23.

[41] Steven J. Sherman, "On the Self-erasing Nature of Errors of Prediction," *Journal of Personality and Social Psychology*, 39 (March 1980), pp. 211–19.

[42] Ibid., p. 218.

that ethics is relative, and many people have not developed the ability to make ethical judgments.

Businesspeople and educators lament the lack of ethical skills among students and the lack of formal ethics in college curricula. It wasn't always that way; in earlier centuries ethics had an important place in the lives of college students. It is paradoxical that businesspeople have learned precise decision rules for inventory, financing, and other business problems but have almost no models for ethical decision making. If actions eventually reflect this lack of knowledge, the business world could become an ethical jungle. The theories of moral development that we considered in the last chapter show that unethical behavior is more typical of adolescents and young children than of mature men and women.

Ethical values, norms, and language can be developed, learned, and used by businesspeople and can thus become more helpful in the making of business decisions. The ethical principles presented above can be used to solve many ethical dilemmas. The decision rules can be expanded to handle more difficult cases, including cases in which the norms conflict. Moreover, there is evidence that making ethical judgments in the classroom helps to bring about more ethical behavior in the real world. Given all the above, it is not surprising that in the better business schools social policy is well integrated into the curriculum and that business ethics is growing in importance.

DISCUSSION QUESTIONS

1. What is the principal difference between utilitarian norms and rights? Do an individual's intentions have any role in utilitarianism? Do intentions have a role in the theory of rights? Explain.

2. What does John Rawls add to the traditional theory of justice? Compare Rawls's theory and the traditional theory with utilitarianism.

3. Indicate the strengths and weaknesses of using the norms of (a) utility, (b) justice, and (c) rights.

4. Outline the criteria for whistle-blowing. If you were an insider and knew of the payments by defense firms to Pentagon officials for insider information, would you feel that you should blow the whistle? Apply the criteria in deciding this question.

5. How many college students take a course in ethics in the United States? Have you had such a course? What is the advantage of such a course? What is the disadvantage of not having ethics taught?

6. How do the market values and social values of the second model compare with the norms of utility, rights, and justice?

7. Ethically assess the actions of Ivan Boesky. What is the ethical problem with using insider information about financial deals? Which ethical norm is most helpful here?

8. Do you agree with John Shad's assessment of the roots of the lack of ethics today? From your experience, which is the greatest contributing factor? Do you agree with his suggestions regarding television and business schools?

9. Is the primary purpose of studying ethics to influence good behavior or to develop ethical decision-making skills? Does the latter ever affect the former? How?

CASES

Double Expense Account

Frank Waldron is a second-year MBA student at Eastern State University. Although he has had many job offers, he continues to have the university placement office arrange interviews. He reasons that the interview experience will be valuable and a better offer may even come along. Frank has also discovered a way to make money from job interviews.

On one occasion, two firms invited him to New York City for visits to their home offices. He managed to schedule both visits on the same day and then billed each of them for his full travel expenses. In this way he was able to pocket $700. When a friend objected that this was dishonest, Frank replied that each firm had told him to submit an expense account and that therefore he was not taking something to which he had no right. One firm had not asked for receipts, which he interpreted to mean that it intended to make him a gift of the money.

What advice would you give Frank? Is what he is doing unethical? Which norms are most helpful in deciding the question?

Tax Assessment Kickback

You own a large building in a major city. The real estate assessor offers, for a fee, to underestimate the value of your property and save you a substantial amount in real estate taxes. Assume that this is a usual practice in this city. Do you pay the fee? Which norm is most helpful here?

EXERCISE: MEMO TO THE CHIEF EXECUTIVE

You are assistant to the CEO of a firm in a very competitive industry. A competitor has made an important scientific discovery that could give it an advantage that would substantially reduce, but not eliminate, the profits of your company for about a year. A scientist who knows the details of the discovery applies for a job at your firm. There are no legal barriers to hiring the scientist.

The CEO knows that you had some ethics in your MBA program and so asks you to present your advice. In a single page memo to the CEO, indicate the major issues and ethical norms to be used, and present a recommendation.

CHAPTER EIGHT
VALUES, ETHICS, AND CORPORATE PERFORMANCE

Practical men, who believe themselves to be quite exempt from any intellectual influences, are usually the slaves of some defunct economist.

John Maynard Keynes

Making a profit is no more the purpose of the corporation than getting enough to eat is the purpose of life.

Kenneth Mason, when CEO of Quaker Oats

The activities and policies of a business firm and its managers are the clearest demonstration of their values and ethics. We understand much about a person by watching how the person acts; this is also true of a firm. Actions tell us more about business values than do eloquent executive speeches or self-promoting advertising.

Let us examine some well-known examples of business activities and policies:

In 1988, Ford for the second straight year reported higher earnings than General Motors. Ford provided all its workers with a $2,100 profit-sharing bonus. GM allocated $169 million for profit sharing for executives, despite the fact that profits dropped by 26 percent. GM hourly and salaried workers received no bonus.[1]

John J. Nevin, chief executive of Firestone Tire, received a $5.6 million bonus in 1986. Firestone has shrunk from 110,000 employees in 1979 to 53,500 today. But Nevin says he is not embarrassed by the size of the bonus, even though he spent

---

[1] "GM's Bonus Babies," *U.S. News & World Report*, March 2, 1987, p. 42.

about half of the annual shareholder meeting defending it. In 1988, Nevin sold majority interest of Firestone to the Japanese firm Bridgestone.[2]

Investment banking firm Lazard Freres announced that it was raising a $2 billion fund to make investments to aid companies that might be targets of hostile takeovers. Said the firm, "We think there is a major investment opportunity to work cooperatively with managements to bring about change in an orderly fashion and not when forced by a raider."[3]

From 1975 to 1988, Japan's spending for civilian research and development increased from 1.9 to 3.0 percent of its gross national product and continues to rise. During the same period American research and development spending remained at about 1.7 percent of the U.S. gross national product.[4]

These actions and policies stem from the goals, priorities, and values of the firms involved. All of them will be discussed later in the chapter.

The poor economic and poor ethical performance of American firms alarm many. Poor productivity and poor quality generally stem from management weaknesses: preoccupation with short-term financial results, parochialism, lack of cooperation within and among American firms, failure to train and motivate workers, and a chronic inability to rapidly convert innovations into reliable, reasonably priced products.[5] These management limitations are often rooted in the self-centered values of concern for self-fulfillment and personal success and in the measuring of success by personal salary and status.

In this chapter we will examine the effect of values and ethics on a firm's performance. We will note some executives and firms who stand out for their ethics and their concern for people, along with others who seem to show little concern. We will then examine strategies for encouraging better performance among managers and firms.

MANAGEMENT STYLES: FOR SELF OR OTHERS

We will here consider different kinds of managers, management styles, and management actions. The intention is to present good and effective behavior that should be imitated and ineffective management styles that should be avoided.

[2]"How Four Executives View Issue of Compensation at the Top," *Wall Street Journal*, March 28, 1988, p. 6.

[3]Leslie Wayne, "Lazard Seeks To Build an Anti-Takeover Fund," *New York Times*, August 28, 1987, p. 27.

[4]National Science Foundation data, from "Can Japan Keep Its Economy from Hollowing Out?" *Business Week*, Nov. 7, 1988, p. 83.

[5]See *Massachusetts Institute of Technology's Commission on Productivity Report*, (Cambridge, Mass.: MIT, 1988); quoted in "The 21st Century Executive," *U.S. News & World Report*, March 7, 1988, pp. 48–50.

TABLE 8-1   Change of Values Which Undergird the Business System

PROTESTANT ETHIC . . . has shifted to . . .	PLURALISM AND SELF-FULFILLMENT
1. Hard work	1. Salary and status
2. Self-control and sobriety	2. Self-fulfillment
3. Self-reliance	3. Entitlement
4. Perseverance	4. Short-term perspective (if not successful here, move on)
5. Saving and planning ahead	5. Immediate satisfaction (buy on time, little savings)
6. Honesty and observing the "rules of the game"	6. Obey the law (in any case, don't get caught)

To gain some perspective on current management values, recall from Chapter 3 the traditional values that prevailed in the United States. The Protestant ethic urges hard work, self-control, self-reliance, perseverance, saving and planning ahead, honesty, and observing the "rules of the game." Are these traditional values still in place or have a new set of values been embraced by Americans?

From what we have seen in earlier chapters, the values of Americans may have shifted toward short-term goals, such as a high salary, high status, self-fulfillment, entitlement, and immediate satisfaction (See Table 8-1).

Self-Centered Management

American industrial productivity has not risen as fast in the past decade as the productivity of competitor nations.[6] Asian nations have taken entire markets away from American and European firms—cameras, watches, television sets, autos, video cassette recorders—and they are rapidly capturing the computer and computer chip markets. With their earnings, Japanese are now purchasing many American businesses (e.g., Firestone) and much urban and rural real estate.

Executives and managers often blame lessening productivity on unmotivated workers, labor unions, and the intrusiveness of the government. Outside observers, however, point to American managers (their practices and values) as the principal culprits.[7] Following are some of the current failures of many American managers:

> Managers often focus on their own personal careers. Knowing that they will be at their particular jobs only a short time, they do not pursue the long-term benefit of their firms.

[6]See, for example, Thomas Peters, *Thriving on Chaos* (New York: Knopf, 1987).
[7]*Commission on Productivity Report.*

They choose measurable, short-term returns, because they are pressured by superiors and institutional investors to show immediate results.

They allow competitiveness and defensiveness to prevail over cooperation and better communication among workers. Others take their cue from their managers' desires for quick results, money, status, and power.

Quality improvements and productivity gains stem from a cooperative, goal-oriented climate in a firm; from encouraging the new ideas of the average worker; from research and development; and from investing capital and time in long-term efforts to raise productivity. Research and development brings forth new ideas and products. When we sacrifice research to cut costs, we sacrifice future markets and long-term profits. Focusing primarily on quarterly or year-end increases in market share or return on investment does not provide a long enough time horizon to generate gains in quality and productivity. In fact, as concern for personal success and power has increased, productivity gains have decreased.

Rather than develop new products and engage in research and development, companies have added lawyers and accountants to their staffs. These "paper entrepreneurs" do not devise better products or services. Rather, they provide information and advice on less risky uses of already existing resources. And they add to overhead costs and thus drag down productivity.

Executive Compensation as a Corporate Strategy

American CEO and top management salaries are higher than those of any other nation. Given that self-esteem is often measured by salary and that CEOs help decide their own salaries, it is not surprising that their salaries are so high. In the ten years prior to 1987, CEO salaries rose an average of 12.2 percent annually. During the same period, hourly workers' pay rose an average of 6.1 percent annually, inflation averaged 6.5 percent, and profits rose a mere 0.75 percent. Consultant Tom Peters says, "The executive compensation system has no coherence, makes no sense, and, at a time when there's a requirement for violent restructuring in companies, has a very negative impact."[8]

The current attempt of American firms to encourage better communication and more trust and cooperation is undermined by compensating executives at such a high rate. When trying to cut costs, top managers urge restraint on the part of hourly and salaried workers. Managers urge workers to settle for little additional compensation. CEOs have also cut wages, closed plants, and urged early retirement. Some of this has been necessary, but increasing

[8]"Corporate Chiefs' Pay Far Outpaces Inflation and the Gains of Staff," *Wall Street Journal*, March 28, 1988, pp. 1, 6. The executive compensation figures are from a study by Sibson & Co.

executive compensation does not convince workers of the need to cut costs. Since higher CEO compensation is often public knowledge and is so clearly self-serving, it supports an attitude of "everyone for himself" and "get what you can, while you can." Comparing the Japanese system of executive compensation with our own, Peters says:

> I'm swayed by one Japanese practice—in hard times management takes the hit first, and then the workers. [Here], in general, management doesn't take the same hit that the work force does—which is a total disgrace. [It is a] grotesque inequity.[9]

James F. Bere, chief executive of Borg-Warner, says that the pay system as a measure of executive performance "is creaking." Huge pay packages also disturb Donald Frey, chief executive of Bell & Howell. He says that nobody is worth the multimillion-dollar pay packages that some are getting, and he points to a problem:

> More in executive suites than elsewhere, pay means status. A lot of CEO's rate themselves—their sense of self-worth—by how much money they're paid. Being on the list of the top 10 salaries is an ego trip. It has nothing to do with what they are going to spend that money on.[10]

High executive compensation has several justifications. It can be (1) a reward for superior performance, (2) an amount that reflects the CEO's worth on the market, (3) a signal to others in the firm about relative worth to the firm, and (4) a just return for contributions. Executive compensation packages are often decided on the basis of the first two purposes, with the second two largely neglected. But determining compensation for managers is but a small portion of a chief executive's responsibilities. Let us now examine other management style and ethical issues.

Managing People and Capital

When managers speak of the tendency to seek immediate fulfillment in the workplace, they often blame blue-collar workers for absenteeism, tardiness, substance abuse, a lack of willingness to work overtime, and a lack of pride in work. Nevertheless, an excessive focus on immediate personal goals begins with managers. In addition, managers often use a narrow criterion for

---

[9] Ibid., p. 1; see also Kenneth Mason, "Four Ways to Overpay Yourself Enough," *Harvard Business Review* 88 (July-August 1988): 69–74; Warner Woodworth, "The Scandalous Pay of the Corporate Elite," *Business and Society Review*, Spring 1987, pp. 22–26.

[10] "How Four Chief Executives View Issue of Compensation at the Top," *Wall Street Journal* March 28, 1988, p. 6.

success—this year's or this quarter's return on investment and increase in market share.

Bonus plans are generally based on last year's performance. However, managers often expect to be in their current job just a few years and then to move to a better position elsewhere. A newcomer who takes a manager's place will reap the reward of better performance. Thus there is little incentive to plan for the long term. Nevertheless, substantial growth is only accomplished when a firm and its managers plan for the long term.

The larger and more diversified a firm is, the less able top management is to know specific products, markets, and employees. Because of its distance from customers, production, new product ideas, and the public, management turns to what it *can* understand—the only control mechanism that is then available—"the numbers". Managers then rely on return on investment, return on equity, and other quantitative indices of success. This reliance also tends to focus attention on short-term results. Moreover, not only does this short-term thinking tend to reduce productivity, research, and risk taking, but it also makes managers less likely to examine the ethics of management decisions. That is, the same pressure to achieve short-term results in the "numbers game" also short-circuits attempts to examine ethical issues.

Takeovers and mergers have resulted in the closing of facilities and the loss of thousands of jobs. A quick multimillion-dollar profit for a few people often coincides with the loss of family income for thousands.

To summarize this section: the principal underlying cause of poor quality and lessened productivity is the shortsightedness of managers. Managers often take the easy way out; they prefer measurable, short-term results so that they appear to be doing their job well. This is the same sort of motivation that leads to unethical behavior. Therefore, it is fair to conclude that many of the values that bring lower productivity also undermine ethics in the workplace. The claim is not that insuring long-run profitability will automatically bring about better ethics. However, it *will* carry us some distance in the right direction. Some executives, noted for their ethics, run very profitable firms. Let us look at some of them.

LEADERSHIP DETERMINES ETHICS AND VALUES

James E. Burke is CEO of Johnson & Johnson (J&J), whose products include bandaids, baby oil, and Tylenol. He became known to Americans when someone placed cyanide in Tylenol capsules, replaced the bottles on store shelves, and waited for a customer to consume the poison. When seven people died, James Burke and J&J were faced with how to respond. The options were these: (1) Since J&J was not responsible for the poisonings, the company could try to ride it out and work to limit damage to the product's image, (2) J&J could stop manufacturing Tylenol (because its image had been ruined) but not recall the product. (3) J&J could recall all unused Tylenol (at a cost of $100 million), be honest with customers, and try to win them back with safer redesigned packaging. The FBI recommended not recalling the unused Tylenol, since that would encourage future poisoners. In making their decision, James Burke and other managers relied on J&J's much valued Credo (See Figure 8–1).

Most company ethical codes state a set of rules, but the J&J code states the moral obligations the company considers itself to have. These obligations in order of importance, are to (1) customers, (2) employees, (3) the communities in which the company works and lives, and (4) stockholders. The credo outlines obligations to stakeholders in a practical, ethical fashion. Burke says that at J&J "we believe strongly in three things: decentralization, managing for the long term, and the ethical principles embodied in our Credo." Regarding the credo, Burke says, "The Credo is our common denominator. It guides us in everything we do. It represents an attempt to codify what we can all agree upon since we have highly independent managers."[11]

Given its credo, J&J had but one real option in the Tylenol poisoning case. Since they believed that their first obligation was to people who use their products, they recalled the Tylenol at considerable expense. They took a $100 million loss but were able to retain the Tylenol brand name. Burke agreed to be interviewed on "60 Minutes" and several TV talk shows; he became a one-man campaign for the rescue of the image of big business in America. According to Burke's own summary, the reason the Tylenol rescue succeeded was "not that we did anything dazzling or clever, but just that we are a company that tries to do the right thing."[12] Because of their honesty in this crisis, Burke and J&J gained even greater stature. Burke reflects on the aftermath of the decisions regarding Tylenol:

> Even in the response to our handling of Tylenol, there were things I found discouraging. All we did was what we thought any responsible company would have done in our position—and people reacted as if this were some radical new departure for American business. My God, what did people *expect* we'd do? The amount of mistrust and cynicism out there is really depressing.[13]

People skills are vital for managers at J&J. According to Burke, "An important skill is to be able to help people to believe that they can accomplish

[11] Laura L. Nash, "Johnson & Johnson's Credo," in *Corporate Ethics: A Prime Business Asset* (New York: The Business Roundtable, 1988), pp. 80–82.

[12] Laurence Shames, *The Big Time: The Harvard Business School's Most Successful Class and How It Shaped America* (New York: Mentor, 1986), p. 159.

[13] Ibid.

Our Credo

We believe our first responsibility is to the doctors, nurses and patients, to mothers and all others who use our products and services. In meeting their needs everything we do must be of high quality. We must constantly strive to reduce our costs in order to maintain reasonable prices. Customers' orders must be serviced promptly and accurately. Our suppliers and distributors must have an opportunity to make a fair profit.

We are responsible to our employees, the men and women who work with us throughout the world. Everyone must be considered as an individual. We must respect their dignity and recognize their merit. They must have a sense of security in their jobs. Compensation must be fair and adequate, and working conditions clean, orderly and safe. Employees must feel free to make suggestions and complaints. There must be equal opportunity for employment, development and advancement for those qualified. We must provide competent management, and their actions must be just and ethical.

We are responsible to the communities in which we live and work and to the world community as well. We must be good citizens—support good works and charities and bear our fair share of taxes. We must encourage civic improvements and better health and education. We must maintain in good order the property we are privileged to use, protecting the environment and natural resources.

Our final responsibility is to our stockholders. Business must make a sound profit. We must experiment with new ideas. Research must be carried on, innovative programs developed and mistakes paid for. New equipment must be purchased, new facilities provided and new products launched. Reserves must be created to provide for adverse times. When we operate according to these principles, the stockholders should realize a fair return.

Johnson & Johnson

FIGURE 8-1   Johnson & Johnson's Corporate Credo

much more than they think they can. I believe that all of us can do 10, 20, 30 times more than we might think."[14]

Burke tells a revealing story about himself. In 1953 he was twenty-eight, had been a brand manager at Proctor & Gamble for three years, and was

[14] Thomas R. Horton, *What Works for Me: 16 CEOs Talk About Their Careers and Commitments* (New York: Random House, 1986), p. 22.

offered the opportunity to run the Munich office of Radio Free Europe. Most of his friends thought it was a terrific opportunity and a great adventure for a talented young man. But Burke still had doubts and asked an experienced friend who was with the government in Washington. Burke goes on:

> He asked me how much time I had, and I said, "As much as you want, sir." Then, for the next two and a half hours, he absolutely tore me apart, completely eviscerated me for even considering taking on the Radio Free Europe assignment. Among other things he said, "One of the troubles with this world of ours is people like you have the pretensions that you are ready to take on an important public service job with no real background that qualifies you. The fact is that you graduated from Harvard Business School, have three years of business experience, and that's all you've got. To take that job at Radio Free Europe would be a great disservice to this country."
>
> I was somewhat shaken, but I knew immediately that he was right. I simply was not mature enough to think of anything other than the fun of being a big shot and making more money than I'd ever dreamt of making at that age. As I left his office, he put his arm on my shoulder and said, "Son, stay in business until you have demonstrated what you are capable of doing. Then, if you still want a Washington job, let me know...."
>
> I learned several things from that interview. One was about myself, for he gave me a sense of reality. But I also learned something about giving advice to young people. You need to tell them not what they want to hear, but what you really believe. He had been forthright enough to tell me the truth, and that meeting was an important turning point for me.[15]

James Burke is a man of integrity. Moreover, he builds on a company tradition of respect for family values and the dignity of all men and women.

Executives as Moral Leaders

We will now spotlight a few additional business leaders because of their contributions to business, business values, and business ethics. They have not been selected because of the financial success of their firms, although these firms are generally the leaders in their industry. They are discussed here because their values and actions may serve as models for all businesspeople.

Physician and biochemist *Roy Vagelos,* CEO of Merck & Co., heads a very successful pharmaceutical company. Merck spends more money on research and development than any of its competitors (11 percent of sales, or $530 million in 1987).[16] Among Merck's winners is the drug Mevacor, an anticholesterol drug. Of Merck's business successes, *Business Week* had this to say:

---

[15] Ibid, pp. 22–23.
[16] "The Miracle Company," *Business Week,* October 19, 1987, pp. 84, 90.

Merck's management has done a better job of managing its business than anyone we can think of in its industry or, for that matter, in U.S. business. Merck management has not been pressured into quick-fix strategies by Wall Street the way so many others have. Its reward: Investors now can't seem to get enough of Merck.[17]

Merck developed a drug called ivermectin twelve years ago for treating parasites and ticks common in dogs and farm animals. After years of testing by the World Health Organization, a version of the drug was found to be effective in combating a disease called *river blindness*, which is common in some third world countries. River blindness results from the bite of a fly, which deposits a parasite under the skin. That parasite can grow to two feet long and can generate millions more parasites; when it gets to the eye, it causes blindness. The disease afflicts an estimated 18–40 million people in Africa, the Middle East, and Latin America; roughly 340,000 have gone blind. The disease had been untreatable. But now a dose of Merck's tablets every six months can prevent the ravages of the disease. The problem: Most people who need the drug are extremely poor and cannot pay for it.

Merck decided to donate the drug as long as legitimate local medical personnel administered it. Both Merck and WHO monitor its use. The cost to Merck is substantial, and the firm does not want to set a precedent so that poor nations will expect drug companies to donate drugs. This would discourage research into similar drugs.[18]

Vagelos describes what gives such zeal to Merck employees:

It's understanding that the most important thing you can contribute as a human being is improving the lives of millions of people. We do that every year, introducing drugs and vaccines that will change the course of diseases or prevent diseases. And what could be better than that?[19]

It is this vision that lead Vagelos and Merck to donate the drug to millions of poor to prevent river blindness. Merck and Vagelos have received much favorable attention for their generosity.

Thomas S. Monaghan is the founder and owner of Domino's Pizza, the largest pizza delivery firm in the world. Domino's has 4,500 stores, 180 of them outside the United States in ten countries. Sales rose 35 percent to top $1.9 billion in 1987.[20] Tom Monaghan's father died when he was four years

[17] "Merck's Miracle Was Hard-Earned," *Business Week*, October 19, 1987, p. 154.

[18] Michael Waldholz, "Merck to Donate Drug for 'River Blindness,'" *Wall Street Journal*, October 22, 1987, p. 38.

[19] "Let's Hear It from the Winner," *Fortune*, January 19, 1988, p. 38.

[20] "Tom Monaghan: The Fun-loving Prince of Pizza," *Business Week*, February 8, 1988, p. 90.

old, and his mother was forced to place him in foster homes and a Catholic orphanage. Although Monaghan disliked the discipline of the orphanage, he credits Sister Berarda with giving him a sense of himself and helping him form his strong human and religious values.

Domino's has been successful because of its formula of quality products, quick delivery, and good customer treatment. Monaghan also emphasizes the Golden Rule to all Domino's employees: Do unto others as you would have them do unto you. Tom Peters says of Monaghan and his autobiography, "*Pizza Tiger* has it all—a terrific tale, simple virtues, and practical lessons for a complex business world. If there were 500 Tom Monaghans to run the *Fortune 500*, America's competitive woes would be over."[21] (The title of the book alludes to the fact that Monaghan owns the Detroit Tigers.)

Domino's promotes people from within the organization, which means that men and women who began as cooks or delivery people have become vice presidents. Domino's has many training programs and encourages good communications, loyalty, and a strong esprit de corps.

Monaghan developed a set of priorities for himself and his organization. For him, a person's spiritual well-being should be the top priority, followed by social, mental, and physical well-being; financial success should be last. Monaghan, on the basis of his priorities, thinks that when any Domino's worker experiences a conflict between family and work, the worker should give preference to family. Monaghan acknowledges that he and Margie, his wife of twenty-seven years, had a rough spot some years ago. They sought outside professional help and found their relationship became stronger and more loving. He recommends the same solution for any Domino's employee with a marital problem.

Tom Monaghan had a deep, active religious faith; his Catholic faith means much to him. He attends Mass, says the Rosary daily, and fasted on Fridays for about six months. There is a Catholic and a Protestant chaplain on the staff at Domino's headquarters outside Detroit. Monaghan urges all people to examine their religious roots in order to make their faith and the values stemming from it real and active.

In the spring of 1987, Monaghan formed a group of Catholic presidents of organizations. The group is called *Legatus* (Latin for ambassador, taken from St. Paul's epistles, "ambassador for Christ"). Legatus, which includes spouses, meets monthly in order to encourage the moral and spiritual development of members and to help them empower others in their organizations to grow. Because of the hard work of Monaghan, Legatus now has chapters in Chicago, New York, Boston, Washington, Pittsburgh, and Los Angeles.

---

[21] Quoted on back cover Tom Monaghan with Robert Anderson, *Pizza Tiger* (New York: Random House, 1986).

The members pray together, share insights, and listen to and challenge guest experts. They hope to generate spiritual, ethical, and human development in their own firms and in business as a whole.

Felix Rohatyn is undoubtedly the best-known and probably the best-connected investment banker in America; he is senior partner at Lazard Freres & Co. Rohatyn is a "soft-spoken man, polite without being warm, who doodles with geometric precision on unlined white paper."[22] He was born in Austria and came to the United States in 1942 to escape the Nazi persecution of Jews. For twenty years he has been the principal deal maker at Lazard. Lazard reports three times the profit per employee as its closest rival, Morgan Stanley, and it leaves other competitors such as Solomon Brothers, First Boston, and Merrill Lynch even further behind.[23] Rohatyn worked as a consultant with Harold Geneen when Geneen put together ITT. Although Geneen has a reputation as a pirate, Rohatyn is slow to criticize him. Geneen gave him his start. Rohatyn was one of the earliest and most skillful consultants to firms involved in giant mergers, yet he feels that the merger mania has now gone too far. In 1975, Rohatyn engineered a deal that made New York City, which faced bankruptcy, solvent again.

He is sharply critical of many of his peers in investment banking. Examining the October 19, 1987, stock market crash, he says that the United States had done practically nothing to prevent a recurrence.[24] He notes that the primary purpose of the stock and bond markets is to provide investment funds for organizations that need capital. Yet the markets do not accomplish that well:

> The fundamental weakness in the securities markets, world-wide, is the result of excessive speculation, excessive use of credit, and inadequate regulation. This speculative behavior is not driven by individuals, as was the case in the 1920s, but by such institutions as pension funds, banks, savings and loans, and insurance companies. In many cases, these institutions are backed by federal government guarantees. Curbing speculation and promoting investment must be the objective of reform.[25]

He points out it is in the self-interest of investment bankers to complete "deals" (mergers or acquisitions), because their fees depend on such deals. The rewards of completing a deal occur even in the case where a banker's

---

[22] "The Last Emperor of Wall Street: How Michel David-Weill Rules the Private World of Lazard Freres," *Business Week*, May 30, 1988, p. 65.

[23] Ibid., p. 67.

[24] Felix G. Rohatyn, "Institutional 'Investor' or 'Speculator'?" *Wall Street Journal*, June 24, 1988, p. 14.

[25] Ibid., p. 24.

own analysis indicates that the merger is not in the best interest of the client. In any case, Rohatyn thinks that investment bankers' fees are much too large. Rohatyn feels, according to one biographer, that he has a "responsibility to save capitalism from itself—that greed, ideological rigidity, or the simple lack of competence outside their narrow arenas of expertise can blind the movers and shakers of the business world to the risks of financial instability they are promoting."[26]

The following are among Rohatyn's suggestions for encouraging investment and cooling speculation:

> Impose a 50 percent tax on the profit of securities held for less than a year. This tax would apply to individuals, corporations, partnerships, and currently tax-free institutions. At the same time, reduce capital gains taxes on securities held for more than five years to 15 percent.

> Sharply limit the type and proportion of speculative investments held by federally insured institutions.[27]

Rohatyn's firm is building up a fund to help companies faced with hostile takeovers, as was mentioned at the beginning of the chapter. Rohatyn has had considerable influence on the firm's policies. He takes into account the public interest, even in cases where it would mean limiting his own and his firm's fees. That is the earmark of good leadership.

Executives and Firms That Pursue Self-Interest

Most executives take their responsibilities seriously and are concerned about all the stakeholders of their firm. On the other hand, there are some executives who focus exclusively on dollar return or personal gain—and that often hurts society and ultimately hinders the efficient operation of the firm. Some conglomerates, such as Litton Industries, Gulf + Western, and ITT, have a long-standing reputation for self-interested behavior. Whether you are a customer, employee, or supplier of these firms, it is wise to check your contract closely and leave little to a handshake.

Thomas V. Jones was born in 1920 and has been CEO of Northrop since he was thirty-eight years old. Educated as an engineer, for decades he has been the primary salesperson for the firm. Northrop's main business is defense, and its customers are mostly governments. Jones is on a first-name basis with many foreign heads of state. He is also a friend of Ronald Reagan. Before joining Northrop, he spent four years in Brazil advising its military on aircraft needs. Northrop's main products are the F-20 Tigershark fighter

---

[26] Ralph Nader and William Taylor, "Felix Rohatyn: The Interstitial Man," in *The Big Boys* (New York: Pantheon, 1986), p. 210.

[27] Rohatyn, "Institutional 'Investor' or 'Speculator'?" p. 14.

plane, the Stealth bomber, and the guidance system for the MX missile. CBS's "60 Minutes" criticized the MX guidance system for being unreliable.

The F-20 Tigershark was developed at Northrop's own expense ($800 million) and was designed as a lower-cost, reliable aircraft. This was a risky venture. Most military aircraft are developed with government funds, and governments have very deep pockets. Northrop's earlier fighter aircraft, the F-5, was relatively simple. From 1962, hundreds were sold to Iran, Korea, Greece, South Vietnam, Canada, Norway, Saudi Arabia, Taiwan, and many other countries. Jones did much of the selling himself, being a personal friend of the king of Saudi Arabia.[28]

For two decades Jones has criticized the defense industry's failure to design military hardware that was reliable and affordable and its obsession with technical sophistication. Military brass always want the latest in sophisticated electronic gear. Military contractors oblige them. This generally means that the plane, missile, tank, or gun is high cost, difficult to operate and maintain, and unreliable. Jones has also long urged fixed-cost contracting, in which contractors could not pass on increased costs to the government.

In the defense business, a single contract with a single buyer (a government) can mean the survival of a firm. So U.S. defense firms have learned how to do such business: They give cash payments to government officials and intermediaries who provide access. However, such payments are bribes, are illegal, and undermine the free market system. When Lockheed acknowledged that it had spent millions of dollars in overseas payments, the board of Lockheed forced the resignation of its chairman and president.

As early as the 1960s, Jones established a secret fund in Paris to launder money for illegal political contributions in the United States. Northrop was involved in a public scandal in the 1970s when it gave a bribe of $450,000 to two Saudi Arabian generals. In 1974, Jones pleaded guilty to illegally contributing $150,000 to the Nixon campaign. He could have been sent to prison for five years but instead was fined $5,000.

In 1983, Northrop hired a Korean lobbyist, a former South Korean presidential aid and national assemblyman, Park Chong Kyu, to obtain orders for its F-20 fighter aircraft in Korea. In 1980, before his connection with Northrop, Park spent time in jail in Korea for "influence peddling." He was scheduled to receive $55 million for getting Korea to purchase the F-20s. Park had already been paid $6 million when he died in 1986. The case is still being investigated.[29]

---

[28] Ralph Nader and William Taylor, "Thomas Jones: Life of a Salesman," in *The Big Boys* (New York: Pantheon, 1986), p. 352.

[29] "Northrop Signed on Secret Lobbyist to Try to Sell F-20 to Korea," *Wall Street Journal*, June 8, 1988, pp. 1, 10. By permission of *Wall Street Journal*, © Dow Jones & Company, Inc. (1988). All rights reserved worldwide.

As an admirer of Jones put it, "Jones did a phenomenal job with the company. When I joined in 1963, the company had just broken the $300 million mark. Now it sells more than $3 billion. I do think he tends to cut corners a bit ethically sometimes.... He'll do absolutely whatever is required for his company."[30] The imprint of Jones on Northrop is summed up in the comments of a high-ranking Air Force procurement officer: "Jones ran the company from stem to stern. When Tom Jones drops dead, that's going to be the end of the company."[31]

In 1988, Northrop was fighting several suits brought by its own employees. One suit claimed $400 million in false labor charges for work purportedly done on the secret B-2 Stealth bomber; another claimed false billings and product testing on equipment for the MX missile and the air-launched cruise missile. In the latter case, Northrop acknowledged "irregularities in the testing" of the equipment. Northrop also admitted that "there have been management lapses and errors of judgment" in making guidance equipment for the MX missile.[32]

When Northrop, as part of the settlement of a shareholder suit, acknowledged its large-scale overseas payments in the 1970s, it agreed to elect a majority of outside directors and to have the executive committee be entirely made up of outside directors. The new executive committee then investigated the illegal domestic and foreign political contributions. They issued a sixty-page report that contained several reservations:

> The Executive Committee is not convinced that Mr. Jones has communicated fully and openly with the Auditors, with the Committee and with the Board of Directors itself or recognizes the seriousness of his involvement in the matters addressed by the committee. The Committee is disappointed that Mr. Jones failed to concede his lack of knowledge regarding certain of the matters discussed in this Report. The Committee also is concerned that Mr. Jones failed to acknowledge his familiarity with matters which the committee is persuaded that he knew or should have known.[33]

Jones is still chair of Northrop. He weathered the storm following Northrop's unethical activities in the 1970s, and he undoubtedly feels that he can survive the latest crises.

Paul A. Bilzerian was thirty-eight years old when he named himself chairman (CEO) of the Singer Company after a successful $1.8 billion hostile

[30] Nader and Taylor, "Thomas Jones..." p. 373.

[31] Ibid., p. 375.

[32] "Northrop Ex-Workers Win Round in Suit Alleging Phony Billing on Stealth Project," *Wall Street Journal*, July 6, 1988, p. 24. By permission of *Wall Street Journal*, © Dow Jones & Company, Inc. (1988). All rights reserved worldwide.

[33] Nader and Taylor, "Thomas Jones..." pp. 377–78.

takeover. Since then he has actively sought buyers for his firm so that he could parlay his money into additional millions.[34] He had never run a successful company and said, "I don't think I want to be a manager."[35]

Bilzerian, a "high-school dropout, Vietnam veteran, Harvard Business School misfit, real-estate speculator, multimillionaire raider," has also "ridden roughshod over the securities laws of the U.S." The United States Securities and Exchange Commission (SEC) is investigating Bilzerian for "insider trading, 'parking' of stock in accounts to conceal its true ownership, false public disclosure documents filed with the SEC, aiding and abetting the keeping of false books and records, conspiracy to violate the securities laws, and tax fraud."[36] For example, he secretly purchased and parked 58,000 shares of H. H. Robertson Company stock with Jefferies & Company. Boyd Jefferies, the chairman of that firm, has pleaded guilty to two felony securities law violations.

Bilzerian made his money early in real estate speculation, sometimes in partnership with Edward DeBartolo, the Ohio shopping center builder, who is presently under indictment in federal court by the SEC for alleged securities law violations. Bilzerian "often voiced contempt for the Eastern establishment he encountered at Harvard" but felt comfortable with the "wealthy veterans of the rough and tumble real-estate world."[37] He is presently building a new $3,000,000 house which will be ten times larger than his present one. The new house will feature two pools, basketball and tennis courts, and a 2,000-square-foot game room; the grounds will feature a lake for water skiing.

Bilzerian garnered $82 million in a failed bid for Cluet Peabody. He drove the price of the stock up and then sold his shares. In this raid and subsequent raids on Hammermill, Armco Steel, and other firms, Bilzerian concealed the amount of stock he had purchased, "parked" stock with Jefferies & Company and others, and concealed his relationship with DeBartolo, even though SEC securities regulations demand full disclosure of these items.[38]

Bilzerian was probably careless when he forced control of Singer. He is now losing money rapidly paying the high interest on the bonds he negotiated to purchase the firm.

Steven O'Neil was president and part owner of Film Recovery Systems, a small company in the Chicago metropolitan area that specialized in recov-

---

[34] "Can Paul Bilzerian Fatten Singer for the Kill?" *Business Week*, May 16, 1988, p. 43.

[35] "Boone's New Partner," *Fortune*, March 28, 1988, p. 92.

[36] "Secret Dealing Helped Paul Bilzerian Make Takeover Bids Work," *Wall Street Journal*, May 10, 1988, p. 1.

[37] "Paul Bilzerian Still Don't Get No Respect," *Business Week*, November, 23, 1987, p. 62.

[38] Ibid., p. 14.

ering silver from used film. Most of the workers were Polish or Mexican immigrants who spoke little or no English. Stefan Golab, a sixty-one-year-old Polish immigrant who worked at Film Recovery died on February 10, 1983. The Cook County medical examiner determined that his death was due to cyanide poisoning.

In order to recover the silver, Film Recovery mixed the used film with cyanide and water in large open vats. The vats released cyanide into the open air where it was breathed by the workers. Management was aware of the danger but failed to warn workers or equip them with protection from the toxic chemicals. Moreover, some company personnel had defaced the pictorial poison warnings on the chemical drums.[39]

O'Neil, plant manager Charles Kirchbaum, and plant foreman Daniel Rodrigues were all found guilty of murder in the death of Stefan Golab. The court decided that they had responsibility for the safety and lives of their workers. Their responsibility was even greater than normal, since the workers did not understand English. They were sentenced to twenty-five years in prison and fined $10,000 each. The conviction is for murder, so they will not be eligible for parole for twelve and a half years.[40] This is the first time managers have been held responsible for the death of a plant worker.

Each of the above CEOs had a profound impact on the ethics and the values of the firm he led. Any manager has an impact on peers and subordinates that is proportionate to his or her status in the firm. Let us now consider how a climate of responsibility is maintained in a firm.

ETHICS FOR STRATEGIC PLANNING

This section examines methods for making social responsibility and good ethics a part of the fabric of the organization. Our objective is to understand how to achieve responsibility and accountability in the firm. Ethics and corporate strategy cannot be divorced. To do so is an ethical act itself—a wrongful act. Management scholar Edwin Murray puts the point well:

> As an executive of a company, however small, the strategist becomes a leader of a social institution and bears a responsibility to society for which he or she will be held accountable by other modern-day economic, political, and social institutions. Moreover, in selecting economic and other social goals and policies to pursue, the strategist implicitly is acting upon a moral philosophy and is com-

---

[39] "Job Safety Becomes a Murder Issue," *Business Week*, August 6, 1984, p. 23.

[40] "Ex-Officials Get 25-Year Sentences in Worker's Death," *Wall Street Journal*, July 2, 1985, p. 14.

municating his or her values and expectations to organizational subordinates. The moral responsibility of the leader is *intrinsically* part and parcel of the strategist's role. Therefore, the challenge for the manager is not whether to include ethical theory and criteria in strategic choice, but rather when and how.[41]

An executive or a firm cannot develop a strategic plan without a clearly conceived purpose. "Purpose is fundamental to any coherent account of strategy that recognizes the importance of choice."[42] Management ethics scholars Freeman and Gilbert tie strategic planning and ethics together; they argue that "the key to understanding the revolution in management is values and ethics, and the role that they play in organizations."[43]

An effective and successful firm such as IBM, McDonald's, 3M, and Domino's, has a strong set of values, a clear mission, and employees dedicated to achieving that mission.[44] Values and ethics are important to any firm. Responsible dealing with public issues (e.g., employment opportunity, pollution, relations with the local community) is vital for CEOs and managers. Many firms have a high-level committee or a staff that works on these issues.[45]

Most firms have integrated dealing with issues that involve ethics and social responsibility into planning and strategy.[46] Evidence shows that successful firms are also more ethical. Many investigations of corporate social responsibility and good financial performance have shown that the two go together. A recent study of 130 large firms showed that those which were generous in contributing to social causes and did not break the law were the best financial performers. Firms which did not contribute and which were repeat illegal offenders were the poorest performers.[47]

---

[41] Edwin A. Murray, Jr., "Ethics and Corporate Strategy," in *Corporations and the Common Good*, ed. Robert B. Dickie and Leroy S. Rouner (Notre Dame: University of Notre Dame Press, 1986), p. 115.

[42] R. Edward Freeman and Daniel R. Gilbert, Jr., *Corporate Strategy and the Search for Ethics* (Englewood Cliffs, N.J.: Prentice-Hall, 1988), p. 19.

[43] Ibid., p. 6.

[44] Peters and Waterman, *In Search of Excellence*.

[45] See, for example, Michael Useem, "The Rise of the Political Manager," *Sloan Management Review* 27 (Fall 1985): 15–26; see also the following series of articles: Stephen E. Littlejohn, "New Trends in Public Issue Identification and Resolution," *California Management Review* 29 (Fall 1986): 109–123; Steven L. Wartick and Robert E. Rude, "Issues Management: Corporate Fad or Function?" ibid., pp. 109–140; Thomas G. Marx, "Integrating Public Affairs and Strategic Planning," ibid., pp. 141–160.

[46] Edwin M. Epstein, "The Corporate Social Policy Process," *California Management Review* 29 (Spring 1987): 99–114.

[47] Richard E. Wokutck and Barbara A. Spencer, "Corporate Saints and Sinners," *California Management Review* 29 (Winter 1987): 62–77.

Public Affairs Efforts Can Be Abused

Effectively dealing with public issues that touch on the concerns of the firm has become a part of strategic management. However, lobbying the government and using "issues management" in an ill-informed way create dangers for a firm, for business as a whole, and for society. Often the government is asked to provide immediate aid, and the long-term effect of this intervention is not examined. An issues manager who worked at Ford is highly critical of the process:

> My colleagues believed that whatever would benefit the company was all right for them to seek. They believed that any method that would secure those benefits was all right for them to use. They believed that pursuing corporate advantage through the public-policy process was their duty and right. Whatever my colleagues felt like doing, they did.
> Corporatism made my colleagues complacent as well as self-indulgent. They had an unquestioning faith in their approach to public policy. They thought their corporatist schemes were good for God and good for society. They didn't think that Ford's getting what it wanted meant that others would get less.[48]

The message again: Short-term advantage can blind managers to long-term goals. What was good for Ford in the short run was not good for society, nor even for Ford in the long run.

Strategic planning and public affairs are only a part of the responsibilities of the CEO. Let us now turn to the CEO and the board which the CEO must report to.

Role and Responsibilities of the CEO and the Board of Directors

The *CEO* of a firm is ultimately responsible for the firm's success or failure. The CEO sets policy, decides on new products or services, establishes budgets, and sets the mission and tone of the firm. The CEO is the person most responsible for the values, ethics, and climate of the firm. A generation ago, a CEO did not have to be overly concerned with the attitudes of employees or citizens. Today this is no longer true.

The responsibility of the *board of directors* is (1) to hire, evaluate the performance of, and possibly fire the CEO, and (2) to approve major policies and actions. The oversight role of the board is vital to the effective functioning of the corporation. It is also necessary if that firm is to act ethically.[49] Yet the current constitution of corporate boards presents serious problems. Har-

---

[48] Paul H. Weaver, *The Suicidal Corporation* (New York: Simon & Schuster, 1988); excerpted in *California Management Review* 30 (Spring 1988): 136.

[49] E. Eugene Arthur, "The Ethics of Corporate Governance," *Journal of Business Ethics* 6 (January 1987): 59–70.

old S. Geneen, who is a member of many boards and was a tight-fisted, hard-nosed CEO himself at ITT, is sharply critical of boards: "Among the boards of directors of Fortune 500 companies, I estimate that 95% are not fully doing what they are legally, morally, and ethically supposed to do. And they couldn't, even if they wanted to."[50]

Geneen and others before him have pointed out why board members are unable to effectively discharge their responsibilities.[51] The principal reasons are these:

1. Many board members, sometimes a majority, are in the full-time employ of the firm ("inside" board members).
2. The CEO is also the chairperson of the board in most American firms.

As a result, there are many conflicts of interest. First, inside board members are often the presidents and vice presidents of firms. Being a full-time employee of a firm makes it difficult for a board member to objectively critique company plans and proposals at board meetings. There will be proposals from the CEO, the very person responsible for the performance appraisal of any other inside members. It is the CEO who will decide whether they get additional responsibilities and promotions, including perhaps advancement to the CEO position.[52] James Burke, chairman of J&J, inherited a board entirely of insiders when he became chairman. One of the first things he did was to bring outsiders onto the board:

> This was an unpopular decision, and many of the former directors are still somewhat critical. I did it because I felt an all-insider board was wrong. While the Credo was a protection for the company...it also needed strong outsider directors...particularly as it got bigger.... I felt that a majority of outside directors gives the company added protection for the future.[53]

[50] Harold S. Geneen, "Why Directors Can't Protect the Shareholders," *Fortune*, September 17, 1984, p. 28.

[51] See Harold M. Williams, "The Role of the Director in Corporate Accountability," address to the Economic Club of Detroit, May 1, 1978. Williams was also CEO of Norton Simon and later chair of the SEC.

[52] Note that some researchers find that more outside directors do not result in better corporate ethics. See Frederick H. Gautschi and Thomas M. Jones, "Illegal Corporate Behavior and Corporate Board Structure," in *Research in Corporate Social Performance and Policy*, ed. William C. Frederick, vol. 9 (Greenwich, Conn.: JAI Press, 1987), pp. 93–106; Idalene F. Kesner et al., "Board Composition and the Commission of Illegal Acts: An Investigation of Fortune 500 Companies," *Academy of Management Review* 29 (December 1986): 789–99. Many defense firms were forced to add outside directors after being caught providing kickbacks and committing fraud and other crimes. This may have influenced the findings.

[53] James Burke in Thomas R. Horton, *What Works for Me*, (New York: Random House, 1986), p. 33.

Second, a CEO who chairs the board thus directs the very body that is charged with evaluating his or her performance. The chair of the board determines what is discussed at the meeting, what information is sent to the members, and the order and pace of the board's discussions. The chair thus controls the agenda of the board meeting. The conflict: The board's primary role is to assess the performance of the CEO, yet the CEO has vast influence over the very group that sits in judgment. In Japan, very few CEOs chair their own board.[54] Note a contrast: In 75 percent of American businesses the CEO is the chair, whereas in most universities the CEO is not the chair. Yet, where the profit motive operates and large sums of money are involved, there is even greater danger of conflict of interest. Most outside experts argue that the CEO should not chair the board. Some go further and maintain that because of the conflict of interest the CEO should not even be a member of the board.[55]

Compounding the above problem of objectivity and accountability, is the current tendency of American board members to perform their function with less data and less formality. The trouble, according to Walter Wriston, who was CEO of Citicorp for many years, is that business firms are risk-taking enterprises and businesspeople like to move rapidly and avoid bureaucracy. But boards tend to exhibit a legal mentality. They want memos and data to document moves and affix responsibility. In contrast, businesspeople do not want to leave a paper trail. Documentation takes time and allows more opportunity for insider trading on publicly held shares. Wriston says that these two points of view clash in the boardroom and "that some legal authorities would much rather have a paper trail of a failed corporation than no trail for a successful one."[56] Hence, in order to limit liability and insider trading, board deliberations are becoming more informal. The CEO will often contact individual board members for their judgments outside the meeting. Less data are prepared for fewer formal discussions at the board meeting itself. Ironically, this brings about the reverse of what corporate laws try to achieve: greater accountability for corporate actions.

Social Audits, Ethics Training, and Ombudsmen

A firm with a clear, motivating mission statement and clear-cut values must communicate its mission and values to members of the firm. They are of little use if people are not aware of them. A firm chooses individuals who

---

[54] Dan R. Dalton and Idalene F. Kesner, "Composition and CEO Duality in Boards of Directors: An International Perspective," *Journal of International Business*, Fall 1987, pp. 35, 40. The 75 percent figure is from Heidrick & Struggles, Inc., *Profile of a Chief Executive Officer*, 1980.

[55] Murray L. Weidenbaum, "Battle of the Boardroom: Controlling the Future Corporation," *Business and Society*, Summer 1986, p. 12; Geneen, "Why Directors Can't Protect the Shareholders," p. 29.

[56] Walter Wriston et al., "Words from the Wise on Corporate Boards," *Across the Board*, March 1988, p. 30.

perform activities that embody its values and gives them publicity and prizes to encourage such activities. Firms which are open about their operations tend to be more socially responsible. On the other hand, unethical business behavior thrives in secrecy. Firms that are excessively secretive are rightly treated with suspicion.

Disclosure requires two efforts: (1) communication of the mission, values, and models of behavior to members of the firm; and (2) communication of policies, actions, successes, and yet-to-be-achieved goals to external stakeholders. We discussed internal communication earlier. We now focus on external disclosure. Thomas Clausen, who returned after a term as head of the World Bank to become chair of the Bank of America again, made a strong plea for voluntary external disclosure. In his view, business can best demonstrate its accountability "by adopting a sufficient openness to public inquiry... to make clear that we recognize that what once we might have been disposed to call 'our' business is in fact the public's business and that the public, having a stake in our decisions, should have a voice in them as well."[57]

The case for disclosure to external stakeholders (customers, employees, suppliers, and the community, as well as stockholders) is based on the fact that information is required for free markets to operate effectively. Without accurate information, there are misallocations and inefficiencies. As Clausen put it, "a company's actions simply cannot be judged 'efficient,' 'responsive,' 'accountable,' or 'consistent with the public interest,' unless sufficient information about its activities is available." Clausen maintains that if government regulation or even socialism ever becomes predominant, it will be because business leaders were not sensitive to the needs of their stakeholders.

A firm's internal auditor, the external auditor, and the audit committee of the board oversee finances to insure honesty, and this information is reported in the annual financial report. The internal auditor sometimes must decide whether information that has been ignored by management should be brought to the attention of others outside the firm.[58]

As we indicated earlier, among the more important means of implementing socially responsible policies and adequate disclosure is oversight by the board of directors, which is best done with the help of an ethics or social policy staff or a social policy committee of the board. More than 100 large firms now have ethics, social policy, or public policy board committees.[59]

[57] Thomas Clausen, "Voluntary Disclosure: An Idea Whose Time Has Come," in *Corporations and Their Critics*, ed. Thornton Bradshaw and David Vogel (New York: McGraw-Hill, 1981), pp. 61–70.

[58] "U.S. Congress Looks at Internal Auditors," *Internal Auditor*, October 1987, pp. 4–7.

[59] Rob Gray, David Owen and Keith Maunders, "Corporate Social Reporting: The Way Forward," *Accountancy* 98 (December 1986): 108–9; U.S. Department of Commerce, "Business Strategies for the 1980's," in *Business and Society: Strategies for the 1980's* (Washington, D.C.: U.S. Department of Commerce, 1980), pp. 33–34.

Among the firms with active ethics or social policy board committees are General Electric, Levi Strauss, Mead Corporation, Norton Company, General Motors, and Bank of America. These committees oversee the implementation of the corporate code of ethics. In addition, some firms have a public policy staff and a social issues planning group, whose purpose is to be alert to changes in community attitudes and values, follow government activities, do political and social planning, and outline corporate policy options for management.

Corporate reports on public interest issues provide disclosure on social issues. These periodic reports contain descriptions of corporate activities that have a social impact (e.g., waste disposal, energy saving, equal employment opportunity, South African operations) and systematic assessments of the success of these activities. Equal employment opportunity and pollution control can be quantitatively measured and reported. Clear targets and measurable results can be obtained in these two areas, since it is possible to count the numbers of people in various jobs and the parts per million of pollutants. Hence many firms have been measuring performance in these areas for decades. The reporting is generally in the form of a description of activities.

Social reporting requires a firm to state clear policies on the social response it intends to make. Thus social reporting demands that the goals of the firm and their impact on society be articulated and publicly stated; such goals are heavily influenced by value judgments. About 40 percent of Fortune 500 firms report on social performance.[60] Thirty-two publish separate reports on it. Others describe their social activities briefly in their annual financial report (Ford, IBM, Xerox, CDC) as well as in executive speeches and advertisements (Exxon, W. R. Grace).

Among firms that produce a detailed report on their social activities are General Motors, Control Data, Aetna Life and Casualty Company, Norton Company, and Atlantic-Richfield. The reports of the first three are prepared internally and go into some detail on what the firm is doing on socially important issues. For example, *General Motors Public Interest Report—1988* presented equal employment opportunity statistics for the corporation and described GM's efforts regarding clean air, alternative fuels, auto safety, and prevention of ozone depletion. These social reports provide information to shareholders and other stakeholders.

While also prepared by in-house staff, the Norton Company report goes a step further by acknowledging some social targets that have not yet been reached. Atlantic-Richfield asks an outside expert to assess the corporation's

---

[60]W. Michael Hoffman et al., "Are Corporations Institutionalizing Ethics?" *Journal of Business Ethics* 5 (August 1986): 88–89.

performance.[61] Migros of Switzerland, a large food retailer, has published what is probably the most candid social report. For example, Migros acknowledges exaggerations in advertising and admits that it does not sufficiently promote healthier foods.[62] The Migros report is also done by an outside management consulting group. When a firm acknowledges its own failures and publishes assessments that are critical of its own activities, its reports gain credibility. They are thus more likely to be believed when they report on the firm's positive accomplishments.

An outside agency, the Council on Economic Priorities, has for decades done comprehensive, objective reports on the social actions and policies of firms. In a recent book, *Rating America's Corporate Conscience*, the agency evaluated and compared the record of most of the large firms in the United States on equal employment opportunity, contributions to the local community, dollar contributions to politicians, military contracts, and a number of other issues. The agency obtains its information from the firms themselves and from other sources.[63]

Chemical Bank, McDonnell Douglas, and General Dynamics do continual ethical training for all managers. Top managers initially spend a day, and middle managers several hours, in ethics training, and there are periodic follow-up programs. About 44 percent of large firms have some sort of ethics training.[64] In addition, General Dynamics has established an ethical hotline and an ombudsman who can be spoken to anonymously by any employee on ethical issues. Another approach is to place the responsibility on the individual who discovers an ethical problem to negotiate with managers so as to reach a successful and ethical solution.[65] Each of the above strategies depends

[61] See Atlantic-Richfield, *Participation III* (Los Angeles: Atlantic-Richfield, 1980), pp. 77–82. A good handbook to aid in preparing a social audit is American Institute of Certified Public Accountants, *The Measurement of Corporate Social Performance* (New York: American Institute of Certified Public Accountants, 1977); see also U.S. Department of Commerce, *Corporate Social Reporting in the United States and Western Europe* (Washington, D.C.: U.S. Department of Commerce, 1979); David H. Blake, William C. Frederick, and Mildred S. Myers, *Social Auditing: Evaluating the Impact of Corporate Programs* (New York: Praeger, 1976).

[62] See "Migros of Switzerland Prepares a Social Audit," *Responsive Capitalism: Case Studies in Corporate Social Conduct*, ed. Earl A. Molander (New York: McGraw-Hill, 1980) pp. 250–263. For a view by the director of that audit, see Meinholf Dierkes, "Corporate Social Reporting and Performance in Germany," in *Research in Corporate Social Performance and Policy*, ed. Lee E. Preston, vol. 2 (Greenwich, Conn.: JAI Press, 1981).

[63] Steven Lydenberg, Alice Tepper Marlin, and Sean Strub, *Rating America's Corporate Conscience* (Reading, Mass.: Addison-Wesley, 1986).

[64] For a useful overview of corporate ethics in ten leading American firms, see Business Roundtable, *Corporate Ethics: A Prime Business Asset* (New York: Business Roundtable, 1988); see also Ronald E. Berenbeim, *Corporate Ethics* (New York: The Conference Board, 1987); Hoffman et al., "Are Corporations Institutionalizing Ethics?" p. 88.

[65] Richard P. Nielsen, "Alternative Managerial Responses to Ethical Dilemmas," *Planning Review*, November 1985, pp. 24–29, 43; idem., "What Can Managers Do About Unethical Management?" *Journal of Business Ethics*, May 1987, pp. 309–19.

on managers within the firm. But outside stakeholders, especially shareholders, can also have an influence on the values and ethical performance of those inside the firm.

The Influence of Institutional Investors

Institutional investors (pension funds, trust funds, university endowments, and banks) have a large and increasing influence on publicly held corporations in the United States. This was not true two decades ago, when institutional investors did not try to exercise any control over the firms they invested in. They were content to receive dividends and to watch capital gains. Institutional investors currently own a large and determining share of most firms, in many cases well over 50 percent of the outstanding common stock (see Table 8–2).

The influence of institutional investors on business managers is exercised in two ways: (1) by means of the actions of the institution's portfolio manager, who tends to be anxious for short-term gains in the institution's investments; and (2) by means of voting shares at the spring shareholder

TABLE 8-2   Institutional Investors and Their Corporate Stock Holdings

COMPANY	VALUE (in billions)	PERCENTAGE OF SHARES HELD
Companies Listed by Dollar Value of Stock Held by Institutional Investors		
IBM	$29.64	46.1%
Exxon	19.05	31.8
General Electric	16.27	44.0
Philip Morris	12.26	57.8
Ford Motor	12.01	53.1
Merck & Co.	10.79	50.2
Digital Equipment	8.83	55.0
Companies Listed by Percentage of Stock Held by Institutional Investors		
Allegis Corp.	$1.88	98.0%
CNA Financial	3.41	93.9
NWA Inc.	1.22	93.3
St. Paul Cos	1.71	84.8
AMR Corp.	2.13	83.7
Tele-Communications	2.60	82.4
Continential Corp.	1.86	80.4

A survey of the investments of institutions that manage $100 million or more in discretionary equity assets. Figures as of March 31, 1988.

Sources: *New York Times*, July 5, 1988, p. 29; and CDC Investment Technologies. Copyright © 1988 by the New York Times Company. Reprinted by permission.

meeting on social issues that have been brought to the meeting by various activist groups.

The actions of portfolio managers were treated earlier. These actions can include pressuring company management for short-term returns and supporting the attempts of corporate raiders when the likely result will be an increase in share value. Such actions are often damaging to a firm that is trying to work for the long term, as was indicated in Chapter 1.

The second way of exercising influence will be discussed here. Institutional investors began voting their shares in the 1970s.[66] Any shareholder, by following SEC rules, can place an issue on the ballot for vote at the shareholder meeting of any publicly held firm. Among the many issues presented to shareholders in recent years are nuclear power, operations in South Africa, disposal of toxic wastes, equal employment opportunity, and the sale of infant formula. By placing these issues on the ballot, the initiating group is able to focus top management's attention, inform the general public, and often negotiate an agreement with management that will achieve its ends.

For example, the Project on Corporate Responsibility pressed General Motors for reform through the use of shareholders' resolutions throughout the 1970s. It is rare for a shareholder resolution opposed by management to obtain anything near the 51 percent vote which would compel management to comply. Nevertheless, even a small percentage can represent hundreds of thousands of shares and many prestigious institutional investors who are questioning management policy. The embarrassment of having these shareholders vote against management is often pressure enough. For example, while the proposals of the Project on Corporate Responsibility to General Motors received less than 3 percent of the shareholder vote, they did help to produce some significant results at GM: publication of an annual social report, establishment of a public policy board committee, increased numbers of minorities in management positions, the appointment of black activist Reverend Leon Sullivan to GM's board, increased purchases from minority suppliers, and the use of minority banks.

The Interfaith Center for Corporate Responsibility (ICCR) is the most active agent for placing social issues on shareholder ballots. The ICCR is a division of the National Council of Churches. It represents 14 Protestant denominations and about 170 Roman Catholic orders and dioceses. In 1988, 182 resolutions were presented to more than 130 firms. Of these, 31 resulted in successful negotiations with management and were withdrawn. The other 151 were voted on, but no contested resolution won. However, 125 received

---

[66] Theodore V. Purcell, "Management and the 'Ethical' Investors," *Harvard Business Review*, September-October 1979, pp. 24–44. Some ethical investors now place their money in funds that use that capital only for socially responsible investments. See "Investing with a Social Conscience," *Business Week*, May 13, 1985, p. 149; Alice Tepper Marlin, "Social Investing: Potent Force for Social Change," *Business and Society Review*, Spring 1986, pp. 96–100.

a sufficient number of votes (3 to 10 percent) to be eligible to be resubmitted the following year.[67]

To help institutional investors reach a judgment on the merit of the various proposals, the Investor Responsibility Research Center (IRRC) was set up "at the instigation of President Derek Bok at Harvard and with the assistance of the Ford, Carnegie and Rockefeller Foundations."[68] The IRRC (not to be confused with the ICCR) presents the position of both management and the activist group which introduced the proposal. The IRRC then analyzes the proposal and poses any critical questions that seem to merit consideration. The IRRC does not recommend how to vote; that is the investor's decision. At the end of the proxy season, the IRRC publishes a summary of the season's voting. It lists the firms, the issues, and the percentage of shareholders supporting the proposal; it also often indicates which institutional investors supported or opposed individual proposals and why.

The shareholder resolution as an instrument for raising social policy issues is now accepted by most institutional investors. The "Wall Street rule" of blindly supporting management or selling all shares is no longer held in repute. This change reflects the fact that ownership carries with it a responsibility to express judgment on major policy issues. The shareholders resolution can also be an aid to management. It brings to the attention of management many questions that could easily be overlooked. Moreover, it provides an early warning system that alerts management that certain issues may become more important in the future and more deserving of attention. The ethical investor movement can help stakeholders catch the attention of management. Management is thus less likely to be locked into a narrow and bureaucratic mindset. Now let us consider one means that a firm itself has for making explicit its own values and ethics: the code of ethics.

A CODE FOR CORPORATE PERFORMANCE

Most managers want a code of ethics for their firm. This was shown more than two decades ago in what is still the most careful empirical study of business ethics ever done. Raymond Baumhart's study, which included almost 2,000 business managers, revealed that more than two-thirds thought a code of ethics would raise the ethical level of business practice.[69] More than three-fourths thought that a code would be welcomed by business people as

[67] "How 182 Shareholder Resolutions Fared," *News for Investors* 15 (June 1988): 119.

[68] Purcell, "Management and the 'Ethical' Investors," p. 26.

[69] Raymond C. Baumhart, S. J., "How Ethical Are Businessmen?" *Harvard Business Review* 39 (July-August 1961): 166–71; see also idem., *Ethics in Business* (New York: Holt, Rinehart and Winston, 1968).

a help in specifying the limits of acceptable conduct, and most wanted a code of ethics to help clarify their own ethical standards and decisions. In many instances, they did not even *know* what was ethical and so felt they needed help. Cases of overseas bribery (Exxon, Lockheed, ITT, Northrop), of using privileged information for private gain (Texas Gulf Sulfur, Penn-Central Railroad), as well as other transgressions, have underscored the problem.

When an ethical code is designed for a firm, the CEO is most often the initiator. Three-fourths of all firms have a code; among the largest firms, the percentage that have codes rises to 90 percent. Moreover, the discussion of ethics in business over the last five years has had considerable influence on the design of those codes.

Two firms that have developed model ethical codes and systems of monitoring are Caterpillar Tractor and Weyerhaeuser. Caterpillar's code is distributed to all managers worldwide, and these managers must report annually to the home office on "any events or activities that might cause an impartial observer to conclude that the code hasn't been fully followed." The code's provisions are highly ethical: "The law is the floor. Ethical business conduct should normally exist at a level well above the minimum required by law.... We intend to hold to a single standard of integrity everywhere. We will keep our word. We won't promise more than we can reasonably expect to deliver; nor will we make commitments we don't intend to keep."[70] Weyerhaeuser not only established a code of ethics but also set up a Business Conduct Committee (BCC). The BCC, which consists of a small representative group of managers and workers, is charged with promulgating the code, answering questions on borderline cases, and helping to develop and update the code.[71]

Traditional codes of ethics may be of limited use in bringing about more ethical conduct in corporations, however. Recent evidence shows that firms with a code are not much more ethical than those without. This is partly explained by the fact that most corporate codes are really designed to protect firms from their own employees. Codes generally cover relations with customers, keeping honest books and records, and potential conflicts of interest. On the other hand, fewer than one-fourth of the codes deal with such items as product safety, environmental affairs, product quality, matters of personal character, and civic and community affairs.[72]

---

[70] Caterpillar Tractor Co., *A Code of Worldwide Business Conduct and Operating Principles* (Peoria, Ill.: Caterpillar Tractor Co., 1985), p. 4.

[71] Earl A. Molander, "Weyerhaeuser's Reputation—A Shared Responsibility," in *Responsive Capitalism*, (New York: McGraw-Hill, 1980), pp. 224–37.

[72] M. Cash Mathews, "Codes of Ethics: Organizational Behavior and Misbehavior," in *Research in Corporate Social Performance and Policy*, ed. William C. Frederick, vol. 7 (Greenwich, Conn.: JAI Press, 1987), pp. 107–130.

Progress or Cynicism

Economic indicators provide conflicting signals on the health of the American economy. Some suggest a healthy economy: Total employment is higher than ever before, the unemployment rate is down, and American firms are competing better in world markets. Freedom of choice still encourages initiative and innovation. Other economic indicators are not good: We have the largest foreign debt of any nation in the world, our federal budget deficit is immense (most of it accumulated during the 1980s), and delayed gratification is no longer one of our values. Moreover, our cities are decaying, and white-collar crime is higher than ever before.

Moral indicators provide conflicting signals on the health of American society. On the positive side, we still value family, honesty, and integrity. Church attendance is higher in the United States than in other industrialized countries. Fraud, kickbacks, and unethical activities, whether in business or in government, still cause scandal and outrage. Yet there is increasing evidence of insider trading, bribery, and selfishness among businesspeople, along with alcoholism, drug addiction, street crime, murders, and white-collar crime—not to mention the ever-present danger of a mistake triggering a nuclear holocaust.

People motivated by self-interest, when faced with such large problems, often focus on protecting what they already have. In the political sphere, special interest lobbying groups have fractured the society into competing camps. Witness, for example, the success of gun owners, used car dealers, and banks in achieving their goals—even when the goals are contrary to the good of the community. Among world democracies, the United States has one of the lowest rates of voting. For example, Ronald Reagan was elected by less than one-third of the voters. About half didn't even bother to vote.

Most of the changes required in American society (e.g., balancing the budget, dealing with crumbling cities, helping poor and underprivileged people, decreasing the hostility of labor-management relations, and limiting our voracious use of energy) will require intelligence, careful planning, and good leadership but also honesty, humility, and sacrifice. History tells us that little can be accomplished without sacrifice, but we now hear little mention of it. Yet faced with these problems, some are ready to acknowledge our personal and national weaknesses, along with our strengths, in order to create a better society. We will discuss more of what to expect in the future in the next chapter.

SUMMARY AND CONCLUSIONS

Business activities evidence an underlying set of goals and values. Values and ethics are communicated to members and to outside stakeholders by the

CEO. Some CEOs are concerned for the long-term good of the firm and its stakeholders. Humane, cooperative, and ethical values can create a more participative, attractive, and effective climate. In such a climate, employees are more likely to use their abilities to the best advantage in achieving the goals of the firm. Some executives, however, are oriented toward the short term, which seriously harms other people, the firm, and society.

Individualism and the Protestant ethic have carried Americans fast and far, but now delayed gratification has given way to the consumer ethic of "buy now, pay later." Individualism encourages "get rich quick" schemes that are not always to the benefit of society.

Traditional American flexibility and certain incremental changes offer a sign of hope. Public affairs and social responsibilities are now a part of corporate strategic planning. Pension funds, endowments, and foundations now exercise more influence as part owners and often bring pressure on management through their voting on various social issues at shareholder meetings.

Boards of directors now take their responsibilities more seriously. Implementation of social policy and ethics demands a statement or code of ethics. Most American firms have such a code of ethics. Most also consider social issues in evaluating the performance of managers and inform their stakeholders about their social and ethical activities, whether in a social report or some other form.

Executives recognize that most stakeholders want more from a firm than merely return on investment. Quality products, long-term planning, and involvement with local communities are but a few of the additional obligations that firms have been charged with. To the extent that firms do not respond willingly, government will step in to legislate or regulate. Hence the only alternative to regulation is for management to voluntarily initiate policies to insure their obligations are met.

DISCUSSION QUESTIONS

1. Evaluate the GM and Ford compensation schemes described at the beginning of the chapter using the norms developed in Chapter 7. Are they good long-term strategies?

2. How would you evaluate the pay of Firestone's John Nevin? Do you agree with Peters that the amount represents an inequity?

3. What does the difference in research spending in Japan and the United States tell us about priorities? How will the difference influence the future?

4. Do you think that American values have shifted as indicated in Table 8–1? How does this shift affect the values of managers?

5. What does the data on the annual increase of executive salaries versus hourly worker salaries, inflation, and profits tell you?

6. How would you characterize the values, ethics, and management style of James Burke (J&J)? And those of Roy Vagelos (Merck)? Tom Monaghan (Domino's)? Felix Rohatyn (Lazard Freres)?

7. How would you characterize the values, ethics, and management style of Thomas Jones (Northrop)? What are the strengths and weaknesses? Does a defense contractor require a different sort of ethics than a consumer goods manufacturer?

8. Identify the values and ethics of Paul Bilzerian. Likewise for Steven O'Neil of Film Recovery Systems.

9. What problems arise when a board is made up mostly of insiders? What problems arise when the CEO is the chair of the board?

10. Why are the mission, goals, values, and ethics of a firm integral to corporate planning? Describe how to make ethics an effective part of planning.

11. Describe the influence institutional investors have on firms in which they hold stock. What are the advantages and disadvantages of this involvement from the standpoint of the firm? From the standpoint of society?

12. What is the argument for disclosure of financial information? What is the argument for social issue disclosures? Describe the ways in which social issue disclosures are made.

CASES:

Stock Purchase Deal

Through his banking work, Kenneth McGinty learns that Maco Corporation is about to purchase Digital Optics. Digital Optics is a small publicly held firm which has had an unprofitable year and its stock is much undervalued. The price of the stock is sure to rise when the buyout is announced. Looking only to the ethical issues, can Ken purchase some stock for himself? Can he tell a good friend? Explain.

Company Controller

Carol Goudreau, a company controller, is asked by the chief financial officer (CFO) to "manage earnings" in such a way as to present more favorable financial results for this quarter. The CFO does Carol's performance appraisal. What should Carol do? Why?

CHAPTER NINE
BUSINESS VALUES
FOR THE FUTURE

We do not see the poor of the world's faces, we do not know their names, we cannot count their number. But they are there. And their lives have been touched by us. And ours by them....George Bernard Shaw put it perfectly: "You see things, and say why? But I see things that never were, and I say why not?"

Robert S. McNamara
Conclusion of his last address
as president of the World Bank

Planning for the future is essential to business success. Planning in turn is based on projections of what to expect in the coming decades, coupled with a clear sense of what the organization is and what it can do best. Possibilities and expectations regarding new products, markets, and the future work force are among the important focuses of corporate planning. These possibilities depend on people's values. Thus, being alert to changing values enables a firm to formulate better business policies and to be a more sensitive corporate citizen. This chapter probes the current setting for planning, examines the importance of having a coherent business ideology, presents material on future scanning for business, and attempts to chart the direction of changing values and ethics over the coming decades.

TODAY'S BUSINESS VALUES

How the values of businesspeople developed and how they influence current business practices has been examined in previous chapters. But business is not an isolated institution. It operates in society and is influenced by both government and cultural values. Business, as well as government and culture, exists in society. Within that society, business has relationships with both government and with the local culture, and they influence each other with respect to a broad range of issues. For a schematic view of these relationships, see Figure 9–1. The most visible relationship, and one of the most critical, exists between business and government. The basis of this relationship consists of the government's regulation of business and business's lobbying of government to obtain its goals. The government regulation that we are concerned with here is regulation intended to benefit the public.

How extensive government regulation should be—and how extensively the individual firm should work for the public good even when it runs counter to the firm's own good—is hotly disputed. As we have seen earlier, some take the position that each firm should exclusively pursue its own profit. It is argued that society as a whole will automatically be better off as a result. On the other hand, some hold that the good corporate citizen will

FIGURE 9-1   The Relationships Between Business, Government, Society, and Culture

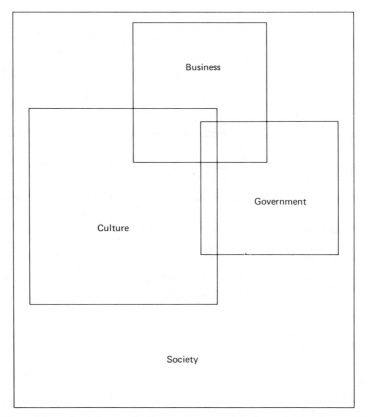

Source: Adapted from the interpenetrating systems model of Lee E. Preston and James E. Post, *Private Management and Public Policy* (Englewood Cliffs, N.J.: Prentice-Hall, 1975).

consider the well-being of others, even in cases where it will cost the firm. The debate between adherents of these two positions was especially heated during the 1980s, when tax cuts for individuals and for businesses and supply side economics arose as specific issues.

However, the arguments do not always make clear that most businesspeople and critics of business agree on certain propositions:

1. Free enterprise is the most efficient, productive, flexible, and innovative socio-economic system yet devised.
2. However, free market mechanisms tend not to provide social goods that are costly to firms, for example, clean air, safe drugs, and truthful advertising.
3. Businesspeople need to pay greater attention to values and ethics and need to increase their ability to make ethical decisions.
4. Some business conditions have a profound impact on business *and* individuals: the balance of trade deficit, the federal budget deficit, the diminishment of nonrenewable resources, damage to the environment (e.g., ozone depletion, the greenhouse effect, pollution from toxic waste dumps).
5. Business, government, working people, and local communities must work together to solve the above problems and to increase competitiveness in world markets.

There is significant agreement on the strengths, direction, and limitations of the U.S. economy. This consensus allows us to deal with more effectively the major business and national problems that face us.

Testimony to Free Markets

All the countries of the world that are developing rapidly have free market economies. The countries of Western Europe, Japan, Korea, Singapore, and Hong Kong all have market systems which encourage innovation and efficiencies. Their success is made possible by their abilities to sell their goods to other countries.

Countries not able to sell their goods on world markets are falling behind. Those goods are either too expensive or of poor quality, or both. In order to boost their international competitiveness, both the People's Republic of China and the USSR have introduced elements of the market system. Both countries, which were autocratic and largely feudal until this century, achieved great progress through their Marxist, communal systems, and both are now initiating market pricing, incentives, and other characteristics of Western economies. The fact that markets are now international has been a challenge not only to American firms but also to Chinese and Russian businesses.[1] If firms anywhere in the world are not able to produce at low cost,

---

[1]Marvin J. Cetron, Wanda Rocha, and Rebecca Luckins, "Into the 21st Century: Long-term Trends Affecting the United States," *The Futurist*, July-August 1988, p. 31.

free markets allow their likely customers to purchase cheaper goods produced in other countries.

But China and Russia are also aware of the weaknesses of free markets. They have not given up trying to encourage people to consider the good of others, including the common good. Even in the United States we know that the free market does not provide parks, libraries, street lighting, symphony orchestras, or clean air and water. The government must provide the services which cannot pay for themselves. For example, in the absence of government regulations, free markets encourage businesses to cut costs by dumping pollutants in local streams.

Aristocratic Society

While the American political system is democratic, the economic system is aristocratic. Politically, every person has only one vote. Some people, however, earn fifty times the average annual income, and they possess as a result fifty times the economic "voting power." They may spend their personal income on expensive clothes, lavish vacations, or second and third homes or to garner political influence. Others who work as hard or harder find it difficult to pay the rent or the food bills. Although we say that wealth is the reward for hard work, we also know that good fortune—especially birth into an affluent family and the resulting opportunities—is even more important. Those who are born in the United States (rather than e.g., Bangladesh) or to college-educated parents have many advantages.

Another weakness of free enterprise is that it encourages selfish activities. According to its ideology, free markets and competition—guided by Adam Smith's "invisible hand"—result in the most economic use of resources. Or, as the seventeenth-century British pamphleteer put it, "Private vices make public profit." In fact, capitalism does reward those who are selfish. Furthermore, it provides a rationalization that promotes and blesses self-seeking, self-centered behavior.

Consumer sovereignty places the consumer in the role of decision maker and policy maker. In the very act of purchasing goods, each consumer sets priorities for him- or herself, for others, and for society. Making consumer sovereignty the basis for setting social goals is convenient, because it distributes responsibility. Who is responsible for the many problems that we have drifted into in the past generation (the trade and the federal deficit, the scarcity of certain resources, the poor quality of the air, pollution due to toxic waste)? Consumer sovereignty leads to undirected, promiscuous economic growth. Coupled with the free market, it is also a convenient principle for those who claim to be value-free, for it presumably enables them to dodge value questions. However, such blind adherence to consumer sovereignty actually values the individual over the community, encourages self-centered behavior, and leads to national stalemates as special interest groups pull in opposite directions. Consumer sovereignty and free enterprise thus enable people to avoid the vital question of what kind of society we want—that is, avoid it until flexibility is gone, options have been narrowed, and crises are upon us.

Capitalism in the United States was built on self-interest and rugged individualism. In the nineteenth century, huge fortunes were amassed before social legislation was enacted. Workers and small businesspeople were often hurt by the actions of the robber barons. Nevertheless, these wealthy barons later used much of their fortunes to benefit the public. Indeed, Andrew Carnegie's defense of large fortunes was based on the claim that rich people better use the wealth created by industry for public purposes (see Chapter 3). John D. Rockefeller built the University of Chicago, Carnegie funded libraries across the United States, and Collis Potter Huntington built a superb rapid transit rail system for Los Angeles (which was dismantled in the 1950s by a combine of GM, Firestone, Phillips Petroleum, and Standard Oil of California). Various foundations were set up by wealthy men (e.g., Carnegie, Rockefeller, and Ford) to serve the public, and these foundations have continued to fund valuable new programs. Are the fortunes made in this decade also used for public purposes?

The Threat of Special Interests to Democracy

There has been a lack of planning in the United States during the past three decades. Fewer libraries, museums, or parks have been built, and suburbs have sprawled haphazardly, paving over land that a generation ago would have been set aside as parks or rapid transit right-of-ways. Vision and planning are required to make cities liveable; both seem to be lacking today. Attention is focused on new homes, new plants, new expressways. Meanwhile, cities are deteriorating, since so many of our parks, libraries, roads, and public transit facilities were built fifty or more years ago. The deterioration of our infrastructure comes as a shock. When individuals pursue their own self-interest, the community as a whole does not always benefit.

This discussion of the strengths and weaknesses of American business brings us to a core question: How does the business system adapt to change? How are inefficiencies and inequities repaired? What does business have at its disposal that enables it to face the future with confidence?

Change in national priorities have been accomplished primarily through the political process: voting and legislation. On public interest issues, Americans are generally committed to an open system and to consensus. This process works slowly, but it does bring changes in law and in life. However, it generally takes a catastrophe to alert us to inadequacies in our social or business system. It took the urban race riots to force us to face the injustice and extent of job discrimination. Lake Erie died before we realized the dangers of water pollution. Millions of birds died from pesticides before we learned how we were poisoning them.[2] It took Three Mile Island and Chernobyl to alert us to the costs and dangers of nuclear energy.

A democracy works slowly and often requires a crisis to awaken its citizens to new public needs. Men and women act when they personally feel a need. This makes long-range planning extremely difficult. The pressure is on legislators to vote on issues in such a way as to benefit home constituents. There is little incentive to trade off present goods for future goods, and any investment policy is just such a tradeoff. On the contrary, special interests, short terms in office, and felt needs back home all militate against the kind of long-term investment of time and capital in research and planning that will pay off a generation from now. Moreover, many of the problems we now face are serious and long-term (e.g., pollution, urban decay, dwindling resources, and lower productivity). If a crisis occurs before we grasp the seriousness of these problems, there will be no time left to find solutions. This may be the most serious flaw of democracy.

Nevertheless, the human spirit is amazingly flexible. If we are able to take the long perspective, we will be able to acknowledge our needs. If we then marshal the talent and initiative that we possess, we can move toward solutions.

Lack of Clear Values

Minds are like parachutes: They only work when they are open. Yet a recent critique of Americans is entitled *The Closing of the American Mind*.[3] The author maintains that all great civilizations were steeped in knowledge of other times and other thinkers. But American universities have virtually stopped conveying a tradition. Since we so rarely examine the most important questions (e.g., What is the good life?), we have become a pragmatic, shallow civilization.

A few years ago a survey found young people critical of the beliefs of their parents and other elders. They were not critical of *what* they believed but of their seeming lack of beliefs and convictions. The values of their elders seemed to be largely inherited and absorbed passively from the surrounding culture. Their elders had very little in the way of thought-out, internalized goals and values.

Young people are often the victims of homogenized mass education and passive entertainment.[4] Not only does mass education directly influence thinking, but it also indirectly influences values through the clothes, food, and TV programs that are currently presented as "acceptable." Mass education, in fact, has as much influence outside the classroom as inside. It substi-

---

[2] Rachael Carson, *Silent Spring*. (Boston: Houghton Mifflin, 1962).

[3] Allan Bloom, *The Closing of the American Mind* (New York: Simon & Schuster, 1987).

[4] Cetron, Rocha, and Luckins, "Into the 21st Century," p. 30.

tutes tastes and fads for critical thinking and the development of personal goals and values. Often young people and adults escape thinking by turning on the TV set. Thus the moral and intellectual fiber of our country has been softened by being pounded for decades by violence, sex, and quick solutions to every problem.

The confusion, apathy, and cynicism that is sometimes found in young people puts an even greater burden on their elders to articulate their own values and ethics. If adults, with more experience and wisdom, have little idea of their own life goals and aspirations, young people are left with no one to turn to. It is especially important that individuals be able to articulate values in a time of rapid change. Otherwise, men and women are left with no rudder and are pushed by events from one job or neighborhood to another. Without values and goals, people are not in control of their own lives, careers, or destinies. Opportunities, challenges, and crises come rapidly, and individuals who have not reflected on why they live, what they do, and why they do it are unable to deal with them. Such people and their families will be confused, frustrated, and hurt. By gaining ownership of their roots and goals, such people and their families will be able to profit and grow.

A major function of education is to encourage students to reflect on their own values and make them explicit so that they may then be able to grow and make clear life choices. Alvin Toffler, in analyzing this problem, is critical of the schools:

> Students are seldom encouraged to analyze their own values and those of their teachers and peers. Millions pass through the education system without once having been forced to search out the contradictions in their own value systems, to probe their own life goals deeply, or even to discuss these matters candidly with adults and peers....
>
> Nothing could be better calculated to produce people uncertain of their goals, people incapable of effective decision-making under conditions of overchoice.[5]

Toffler is speaking of the failure of schools two decades ago; the situation is even more critical today. The need for individuals to search out and make explicit their own values and goals is greater in a period of rapid change, and schools are primary vehicles for this sort of examination and evaluation—yet schools, from kindergartens to universities, have failed in this respect. Educators maintain that education should be "objective" and that values are too controversial for an institution dealing with various kinds of people. What they fail to recognize is that such a position in itself embodies a value. People growing up without internalized goals and values contribute to national confusion, apathy, and cynicism. The resulting individualism and inability to achieve a consensus on public goals create severe strains within democratic societies.

[5] Alvin Toffler, *Future Shock* (New York: Random House, 1970), p. 370.

Basic Beliefs and the Work Ethic

People have a better sense of themselves and are more likely to participate with others when their personal values and goals are explicit. Moreover, goals are clearer and organizations operate better if people probe their basic values and articulate their answers to basic questions such as the following:

What do I see as my fundamental purpose in life?

Are men and women basically self-seeking or are they basically good and generous?

Do men and women have a transcendental and spiritual end or is this present life, with its pleasures and material satisfactions, all there is?

Is there any such thing as a moral absolute or is everything relative?

Does society exist for people or do people exist for society? Or is the relationship more complex?

What is the purpose of the business firm? What is the purpose of the state?

Are the forces of history determined? If so, are these forces moving humanity along the route of inevitable, long-term progress?

The responses to such questions have an effect on the goals of organizations and also on government legislation and regulations.

If you answer the above questions and reflect on the content of those answers, you will be able to learn much about yourself. This will complement the Personal Goals and Values Inventory at the end of Chapter 1. Your answers to these questions may show that you are centered on your own interests and that other people are seen merely as instruments to attain your own goals. On the other hand, your responses may show that you have a concern for others and are often willing to sacrifice your own interests for their sake. To gain yet another perspective, you might imagine yourself in the position of hiring new people. Which responses from a potential employee would make you inclined to hire the person? Or closer to home, which responses would you prefer from a future business partner or a potential spouse?

As for choosing a job, you might ask yourself what sort of a firm you would like to work for—a firm whose employees are centered on their own interests and careers or a firm whose employees are also concerned about others? In which sort of firm would you be likely to do better work and enjoy that work more? In which would you be more successful? In which more satisfied?

A VIABLE BUSINESS CREED

The most salient and precious American business value is freedom: free markets, free competition, free movement of people and capital, and most especially freedom of the individual. Government deregulation is designed to regain the values of the free market.

Important as personal freedom is in American society, it is not unlimited. An individualism that is not conscious of other people leads to mistrust, frustration, and ultimately chaos. One does not have the freedom to shout "Fire!" in a crowded theater. Traffic lights represent restrictions that were undoubtedly objected by by early libertarians. A business firm does not have the freedom to mislead in its product advertising or to dump its waste in a lake. As people live closer together and become more dependent on one another, freedom must be constrained by both self-control and external checks. In fact, real freedom paradoxically emerges only when a people have formed internal constraints: "Freedom is endangered if a free society's shared values are no longer sufficiently vigorous to preserve the moral cohesion on which the discipline of free people rests."[6] Although it may be hard to understand for the individualist, limitations based on a consideration for others (e.g., in the case of traffic lights or truth-in-advertising laws) introduce even greater freedom for all. People have greater trust in the safety of the streets and in what is claimed in advertising, and thus they can act more decisively and with less fear.

One of the strengths of American business has been its pragmatism, its tendency to get the job done while avoiding theoretical and ideological discussions. As Daniel Bell put it, "The ideology of American business... became its ability to perform. The justification of the corporation no longer lay primarily in the natural right of private property, but in its role as an instrument for providing more and more goods to people."[7] Pragmatism thus leads us to accept values and goals simply because they work and often regardless of inequities and undesirable by-products.

Any substantive defense of the values of business and the economic system cannot rest merely on the values of freedom and efficiency, for the following questions arise: Freedom for what? Productivity for what? Freedom, productivity, and the business system they support are not ultimate ends in their own right but are good insofar as they allow people to pursue other more valuable goals. Higher productivity allows a society to provide more jobs, goods, and services and with less effort. This allows its citizens to pursue other goals. In short, higher productivity is a major benefit but not the end of society.

Problems for Future Managers

Some of the problems that already hinder business in the United States have a potential for creating even more trouble in future years. The United

---

[6] Peter Viereck, *Shame and Glory of the Intellectuals* (Boston: Beacon, 1953), p. 196.
[7] Daniel Bell, *The Coming of the Post-Industrial Society* (New York: Basic Books, 1973), p. 272.

States has been running a balance of payments or trade deficit of more than $100 billion annually for several years.[8] We purchase that much more goods and services from foreign countries than we are able to sell to them. Moreover, we must borrow from foreign countries to buy these additional goods and services. The largest single commodity we purchase from foreign countries is petroleum. Even though the United States is still one of the largest petroleum producers in the world, that is not enough to satisfy us; we spend an additional $50 billion each year to purchase more petroleum from other countries.[9] Thus, we are now on the slippery slope of borrowing foreign money to purchase foreign goods, all the while increasing our outstanding foreign debt and interest payments. The United States was the largest creditor nation in the world until 1985. We financed many activities beyond our borders and received interest on those business loans. In the few years since 1985, we have become the largest debtor nation in the world, and we now borrow more capital from other nations than any country in the world. Having a large foreign debt is generally characteristic of poor nations, who need to borrow capital from wealthier nations to finance their own development programs.

In addition to the balance of trade deficit, the United States has an accumulated federal budget deficit of $2.5 *trillion.*[10] To get some sense of the size of what is owed, consider that it amounts to $10,000 for every man, woman, and child in the United States and that to pay the interest on it annually costs each person $800. That is $800 (or $3,200 for a family of four) for which we have nothing to show.

Much of the debt is owed to the Japanese, the Europeans, and the petroleum producers. Japan has moved past Britain and the United States into the top spot among international investors. A list of the world's fifty largest banks by assets demonstrates this. The largest five are all Japanese; the first American bank on the list, Citicorp, is number 7.[11] The second largest American bank, Chase Manhattan, is number 32, and there are seventeen Japanese banks that are larger than Chase! The Japanese are prodigious savers, and they now have the capital to invest around the world. The Japanese take seriously the bank ad to encourage interest on savings: "Let your money work for you."

How will this affect business in the future? It will require increased taxes, which add to the cost of production, to pay for the spending of previ-

---

[8]For 1987, the trade deficit was $135 billion; the deficit for 1988 is only a bit less. See *Economic Report of the President, 1988* (Washington, D.C.: U.S. Government Printing Office, 1988), p. 271.

[9]"Crude Petroleum and Natural Gas," *U.S. Industrial Outlook, 1988—Oil and Gas* (Washington, D.C.: U.S. Department of Commerce, 1988), pp. 10–13.

[10]*Economic Report of the President, 1988*, p. 341.

[11]"International Bank Scorecard," *Business Week,* June 27, 1988, p. 77.

ous generations. It thus adds another hurdle in our attempt to be competitive in world markets. In addition, the trade and federal deficits also illustrate a new American value: If you can obtain the goods today without paying full price, do so, even if your children must pay later. Ted Turner, of Capital Cities, illustrates our spending habits by the following fact: "In the United States we have 2.5 percent of the children of the world, but we spend 60 percent of all that is spent in the world on toys."[12]

Mission Statements and Basic Beliefs

An organization's mission statement and goals reflect the basic beliefs of those who formulate the statement. The J&J credo (see Figure 8–1) reflects the basic values of the firm over the past 40 years. It is "the glue that holds the organization together," according to CEO James Burke. The credo was first stated by the founder's son, General Robert Wood Johnson, when he was head of the company in 1944.

The Parts and Service Division of Ford Motor Company calls itself the "loving and caring division." Vice president Joe Kordick's influence on the division shows in his care for people. His and the division's Ethic of an Anointed Person is as follows:

> With God's help, in each situation, I will always endeavor to treat you the way I would want and expect you to treat me in the same situation. And, with God's assistance, I will always be committed to giving beyond what people and the law require of me in whatever act of service my business and I are involved in.

At the heart of this ethic is a great respect for others. The ethic has enormously influenced the way of doing things in the division.

Tom Monaghan at Domino's encourages all employees to be aware of their religious roots and to build on that foundation. The employees are remarkably obliging to customers. If a customer finds any fault with a pizza, it is replaced with no questions asked. If the pizza is delivered later than the promised thirty-minutes delivery time, three dollars are taken off the bill. When one calls or deals with the employees, one is struck with their consideration and cheerfulness.

Each of these businesses have high ethical and spiritual ideals. The resulting climate then attracts like-spirited people to the organization. The test for any organization is to institutionalize those values so they remain after the retirement of the person who created the statement of ideals. J&J has already passed this test.

---

[12] Ted Turner's address at the University of Detroit, November 25, 1985.

MANAGING SOCIOPOLITICAL FORECASTING

In a recent survey of CEOs, almost 70 percent said that they would be spending more time on strategic planning in the future.[13] But strategic planning can be done only when one has some notion of what to expect in the future. Some information is available from public sources: demographics, availability and price of resources, employment skills, and economic forecasts. Also needed are forecasts of what public policy issues will emerge in the future. Most of the issues discussed in Chapter 8 concern public policy.

Organizing for the Future

Most business firms have established senior staff positions to aid in developing strategic plans and in dealing with public issues.[14] These corporate offices are designed to obtain, analyze, and report information on the social and political environment. The advantages of having such information and using it within the firm are that it (1) lessens managerial surprises, (2) reduces the cost of regulatory compliance, (3) permits "smooth transitions," and (4) enables the firm to focus on opportunities and get ahead of issues.[15]

Various sources of information and techniques for gathering it are available. For example, considerable information can be obtained regarding population characteristics, changes in family compensation, and perceptions with regard to what constitutes quality of life.[16] Several private agencies will, for a substantial fee, provide some of this information, including the Institute for the Future, and some consulting firms.

Capital-intensive firms in stable industries have more need of advance warning of future developments because of their large investment and lessened flexibility.[17] Firms that are flexible with respect to resource deployment can afford to wait for events to take place. One way of obtaining "best guesses" on forthcoming sociopolitical issues is to use the Delphi technique, which is a structured method for arriving at a consensus of opinion among a panel of experts. The Center for Futures Research used this technique with

---

[13] Ben J. Wattenberg, "Their Deepest Concerns," *Business Monthly*, January 1988, p. 33.

[14] William L. Renfro, "Managing the Issues of the 1980's," *The Futurist* 16 (August 1982): 61.

[15] John E. Fleming, "Public Issues Scanning" (Paper presented at the Academy of Management, Social Issues Division, New York, August 1979), p. 12. For an excellent presentation of corporate planning in an ethical context, see LaRue T. Hosmer, *Strategic Management* (Englewood Cliffs, N.J.: Prentice-Hall, 1982).

[16] Fremond Kast, "Scanning the Future Environment: Social Indicators," *California Management Review* 23 (Fall 1980): 22–32.

[17] John E. Fleming, "Public Issues Scanning," in *Research in Corporate Social Performance: A Research Annual*, ed. Lee E. Preston, vol. 3 (Greenwich, Conn.: JAI Press, 1981), pp. 155–173.

business and academic leaders for its twenty-year forecast entitled *The Future of Business-Government Relations*.[18]

Public Issues Scanning

A second technique used by a large number of firms is called *public issues scanning* or *trend analysis*. In this technique, certain critical issues are followed in an effort to determine the direction and speed of their future development. Sometimes the CEO or a group of top managers initially determine which issues will be followed. At other times, corporate staff poll managers or scan media sources to determine which issues are emerging.

Printed media can often provide early indications of new trends. Firms can obtain the results of periodic surveys of selected "opinion leaders," for example, the *Wall Street Journal, New York Times,* or *Washington Post.* Either corporate staff or an outside consultant can do a brief summary of articles on the specified public policy issues. Over time, interest in a certain issue increases, which indicates possible emerging new markets, new pressures on the firm, or new legislation. Public issues scanning provides an early warning system for discovering such potential developments. The life insurance industry has engaged in trend analysis since 1970 and finds it essential for planning. General Electric (GE) was a leader in sociopolitical forecasting for two decades. Ian Wilson set up the office at GE and developed it as a model for corporate social and political forecasting.[19]

Careers with a Future

With the pressure of international competition and the new importance of knowledge and information, new employment needs will surface. There will be fewer jobs in manufacturing. However, contrary to popular belief, manufacturing output constituted roughly the same percentage of U.S. gross national product from 1950 to 1984, and this percentage will probably be maintained. Hence manufacturing productivity and innovation will continue to be important.[20] Also note that although robots will change the nature of work, they will not put large numbers of people out of work. There are only

---

[18] For the results, see James O'Toole, "What's Ahead for the Business-Government Relationship?" *Harvard Business Review* 57 (March-April 1979): 94–105.

[19] Niels Christiansen and Sharon Meluso, "Environmental Scanning and Tracking of Critical Issues: The Case of the Life Insurance Industry," *Business and Society*, ed. P. Sethi and C. Falbe (Lexington, Mass.: Lexington Books, 1987), pp. 423–33. For an account of Ian Wilson's work at GE, see Ian Wilson, "Sociopolitical Forecasting at General Electric," in *Responsive Capitalism: Case Studies in Corporate Social Conduct* E. Molander, ed., (New York: McGraw-Hill, 1980), pp. 239–49.

[20] William Van Dusen Wishard, "The 21st Century Economy," *The Futurist* 21 (May-June 1987): 24.

15,000 robots in operation now, and a decade hence, "for every working robot, there will still be more than 400 people in the labor force."[21]

Most employment will be in the service sector: hospitality, banking, insurance, transportation, and a wide variety of other services. The Bureau of Labor Statistics expects service jobs to compose almost 75 percent of the workforce by 1995.[22] However, most of these jobs will not be as high paying as those lost in auto, steel, and rubber manufacturing.

With more automatic electronic equipment being used in manufacturing and services, there will be a need for people who design, manufacture, and maintain this equipment. Biotechnology will require people with skills in microbiology, biochemistry, and molecular biology. Aerospace is another industry that will continue to grow.

There will be a large demand for people in information processing, including people who can design hardware, write software, and operate and maintain systems. Hazardous waste disposal skills will also be in great demand, along with skills in energy conservation, solar energy, and laser technology. Engineering and business skills will continue to be important as society becomes even more complex.

The dramatic increase in the importance of knowledge and innovation skills will affect education and training. There will be less emphasis on rote learning in large groups and more emphasis on encouraging new ideas, understanding, and creativity among individuals and small groups of learners. Institutions of higher learning serving college-age students will be smaller so as to better meet students' needs.[23] Business will also be more involved in a wide variety of education and training programs.

FUTURE BUSINESS VALUES

American business and its values have shifted over the last decade; earlier chapters of this book charted these shifts. Because changes continue at a rapid rate, it is imperative that we understand the direction and the substance of current changes.

In this final section we will review the changes that are taking place and try to assess their potential impact on American business. We will identify emerging values that will significantly affect people, firms, and American business ideology. Note that these emerging values are extensions of traditional American values; there are few sharp breaks (see Table 9–1). We will attempt to make objective projections by using data and expert opinion.

[21] Sar A. Levitan, "Beyond 'Trendy' Forecasts," *The Futurist* 21 (November-December 1987): 29.

[22] Cetron, Rocha, and Luckins, "Into the 21st Century," p. 34.

[23] Ibid., pp. 33–34.

TABLE 9–1   Future Business Values as Extensions of Traditional Values

FUTURE BUSINESS VALUES . . . stem from . . .	
	TRADITIONAL AMERICAN VALUES
1. Central role of the individual	1. Dignity of the individual
2. Participation in management decisions	2. Entrepreneurship and the democratic spirit
3. Business as servant of society	3. Business as provider of goods and jobs
4. Long-range perspective	4. Planning ahead
5. Lessened expectations of consumers and citizens	5. Empirical realism
6. Efficiency, flexibility, and innovation	6. Growth and productivity
7. Interdependence of people, institutions, and nations	7. Builders of railroads, radio, telephone, television, canals, etc.
8. Harmony with the environment	8. Respect for the land; self-reliance
9. Local control (small is beautiful)	9. Frontier self-sufficiency and initiative
10. Religious roots of business creed	10. Influence of religion and churches on American life
11. Liberation and self-denial	11. Freedom and self-reliance
12. Concern for others	12. Helping neighbors (building barns, labor unions, charitable organizations)
13. New measure of success	13. Centrality of the individual, the family, and the local community
14. Vision and hope	14. Optimism and openness

Central Role of the Individual

The importance of the individual pervades American life, literature, and thought. Individualism, democracy, human rights, the free market, and the courts build on the centrality of the individual. As standards of living and the level of education rise, people are less willing to put up with uninteresting work and allow themselves to be treated, along with capital, as merely an input into the production process. Until recently, organizational efficiency was often described using the metaphor of "a well-oiled machine." Talking of people as replaceable parts in a machine does not do justice to their importance as human beings. A better description, now more commonly used, stems from our religious roots. It compares the efficient firm to a body whose parts work intimately together and are dependent on each other. Each part is vitally important to each of the others and to the whole and is not easily replaceable.[24]

Future demands for greater productivity, coupled with the central role of the individual, will cause a resurgence in programs for upgrading skills

[24]Thanks to Otto Bremmer for this observation, and also for the model in Table 9–1.

and for management development and an increase in flexibility in an individual's workday, workweek, and career. While some workers still possess an exclusive "me first" mentality, many recognize that teams and loyalty bring satisfaction and success. The family will remain the bedrock of America's social structure.

Social commentator Ivan Illich points out that every tool (in the broad sense) should be designed and used to bring people closer together so they can live fuller and happier lives. Yet he finds many tools divisive and disruptive no matter who uses them:

> Networks of multilane highways, long-range, wide-band-width transmitters, strip mines, or compulsory school systems are such tools. Destructive tools must inevitably increase regimentation, dependence, exploitation, or impotence, and rob not only the rich but also the poor of conviviality which is the primary treasure in many so-called underdeveloped countries.[25]

He challenges the notion that progress means more elaborate tools in the hands of a highly trained elite, which would make each individual more and more dependent and helpless. Computers and robots *can* make people more dependent. On the other hand, powerful tools can also relieve people of dreary and demeaning work and give them more responsibility and make their work more challenging.

The firm must provide for the development of its employees. Their creativity and flexibility are the key to future success. Many firms, such as Hewlett-Packard, Ford, and 3M, have launched large-scale education and training programs. The work setting, too, must be such that the individual is allowed to be innovative and is challenged and fulfilled at work. This is, of course, especially true of educated, skilled, achievement-oriented white- and blue-collar workers.

A firm in which the talents of each employee are challenged, in which co-workers communicate and supervisors provide feedback on work, is one in which each individual may grow as a worker and as a person. Numerous programs now focus on product quality, worker input, and job enlargement. Take the auto industry. Volvo assembles its automobiles in teams rather than on assembly lines. Toyota uses robots, and each worker is asked to provide input. Ford and GM now emphasize quality of product by means of worker input. For a business firm to succeed, its workers must be committed to a quality product or service. The firm must enlist all workers in the struggle to attain its goals by publishing its mission statement, creating a cooperative climate, allowing time in the workweek for group sessions on better quality, and rewarding groups and individuals that contribute to reaching the goals.

---

[25] Ivan Illich, *Tools for Conviviality* (New York: Harper & Row, 1973).

Firms now recognize that the best way to succeed is to draw on the full talents of all workers. Workers tend to feel that they are part of the team when they are asked their opinions of products and processes. Workers then develop a sense of ownership with respect to the job and the firm, and they work better, experience less fatigue, and enjoy greater satisfaction as a result.

Participation in Management Decisions

In addition to restructuring the job, managers now encourage participation in decisions. Various schemes have been developed in the United States, Sweden, Japan, Yugoslavia, and elsewhere to obtain worker input and to share the responsibility for decision making with workers. Decision making through consensus at the grass roots level among workers, as opposed to decision making at the top, is now fairly common.[26] The American Catholic bishops devoted an entire section in their letter on the U.S. economy to participation.[27] However, a caution is in order. In the words of Sar Levitan, veteran observer of work,

> In most cases...management preaches worker cooperation but ignores workers' priorities if they conflict with immediate profit-maximization efforts. Employees are encouraged to participate in corporate decision making only if it does not infringe on management perogatives.[28]

Most people find that liking their co-workers is essential to job satisfaction. If co-workers are friendly, cooperative, and provide feedback on job-related and other items, work can be something to look forward to. Large firms that previously would transfer talented, high-potential managers every few years now recognize the need people have to establish friendships and stability and to contribute to the job, the neighborhood, and their children's development. Life on the job and in the suburbs can be alienating, and friendships there can be shallow and superficial. It can be too great a risk to get to know people well, for one might be transferred and thus forced to go

---

[26] Cetron, Rocha, and Luckins, "Into the 21st Century," p. 37.

[27] United States Catholic Bishops, *Catholic Teaching and the United States Economy*, (Washington, D.C.: United States Catholic Conference, 1986), part 4, nos. 295–325. For a chronology of drafts and changes, see Manuel Velasquez and Gerald F. Cavanagh, S. J., "Religion and Business: The Catholic Church and the American Economy," *California Management Review* 30 (Summer 1988): 124–41. For background, see John W. Houck and Oliver F. Williams, eds., *Catholic Social Teaching and the U.S. Economy: Working Papers for a Bishops' Pastoral* (Washington, D.C.: University Press, 1984). For commentary on the Bishops' letter on the economy, see Thomas M. Gannon, ed., *The Catholic Challenge to the American Economy* (New York: Macmillan, 1987).

[28] Levitan, "Beyond 'Trendy' Forecasts," p. 30.

through the pain of leaving real friends. It is simpler and less painful not to get involved. Recognition of the human need for stability has caused firms not to demand that their achievement-oriented executives regularly move. Thus, managers can increase their self-esteem and confidence and become more involved in the local community.

Most American firms now have programs designed to increase employee involvement and satisfaction. For example, Ford reduced the number of defects in its vehicles by 48 percent in a two-year period by enlisting the efforts of workers. Where labor relations are not adversarial, management is able to ask employees to help improve quality by monitoring the product as it is made and by suggesting better manufacturing processes. Ford engineers took a prototype of the Ranger mini–pickup truck to line workers and asked for their suggestions. Larry Graham, an assembly-line worker who had worked on a previous model pickup suggested that the design be altered to allow assemblers to bolt the pickup cargo box from above rather than from below. When bolting from below, an assembler had to lift a heavy pneumatic wrench over his or her head from a pit beneath the truck. Bolts were not firmly tightened, and customer complaints came in. The engineers used Graham's suggestions to redesign the assembly process, resulting in easier assembly and far fewer consumer complaints.[29]

Lessened Expectations

The 1980s have been sobering to Americans. After a generation of growth in employment and wealth, we lost our unchallenged supremacy in world markets. In many cases, foreign produced goods are of higher quality and lower cost. The United States will probably never again attain the supremacy in world markets or the growth rate that it had in the 1950s and 1960s. Many new service and high-tech jobs are less challenging: "High technology has been changing white-collar work to parallel more closely the earlier factory situation of repetitive, tedious, unchallenging tasks, uncontrollable by individuals."[30] Resources are now more expensive. Pollution is rampant, and the cost to clean it up adds to our cost of living. Finally, we face competition for markets from dozens of developing countries, especially those of the Pacific rim. This phenomenon was discussed in Chapters 1 and 8. The economy of the future, methods of organizing work, government policy,

---

[29] "A Better Idea: American Car Firms Stress Quality to Fend off Imports," *Wall Street Journal*, August 26, 1982, pp. 1, 14.

[30] J. H. Foegen, "The Menace of High-Tech Employment," *The Futurist* 21 (September-October 1987): 38.

and personal values will all be heavily influenced by the coming era of lower rates of growth.[31]

Long-Range Perspective

Future business thinking must include plans for the long term. There are few propositions on which there is more unanimity among business executives. In a recent survey of CEOs, 89 percent said that they thought that American companies were too oriented toward the short term.[32] New products and new business depend on R & D, but short-term thinking has resulted in too little time and money being devoted to it.[33] The survival and growth of American business demands an increased attention to long-term concerns. Pressure resulting from short-term financial interests makes long-term planning difficult but does not alter its importance for the future. This issue was discussed in Chapters 1 and 8.

Businesspeople as Servants of Society

The free market model views the business firm as independent, isolated, and competing with other firms to survive and grow. As long as a firm shows a profit, financial analysts and *Fortune* call it a success. The firm is thus judged successful whether it makes high-quality, energy-efficient necessities (e.g., refrigerators and autos) or dangerous, trivial products (cigarettes). The firm's "success" might even be at the cost of unsafe working conditions (asbestos) and the pollution of neighborhoods. The models and ideology of old-school economists and businesspeople urged indiscriminate production and consumption. To them, any increase in gross national product is a sign of success. However, note that a bad accident on the highway or the creation of pollution leads to an increase in the gross national product—as a result of the work required to repair the damage. How can an accident or pollution be considered to constitute success?

Therefore, it is now apparent that these criteria of success are not accurate. Businesspeople and business firms are servants of society. Their purpose is to provide for the needs of citizens—to make their lives safer, healthier, and happier. Conscientious corporate executives have long acted on this notion that the firm should serve society. CEOs have redirected their firms through new goals, new programs, and a new ethical climate to ensure

---

[31] Cetron, Rocha, and Luckins, "Into the 21st Century."

[32] Wattenberg, "Their Deepest Concerns," pp. 27–36.

[33] "A Perilous Cutback in Research Spending," *Business Week*, June 20, 1988, pp. 139–62.

that social objectives are met.[34] New and developing industries that have been identified as having high growth potential are geared to genuine human needs (e.g., robotics, solar power, office technology, energy conservation, cable TV, and genetic engineering).[35]

In contrast to the "cowboy economy," in which gross production and consumption measure success, the newer "spaceship economy" recognizes that all men and women live together on a fragile planet. This planet has only finite resources and a limited ability to cleanse itself of pollution. Thus, if human needs and desires could be met with less use of resources, less production, and less consumption, that economy would be superior. To say this is economic heresy. However, if we can meet human needs with less disruption and waste, are we not better off? Consumption and production, when carried to extremes, harm people and the environment, and they should hardly be considered as absolute goals.

There is resistance to this reformulation of goals and to the new criteria of success that result. The reformulation requires that we make judgments on the type of growth and the type of products we want and on the type of tradeoffs we are willing to accept. Judgments require discussion and the establishment of a consensus—a big task for a fractured democracy. It is easier to allow the "free market" to decide all issues. However, giving all power to the market is wasteful of time, land, resources, and human lives and is thus not a responsible policy.

One of the major criteria of the worth of any skill or work up to the time of the Industrial Revolution was the relative value of the good or service to society. As we have seen in earlier chapters, with the growth of industry and the division of labor, an ideology developed that bestowed value on any work regardless of its outcome. The amount of compensation received became more important than what was accomplished. However a growing number of men and women now question the value of some work no matter how well paid it may be. These individuals would not work for a strip-mining firm, a hard-sell advertiser, a nuclear missile manufacturer, or a junk bond firm with a shady reputation. They are thereby reintroducing criteria that had been pushed aside. The value of a job or position is judged both by the contribution of the worker to a product or service and by the contribution the product or service makes to society. For example, individual transportation vehicles are important for society, and thus an auto worker's efforts take on value beyond the paycheck and benefits.

---

[34] See Business Roundtable, *Statement on Corporate Responsibility* (New York: Business Roundtable, 1981), pp. 1, 8, 12–14. The Business Roundtable is an organization composed of the CEOs of 170 large firms in the United States.

[35] These six industries were selected for separate explanatory pamphlets for job-seeking graduates of the Harvard Business School. See *Wall Street Journal*, April 1, 1982, p. 1.

Does it make any difference whether a manager or a worker is helping to produce canned foods, tractors, cigarettes, throw-away bottles, or nuclear weapons? All goods are not of equal value to society, and judgments can be made on the relative merits of these goods. In a small, primitive economy, these questions do not arise, since there are only enough resources and energy available to provide the necessities. Our society has many goods and diminishing resources, so questions about relative values are forced on us. We must use criteria to determine which goods are more valuable to society. The principle presented here might help in developing these criteria: Goods and services should be judged to be worthy insofar as they support life, build a sense of community, give freedom, and provide joy and happiness.

Quality, Efficiency, and Innovation

Efficiency, flexibility, and the ability to innovate have been prized American virtues over the generations. They will continue to be important in the future. American firms recently have reorganized to encourage increased innovation and productivity.[36]

Increased product and service quality is also essential. Japanese manufacturers have challenged their American counterparts by producing goods of consistently high quality. If we are to remain competitive in world markets, American goods must also be of high quality. This issue has been discussed in earlier chapters.

Interdependence of People, Institutions, and Nations

In this world of increasing population, more elaborate life styles, and faster transportation and communication, people are becoming more interdependent. On the individual level, people depend on each other and require interaction to develop as persons. For example, when people flee the problems of the city, their affluent children, without parks, libraries, and corner stores within walking distance, find little to do and become bored. Bus service is not readily available in some of these communities, leading to isolation for anyone who does not drive. Many children then use alcohol, drugs, drop out of school, and run away from home. On the international scene, a military coup or a war in the Middle East, Latin America, or Asia is brought by TV into our living rooms in a matter of hours. Malnutrition and starvation in Africa is also presented to us quickly, along with the fact that our use of lawn fertilizer, dog food, and red meat may play a role in depriving those Africans of life-giving grain. Narrow chauvinism, such as may

---

[36] Note, for example, the firms that are examined by Thomas Peters and Robert Waterman, *In Search of Excellence* (New York: Harper & Row, 1982). See also Thomas Peters *Managing Chaos* (New York: Random House, 1988).

occur in France or Iran, does not suit the United States. This country can no longer assume that what is good for the United States is therefore good for all peoples.

These problems face most nations: acid rain, the greenhouse effect, malnutrition, toxic waste, a balance of trade deficit, dwindling finite resources, nuclear waste, and the threat of nuclear war.[37] No single nation can solve these problems alone. Too often U.S. officials are insensitive to worldwide reaction to U.S. policies. This country's lone vote against the World Health Organization's code for marketing infant formula and its repudiation of the Law of the Sea Treaty lost the United States much international respect.[38] Trying to stop the European gas pipeline from Russia may seem to be good short-run policy for the United States, but it is not good for the Europeans. Business managers know that the narrow nationalistic attitudes that might have served well a generation ago are no longer sufficient. Managers now operate in world markets and must be responsible citizens of more than one country. As the world gets smaller, all people depend more on each other. Yet, paradoxically, a new nationalism is afoot. Many nations are unwilling to limit their sovereignity or their greed. Hence we see individualism clash with the reality of interdependence.

Sociologist Robert Bellah thinks America's failure lies in its emphasis on the atomistic self and on rational self-interest and in its break with the basic understandings of the Founding Fathers. In early America, there was a strong social, collective emphasis: Citizens were together responsible for the state. Bellah demonstrates how this emphasis derived from the biblical covenant between God and God's people and from the gospel notion of a loving community based on membership in the common body of Christ. Bellah is convinced that the economic system of contemporary industrial America no longer is based on the early American view that economic interdependence is the foundation of the political order.[39] Perhaps our early ideals can be recaptured. The urgency and importance of the problems that face the nations of the world may force leaders to work together for solutions.

Harmony with the Environment

In the course of meeting people's real needs, business firms will have to operate with greater respect for the natural environment. Scarcity of resources, pollution, and undesirable by-products place constraints on the

---

[37] See "Deadly Combination Felling Trees in East," *New York Times*, July 24, 1988, pp. 1, 13.

[38] James E. Post, "Business, Society, and the Reagan Administration," (Chairperson's presentation at the Academy of Management, Social Issues Division, New York, August 17, 1982), pp. 19–20.

[39] Robert N. Bellah, *The Broken Covenant: American Civil Religion in Time of Trial* (New York: Seabury, 1975).

direction and pace of economic and business growth.[40] These physical constraints will become more pressing, and citizens' expectations that firms will
respect those constraints will become more pronounced. Hazardous industrial waste looms as an ever-increasing problem during the coming decade.
Its transportation and disposal, as well as the determination of liability, pose
difficult problems for business in the future. The federal government has
created the multibillion-dollar Superfund (from taxes on chemical firms) to
help clean up toxic waste dumps. However, after $1 billion has been spent,
only 6 of the designated 18,000 toxic waste dumps have been cleaned up.[41]

Is it then surprising that West Africa is becoming the dumping ground
for American and European toxic waste? As the costs of disposing of this
waste go up, it becomes cheaper to pay Morocco, Congo, or Niger to bury it
on their land. For example, in early 1988 American and European private
waste disposal firms offered Guinea-Bissau $120 million annually to bury 15
million tons of toxic waste from tanneries and pharmaceutical companies.
This is slightly less than the African country's gross national product of $150
million.[42] This practice has created a furor in West Africa, with many people
in these nations demanding that the contracts be repudiated.

Local Control: Small Is Beautiful

The small firm has traditionally been preferred to the large one in the
United States. Large size is necessary in some cases: When economies of scale
are required for the purpose of competing with large international firms (e.g.,
steel, autos, and computers). Nevertheless, encouraging entrepreneurship in
the private sector and keeping the government's role limited in the public
sector are traditional American values. Even in providing human services,
such as education, health, and retirement, the independent sector can generally deliver better services at a lower cost than the public sector. As long as
these services are provided to the poor and disadvantaged, local control in
both the public and private sectors has several advantages: (1) It gives people
a sense of more control over their lives and work and thus provides increased
personal involvement in the neighborhood and at work; (2) it more clearly
locates responsibility; (3) it eliminates layers of organizational bureaucracy;
(4) it is less costly; and (5) it is in the American tradition of self-reliance.

Small businesses are encouraged in the United States by lower tax rates.
Except where it can be demonstrated that large size is necessary for world

---

[40] For additional details on these issues, see Lester R. Brown, *Building a Sustainable Society*
(New York: Norton, 1981).

[41] "One Billion Dollars Later, Toxic Cleanup Barely Begun," *U.S. News & World Report*,
April 22, 1985, p. 57.

[42] "West Africa Attracts Toxic Waste Dumpers," *Cleveland Plain Dealer*, July 17, 1988, p. 19.

competition, a graduated corporate tax rate might be devised, with larger firms (measured by gross sales) paying a higher tax rate than smaller firms.

As for work and home life, many are opting for simplification. For example, much time is spent in transportation. Much of the time that was saved in shortening the work day is absorbed in getting to and from work, church, and stores. Whereas even little children could walk in older neighborhoods, in newer suburbs one must drive or be driven. This constant reliance on the automobile wastes not only time but also petroleum and other natural resources. It constitutes, not progress, but a loss of freedom. Similarly, time is lost in filling out forms such as income tax returns, insurance applications, and questionnaires and in listening to advertisements. In speaking of these same issues, Walter Weisskopf urges, "Wherever there is a choice between making more money and simplifying life, the latter road should be taken." His suggestions include

> abandonment of the purely activistic way of life, of getting and doing more and more for the sake of power over and control of the external world including our fellow beings; taking seriously the Kantian maxim that men should never be used as means but always as "ends"; putting more stress on being than on doing by cultivating receptivity to nature, to others, to art, to feelings; more listening rather than talking, also in relation to one's inner life; taking seriously intuition and insight by trying to resurrect what is valid in mysticism and religion; recovering the art of faith by breaking through the value-relativism of technical reason and cultivating the inner powers on which faith rests.[43]

Many of these attitudes have now taken hold in our society. They will have a significant impact on the firm and its activities. The successful firm is alert to changes in attitudes and will gear its actions and policies to new expectations.

Religious Roots of the New Business Creed

Personal and national goals in the United States have been heavily influenced by religion, especially Christianity. We live on a foundation provided by the Judeo-Christian culture. Although our values and attitudes are currently not well anchored, the older roots continue to provide sustenance and life. As our society becomes more pluralistic (each person's values are deemed as good as any other person's) and atheistic (the existence of God is denied), our values become more free floating. Although it soon became secular, the Protestant ethic stemmed from Christianity, particularly Calvinism. Since religious values have had such a profound influence on business

---

[43] Walter A. Weisskopf, *Alienation and Economics* (New York: Dutton, 1971), p. 192.

and economic life in the past, it is appropriate to ask whether religious ideals will have an impact in the future. And if so, what will that impact be?

There has always been a strong streak of moralism in American culture. Witness our outrage at influence peddling and bribery in the Pentagon and the defense industry and our outrage at the selfish activities of so many of the Reagan administration appointees. This sort of reaction is not new; our history is replete with idealistic public reaction to problems. In the last century, the antislavery (abolition) and antitrust (muckracking) movements were morally motivated and received their inspiration from the Gospels.

The civil rights movement in the United States was led by Martin Luther King, Jr., a Baptist minister. He preached "love for the oppressor" and espoused a specific nonviolent technique to gain social justice for blacks. The record shows how effective the movement and his leadership were. A decade ago it would have been unthinkable for a religious figure to run for president of the United States, but the Reverends Jesse Jackson and Pat Robertson had a pronounced influence on both political parties during the last election. Many of the most committed social activists are inspired by the Gospels and the life of Christ. Ralph Nader comes from a religious family with high ideals, and Common Cause appeals to the generosity and moral qualities of Americans. Mahatma Gandhi was an inspiration to many of these people, and he was also inspired by the life of Christ. Moreover, his nonviolent approach to gaining India's independence from England was successful.

Many Catholic priests and sisters are being murdered in Guatemala, El Salvador, Brazil, Bolivia, Chile, and other Latin American countries because they have defended the interests of the poor.[44] Their inspiration comes from Jesus, his love for the poor, and his commitment to bring justice to those at the bottom of the socioeconomic ladder (Matt. 5:3; Luke 6:20). The goal of these Gospel-inspired leaders is liberation. They want the poor, ordinary citizen to have the freedom to own land, to vote, and to be a self-respecting citizen, as well as the freedom to work and earn a fair day's pay. They want everyone to have freedom from the danger of nuclear holocaust. They want self-determination for peoples around the world. Thus they often find themselves in opposition to some multinational business firms and military governments.

Religion views the manager or owner as a steward. Thus wealth and power constitute a trust that is held for others. Based on the understanding that the world and all its goods come from and ultimately belong to God, the

---

[44] "Roman Catholic Priest Has Struggle Changing Lives in Rural Brazil: Father Ricardo Resende Faces Violence, Makes Enemies in Fight to Aid Landless," *Wall Street Journal*, August 28, 1986, pp. 1, 16. For additional examples, see Penny Lernoux, *Cry of the People* (New York: Penguin, 1980); Martin Lange and Reinhold Iblacker, *Witness of Hope: The Persecution of Christians in Latin America* (Maryknoll, N.Y.: Orbis, 1981).

individual businessperson holds all this in stewardship—in trust for others.[45] A new organization of Catholic CEOs, with chapters in eleven American cities, brings the Gospel into the marketplace. Legatus meets monthly to enable these executives together to pray and reflect on their responsibilities.

Fundamentalist Christian preachers have gained much attention in recent years. They cite the Gospels and tend to be conservative on issues such as racial equality, third world poverty, the environment, and the role of business. They insist that the United States is and must remain number one in the world. They present their message to TV audiences in clear, dramatic, and uncompromising terms. These preachers often tell their adherents that they are among the saved and that others are unfaithful, which reinforces existing biases. They spell out exactly what one must do to be saved, which includes contributing money to them and to their churches. They defend the value of the family and the nation and are consistently conservative on social issues. However, a full reading of the Gospels does not lead to the conclusions espoused by these preachers.

Liberation and Self-Denial

Theology is an attempt to understand oneself, other people, and God in the light of personal experience, religious values, and scripture. Business theologian Donald Kirby says that "theology aids the human person in staying human against a culture which constantly tries to shift people from the human" and it "protects human beings from the distortion of the human by contemporary culture."[46] If religion influenced economic life in the past, it will probably help to fill the vacuum in basic values that exists in the United States today.

In Poland and other East European nations, religion motivates many who challenge the government for more freedom. Liberation theology motivates many who try to bring more opportunities to the very poor in Latin America. The Catholic Church thus sides with the poor and powerless, and new theologies are developing that emphasize the Church's entwinement with people's lives.

The new theologies began by reflecting on people in community and on the individual person's relation to God. Such theologies provide the value foundation for self-determination, whether at work, at home, or in the city.

---

[45] For an excellent statement of this and related issues, see the United States Catholic Bishops, *Economic Justice for All: Catholic Social Teaching and the U.S. Economy* (Washington, D.C.: Origins, 1986). For an account of the testimony taken, changes through the three drafts, summary of the content, and critique, see Manuel Velasquez and Gerald Cavanagh, "Religion and Business: The Catholic Church and the American Economy," *California Management Review* 30 (Summer 1988): 124–40.

[46] Donald J. Kirby, "Corporate Responsibility," (Paper presented at Workshop on Teaching Business Ethics, Fordham University, New York, August 9, 1982).

Such self-determination is not the old-fashioned individualistic sort but is hammered out with others, in a community of men and women. Proponents of liberation theology are critical of capitalism. In their experience, capitalism and profit maximization lead to the exploitation of the poor and the concentration of wealth in the hands of a few. They thus work for various forms of participation and worker control. They ask for worker input into all decisions, both short- and long-range.

It is arguably a healthy characteristic for American society to have streaks of utopian moralism, even righteousness. The latter can be arrogant and unbending, but it can also provide the inspiration that allows people to continue to have hope and demand the best from themselves, their society, and their institutions. A new series of cultural "thou shalt nots" may be required in the future.[47] Humankind will not be able to survive if individual humans do not set limits to their appetites, do not develop an habitual willingness to conserve and preserve, and do not maintain a conscientious concern for others. Although these attitudes are difficult to achieve, they are essential if we are to prevent mass starvation, war, and chaos. The development of new spiritual and human values that are integrated into everyday life and institutional decision making is a priority. On this shrinking planet, economic and political planning must consider the larger issues. Paradoxically, it is "old-fashioned" religion that has traditionally urged concern for others, especially poor people in other nations and future generations.

Concern for Others

People who are loved tend to be mature, less turned in on themselves, and more concerned about others. Self-centeredness and insularity are children's vices. Love for others is a basic human virtue. Expressing such love is a matter of giving—often without hope of return. Altruistic love is possible for anyone, although it is more readily achieved by those who have been loved. It is essential for the development of persons, families, and society, yet it is sometimes difficult. Speaking of this sort of love, economist Kenneth Boulding says,

> It always builds up, it never tears down, and it does not merely establish islands of order in a society at the cost of disorder elsewhere. It is hard for us, however, to learn to love, and the teaching of love is something at which we are still very inept.[48]

Much of the energy of the poor is spent on obtaining the necessities of life. Once a person's basic needs are reasonably satisfied, that person is more

[47] Daniel Callahan, *The Tyranny of Survival* (New York: Macmillan, 1974).

[48] Kenneth E. Boulding, *The Meaning of the Twentieth Century* (New York: Harper & Row, 1964), p. 146.

inclined to consider the needs of others in society. Thus, material security is often a foundation for loving and giving. Having food and shelter enables people to reach beyond themselves and their own problems to other human beings and realize the interdependence of people and institutions. Concern for others is an important part of the organizational climate at Hewlett-Packard and IBM. The Ford worker-involvement program encourages all Ford employees to focus on quality. As mentioned earlier, the Parts and Services Division calls itself "the loving and caring division of Ford."

New Measures of Success

To be successful a business firm must be efficient and profitable. However, corporate leaders now no longer claim that enlightened self-interest is the only goal of business or that such a goal automatically benefits society. Chapter 8 described many situations where what was good for a firm was not good for society.

New measures of success for business firms arise when we realize that such firms operate to benefit people. They are essentially instruments of service to people—all kinds of people. Those to be benefited include customers and shareholders but also employees, suppliers, and the members of the local community. Benefits to one constituency are generally not at the expense of another group; business is not a zero-sum game. When J&J states that their first obligation is to customers and their last to shareholders, the shareholders do better than they would otherwise.

Just as a financial audit sketches a firm's financial performance, a social audit outlines the impact of the firm's operations on its other constituencies. Criteria for judging social performance are crucial if we are to decide accurately the degree of success achieved by a firm.[49]

Business firms are aware of the need for corporate social performance measures. The Business Roundtable, composed of the CEOs of the largest U.S. firms, described the importance of social goals and how to structure a firm so that these social goals are achieved.[50] These CEOs also sponsored a handbook that aids firms in the achievement of their social goals.[51] Government policy, too, both national and international, must be assessed using the same criteria: what is better for all people?

The new measures of success focus on the benefits that accrue to people–all the stakeholders of the firm. This focus constitutes a fundamental

---

[49] Cetron, Rocha, and Luckins, "Into the 21st Century," p. 40.

[50] Business Roundtable, *Statement on Corporate Responsibility;* see also the earlier Round-table statement, *The Role and Composition of the Board of Directors of the Large Publically Held Corporation* (New York: Business Roundtable, 1978).

[51] Francis W. Steckmest, ed., *Corporate Performance: The Key to Public Trust* (New York: McGraw-Hill, 1982).

change in perspective for corporate managers. Because achievement of social goals is increasingly among the criteria for measuring the success of business managers, they have a profound impact on the values and perspective of managers.

Vision and Hope

The problems that we face—trade and budget deficits, pollution, food shortages in poor countries, unjust governments, lack of jobs, danger of nuclear war—are so immense that some find it easier to deny them. These problems are the result of trying to achieve other goods or, in some cases, of callously disregarding the welfare of other people. We then must ask: Do we have enough motivation to seek solutions when each solution has a price tag? And are we able to alter our actions to make more ethical tradeoffs with respect to each issue? Can we build the values, structures, and institutions necessary for peace and justice throughout the world?

Vision and hope have always been American virtues. Ever since the days of the frontier, we have disliked defeatists and fatalists. Nevertheless, it would be foolish to underestimate the enormousness of the problems before us. Many people today are concerned mainly with their own personal lives and careers and care little about what they can do to solve these problems. Yet, as has occurred, a single individual or a small group of talented, generous people can have a profound impact on the lives of others and on the world as a whole.

SUMMARY AND CONCLUSIONS

The main problem of the future is to provide decent work and a reasonable standard of living for all people and yet not needlessly exploit finite natural resources or leave the world more polluted than we found it. American business firms have achieved unprecedented efficiency, productivity, and growth. Nevertheless, it is clear that the free market is not able to provide such goods as clean air and water, safe products, or even fair competition. Often a firm that provides jobs and goods also, in the process, destroys natural beauty, harms people's health, and causes dissatisfaction. Its production processes may be demeaning or dangerous, use nonrenewable resources, or cause pollution.

Generating cooperation and providing benefits to society are appropriate goals for American business and government. Pressure from special interest groups, coupled with our apathy and lack of clear goals, has pushed American society into many unfruitful, expensive, and frustrating traps. Note, for example, defective and dangerous products, collapsing railroads and urban public transportation systems, decaying cities, disappearing farm-lands, defective nuclear power plants, and expensive and wasteful defense systems. Exacerbating the problem is the fact that traditional business ideology justifies and rewards selfishness. More humane personal values and an acknowledgment of public goals would help to avoid these costly and frustrating blunders. Most firms forecast future values so that they can gear their product planning, employee participation programs, and advertising to the new attitudes.

Future business values require efficiency and innovativeness on the part of firms. Productivity and growth cannot be taken for granted. Moreover, citizens continue to demand that business decisions contribute to the overall goals of society. A business firm is no longer merely seen as a private enterprise; its role is to serve the needs of society. If business firms are unable or do not choose to act responsibly, prescriptive legislation or tax incentives will be required to encourage such behavior.

Americans want greater independence, even in the face of the dehumanizing factors of modern life. In spite of encompassing corporations and government, individuals still prefer autonomy, personal responsibility, and the ability to share decisions. Businesses will be better structured to encourage such self-reliance and responsibility.

Religion has provided in the past, and probably will provide in the future, a foundation for business values. Traditional religious values generally run counter to self-interest and what has come to be known as the consumer ethic. The Protestant ethic demanded moderation, planning, and self-sacrifice. Budget deficits, pollution, noise, anxiety, crime, and substance abuse demonstrate the failure of current values. Americans now may be ready for some degree of sacrifice for the sake of a larger purpose. Most would sacrifice a Florida vacation or a third automobile if it meant that they would have a more satisfying job, a happier life, and better relationships and that their grandchildren would not inherit a nation ravaged by open-pit mines and cancer-causing chemicals. Western religions have traditionally directed people's attention out beyond themselves. If Americans could regain this perspective, they might share their expertise and resources with poorer peoples of the world so that others may also enjoy some of the humane fruits of industry. Religion urges self-discipline and generosity toward neighbors based on a reverence for God and a loving concern for others.

Clarifying and internalizing values and goals is necessary for any person as he or she grows to maturity. Especially during times of rapid change, internalized values provide a firm foundation on which to build a stable, challenging, and satisfying life. Furthermore, personal values, together with personal needs, will be the building blocks of future business goals and policies. The process of articulating values and goals requires leadership. The problems are pressing and complex. Nevertheless, business, religious, educational, and government leaders have been able to point out directions and inspire confidence in the past, and we must have faith that they can meet the challenges of today and tomorrow.

DISCUSSION QUESTIONS

1. Outline the current major domestic and international evidence on the success of free markets.
2. What are the issues on which there is general agreement between business managers and business critics? What is the major issue on which they disagree?
3. What does it mean to say that free markets are aristocratic? Do you think this is true?
4. What are the strengths and weaknesses of a democratic society in meeting new social needs (e.g., pollution control or energy conservation)? How do special interests undermine the effective operation of democracy?
5. What are the limitations of personal freedom?
6. Outline the techniques of future forecasting.
7. Do you think that each of the "future business values" listed in Table 9–1 is likely to become prevalent? Assuming they all do, what significance would each have for your organization?
8. If these business values did become prevalent, would it increase or decrease the quality of life? Explain.
9. Is any increase in gross national product a mark of success for an economy? Why or why not?
10. Would people be better off if they could meet their needs with less consumption, less pollution, and less use of finite resources?
11. Americans need to save more to provide for investment and to reduce foreign borrowing. How much do you save of your take-home pay? How much does your family save? Why?
12. Upon what basic values might it be possible to build a public policy consensus for the future? Will religion have a role in articulating these values and this consensus?

CASE: AMERICA'S MOST ADMIRED CORPORATIONS

A recent survey of executives and financial analysts to determine "America's most admired corporations" ranked Merck as number one and Philip Morris and R. J. Nabisco among the top ten.[52] Criteria included quality

---

[52] Ellen Schultz, "America's Most Admired Corporations," *Fortune*, January 18, 1988, pp. 32–39.

of management, quality of products or services, financial soundness, and community and environmental responsibility. Manville was rated among the "least admired" because of its involvement with asbestos. The core business of both R. J. Nabisco and Phillip Morris is cigarettes. (1) Do you agree with ranking Merck as number one? (2) Do you agree with the rating of Manville? Of Phillip Morris and R. J. Nabisco? Explain why in each case.

INDEX

National priorities, 97
Natural selection, *See* Survival of the
  fittest
Nef, John V., 68, 70
Nevin, John J., 214
Nineteenth century factories, 83–85
Norm, 41
Norris, William, quoted, 23
Northrop, 226–228
Norton Company, 236
Novak, Michael, 23
Noyes, John Humphrey, 121

O

Obedience, 77
O'Connor, James, cited, 107–108
Olsen, James E., 153
Ombudsman, 136, 237
O'Neil, Steven, 229–230
Opinion survey, American views, 13–
  14, 15
Optimism, 58
Organization, *See* Corporation
Owen, Robert, 121
Ownership, 97, 99–100
Oz, Amos, quoted, 46

P

Palmer, Russell, quoted, 209–210
Participation, 68–71, 261–262
Path-Goal Theory, 144
Patriotism, 57
Personal growth, 139–140
Peters, Tom, quoted, 139, 217, 218, 224
Petroleum, 4–5, 254
Phillip Morris, 206–208
Philippines, 20
Piaget, Jean, 159
Pickens, T. Boone, 7–8
Plato, quoted, 66
Poison pill, 7
Political contributions, 14–15
Pollution, 15, 249–250
  industrial, 108
Portfolio manager, 9–10
Posner, Barry Z., cited, 169
Post, James E., cited, 246, 266
Power, 77
  need for power, 142

Practicality, 55
Pragmatism, 39, 53, 253
Preston, Lee E., cited, 246
Private property, 76
Project on Corporate Responsibility,
  239
Productivity, 3, 89–90, 113
Profit, 71–73
  maximization, 78–79, 102
  productivity increases, 89
Protestant ethic, 80–81, 131, 268
  change to present 215–217
  criticism, 74
  economics, 73
  predestination, 72
  Protestant Reformation, 73–76, 140
  values, 216
Protestant Reformation, 72–76, 140–141
Protestantism, 71
Public interest groups, 109, 118
Public affairs, 232
Public affairs officers, 174
Public issues scanning, 257
Puritans, 2–3
Puritan ethic, 36–38, 131
Put into play, 7

Q

Quality, 265
  of work life, 129–130

R

Raiding, corporate, 6–8
Railroads, 80
Rand, Ayn, 162
Rationality, 57–58
Rating corporations, 237
Rawls, John, 187, 194, 196
Religion, 268–270, 270–271
  influence among immigrants, 35
Research and development, 215, 217
  United States vs. Japan, 5
Resources
  diminishing, 105–106, 264, 266–267
Rights
  individual, 190–193
Robertson, Pat, 269
Rockefeller, John D., 249